The Conservative Collection

WORKS BY GREG LACEY

James Madison and the Virginia Resolution

The Conservative Collection

The World Is Your Playground

The

Conservative Collection

A Guide to History and Politics in Modern America

SECOND EDITION

Greg Lacey

LLF PUBLISHING

First edition published in 2013 by
We Conservatives Believe, LLC.

Second edition published in 2018 by
LLF Publishing,
an imprint of the Lacey Law Firm.

Library of Congress Control Number: 2018901151

Available in the following formats:
Kindle Ebook (ASIN B07CJPBZPN)
Audiobook (ASIN B00HK4Z8PG)
Hardback (ISBN 978-0-9890260-4-8)
Paperback (ISBN 978-0-9890260-3-1)

Printed in the United States.

To David MacKool—
for his persistence.

We are springing to the call of our brothers gone before,
and we'll fill our vacant ranks with a million free men more;
shouting the battle cry of freedom.

—BATTLE CRY OF FREEDOM

CONTENTS

Foreword
by Brian McGovern

ANY BOOK ON POLITICS, especially one as comprehensive as this one, should be refreshed and updated from time to time to reflect changes in the political landscape. Greg Lacey's *The Conservative Collection* is no exception. This newly edited edition is updated to better reflect what "We Conservatives believe."

Politically, a lot has changed since the first edition was published in 2012. One big change is that both houses of Congress have Republican majorities. But the most notable is how the pendulum has also swung to the right in the White House with the election of Donald Trump.

Granted, the president is an unorthodox and even a polarizing figure. And though the public-approval rating of members of Congress as a whole remains at consistent lows, both events still indicate one thing: a widespread rejection of left-wing ideologies.

However, not all Conservatives agree on everything, nor should they. Even within the microcosm of conservative thought, there are varying opinions on how to achieve the ends of liberty, justice, and fiscal responsibility.

One point upon which most conservatives tend to agree is the concept of absolute moral truth, which hinges on the acknowledgment of a Divine Creator. In fact, I personally believe that God's standards are infinitely more reliable than man's. And to that end, He transcends political parties, elephants and donkeys, and divisions based on colors like red and blue.

Lastly, on a personal note, as the narrator of the audiobook edition, it was a pleasure to read a volume with which I agreed so profoundly. Since producing that work in 2012, I have grown to consider Greg a great friend and fellow patriot. He is absolutely sincere and has exhaustively thought through the pillars contained in this book.

BRIAN MCGOVERN
TEXAS

Preface to the First Edition

IN WRITING THE CONSERVATIVE COLLECTION, I attempted to steer away from most current events happening during its penning. To say, however, that various political issues arising throughout the process did not affect its composition would be an inaccuracy, and quite a few hot-button issues came to the political forefront during the book's authoring (particularly because I began writing during the end of a presidential campaign). As a result of my hesitancy to write specifically about current topics, I geared the book more toward the generalities and holdings of America's conservative wing. Nonetheless, I took the liberty to confront certain, never-ending concerns of American life—those affecting Americans regardless of who is in power or when. These include matters such as taxation and gun rights, or, more recently, health insurance mandates. But by sticking primarily to conservative holdings, I hoped to decode the "conservative language," one that is often misquoted, mischaracterized, and misunderstood. It is a way of communication that needn't have an enumerated platform for every contemporary issue of concern, for when one cherishes conservatism, he also relies on conservative principles to guide him through every political storm. The filters conservatism supplies allow modern progressions to advance but not at the cost of time-tested truths.

The sources I have utilized are many and distinct. To the best of my ability, I have tried to preserve the original contexts from which I pulled quotes and paraphrases. As stated in the introduction, I have relied heavily on other Conservatives' viewpoints and arguments, in addition to my own, because we must work together if we wish to overcome our great odds. Whenever I borrowed work, I gave credit where due, as the extensive notes section details. The founders' writings were incredibly resourceful, primarily those of Madison and Jefferson.

One of the most challenging obstacles in writing *The Conservative Collection* was determining what exactly to confront. Obviously, no manmade writing can be all-inclusive and final, but some degree of structure is necessary to provide organization and flow. The eleven main divisions of the book—"Conservative History," "Individual Liberty," "The Legislature," "The Executive," "The Judiciary," "Economic Strength," "Educational Strength," "Military Strength," "Personal Responsibility," "International Leadership," and "Moving America Forward"—are the result of that internal debate. Clearly, as you will read throughout the book, some conversations have little, if anything, to do directly with politics. Instead, they are often about the character of the individual. As Conservatives, we hold ourselves to a standard not tied exclusively to political distinctions or trends. We seek continual individual development and spiritual maturity. Our names are our honor, and our honor is our greatest quality. As we seek to advance our individual pursuits, let us always remember to cherish our combined triumphs—not merely as Conservatives but more importantly as Americans. As Americans, we can accomplish anything, and as leaders in a turbulent world, we can lead the way toward peace and prosperity. WE CONSERVATIVES BELIEVE, throughout our continued quest for "a more perfect Union," we must all couple together with our shared histories and our common interests, perpetually applying America's conservative foundations for ages still to come.

Chronology

April 19, 1775	Commencement of the Revolutionary War
July 4, 1776	Ratification of the Declaration of Independence
March 1, 1781	Enactment of the Articles of Confederation
September 3, 1783	Conclusion of the Revolutionary War
May 25, 1787	Establishment of the Constitutional Convention
June 21, 1788	Enactment of the Constitution
December 15, 1791	Enactment of the Bill of Rights
June 18, 1798	Enactment of the Naturalization Act
June 25, 1798	Enactment of the Alien Friends Act
July 6, 1798	Enactment of the Alien Enemies Act
July 14, 1798	Enactment of the Sedition Act
November 16, 1798	Passage of the first Kentucky Resolution
December 24, 1798	Passage of the Virginia Resolution
December 3, 1799	Passage of the second Kentucky Resolution
1800	Expiration of the Sedition Act
1801	Expiration of the Alien Friends Act
April 14, 1802	Repeal of the Naturalization Act
June 15, 1804	Enactment of the Twelfth Amendment
June 18, 1812	Commencement of the War of 1812
February 17, 1815	Conclusion of the War of 1812
April 12, 1861	Commencement of the Civil War
May 9, 1865	Conclusion of the Civil War

July 9, 1868	Enactment of the Fourteenth Amendment
January 16, 1919	Enactment of the Eighteenth Amendment
October 24, 1929	Commencement of the Great Depression
December 5, 1933	Enactment of the Twenty-First Amendment
	Repeal of the Eighteenth Amendment
August 14, 1935	Enactment of the Social Security Act
1939	Conclusion of the Great Depression
June 23, 1947	Enactment of the Taft-Hartley Act
June 27, 1950	Entry of the United States in the Korean War
February 27, 1951	Enactment of the Twenty-Second Amendment
July 27, 1953	Signing of the Korean Armistice Agreement
November 1, 1955	Entry of the United States in the Vietnam War
December 17, 1963	Enactment of the Clean Air Act
July 2, 1964	Enactment of the Civil Rights Act
July 30, 1965	Enactment of the Social Security Amendments, creating Medicare and Medicaid
January 22, 1973	Supreme Court's decision on *Roe v. Wade*
November 7, 1973	Enactment of the War Powers Resolution
April 30, 1975	Conclusion of the Vietnam War
June 29, 1992	Supreme Court's decision on *Planned Parenthood v. Casey*
January 20, 2009	Commencement of Barack Obama's tenure as the president
March 23, 2010	Enactment of the Patient Protection and Affordable Care Act (Obamacare)

January 20, 2017	Commencement of Donald Trump's tenure as the president

THE
CONSERVATIVE COLLECTION

Introduction

Being a Conservative

I WAS NOT ALWAYS A CONSERVATIVE. The principles of conservatism were present in my life, but perhaps through a combination of naïveté and inexperience, I chose to ignore the values of the Right. As I became aware of the public arena, I fell into the traps of dependence, deception, and entitlement that the allure of the Left laid before me as a smooth avenue upon which I could face my first encounters with politics and legal interpretation. In fact, joining the Left took no effort at all. When I would talk about politics, others *assumed* I was a Democrat, and so in response, I *believed* I was. I learned the talking points, the art of deflection, and the mixing of fact, opinion, and bias. Groupthink threatened to become my foundation.

Yet even during these times, something had not entirely settled in my mind. Insecurity increasingly backed the façade I put forward. My studies of our founders and history were quite often at odds with what I was being groomed to preach. As I became more conscious of our liberties' histories, coupled with a deeper understanding of self, I found that I grudgingly agreed with Conservative Republicans. But even through these growths and recognitions, I kept it all hidden from others. In an increasingly hostile political scene, one which readily demonizes those who step out of rank, I was concerned about the potential backlash that may ensue should I reveal my true political affiliations.

But I did. And I found my newly held beliefs to fulfill the very gaps and shortcomings I had confronted under the thinking of my past. And while the anticipated scorn and disappointment did come from some, it was not as objectionable as I expected, nor was it from everyone I foresaw. Even more and to my great surprise, I discovered many other people who had been, for so long, in the same dilemma as me. Societal pressures have unfairly placed a stigma on those who proclaim conservatism, and that stigma can effectively lead people to suppress or hide their conservative values. Defecting from liberalism has proven to be an enlightening and exciting choice. My respect for American exceptionalism has grown as a consequence, and my hope for our continued greatness seems more plausible through the application of conservative principles.

I provide this simple example not to itemize a sample from my life but rather to suggest that liberalism needn't cemented itself in the minds and hearts of the people. It is, by its admission, a fluid idea, and when matched beside the time-tested convictions of conservatism, its potency shrinks. Liberalism fails where conservatism triumphs. Everyone's story is different, yet for many, liberalism has become a *de facto* political affiliation. But when one breaks that mold, what does being a Conservative mean? We can perhaps best answer this question by comparing the two competing factions of conservatism and liberalism.

America's major political affiliations have, over the last century, grown so absolutely different that nearly every issue requiring bipartisanship will, in some way, violate a principle either party holds dear. Politicians (many on both sides) are so entrenched with special-interest groups and lobbyists that even an *attempt* at bipartisanship will breed a fallout. Furthermore, moral convictions of each member of Congress steer their ability to vote for or against matters of national concern. Abortion, marriage, stem cell research, the death penalty, suicide, the use of firearms, unions, affirmative action, church and state, immigration, drug use, energy production, progressive taxation, healthcare, cloning, language, welfare, and the use of force—these are but some of the innumerable areas of disagreements both sides usually and principally cannot agree on because doing so would necessarily violate baselines of their affiliations and moral compasses. Compromise, as such, is simply unworkable.

True Conservatives (both in the government and the home) have much in common from the start and use these commonalities to filter through all concerns of the country. Some of the most basic and unwavering include:

- An originalist interpretation of the Constitution and other founding documents;

- Limited government, one that respects the individual and free enterprise;
- The appreciation of success and achievement, both financial and familial;
- The acceptance of natural law as provided by God, not government; and
- American exceptionalism.

Not all Conservatives can (nor should) agree on every matter. In fact, as General Patton recognized, "If everyone is thinking alike then somebody isn't thinking."[1] But these fundamental principles of conservatism act as a general groundwork upon which most can rally. They are also the values upon which I wrote this book.

The format of *The Conservative Collection* is unique through its division into several sub-chapters, each attributed to a particular principle of conservatism. The eleven fields of conservatism covered in this volume are diverse and varied. Of these, there is perhaps a no better place to begin than with a strengthening of our historical roots. On being attentive to our past and attaching value thereupon, the Roman statesman Marcus Tullius Cicero wrote, "Not to know what happened before you were born, that is to be always a boy, to be forever a child."[2] Practically all life's studies and knowledge relies on experiences, events, and discoveries prior to the present day, resulting in an ever-growing fortress of comprehension and awareness. The first part of this work focuses on that perception, for it is impossible to truly grasp American political structures without an understanding of our past—"Conservative History" will attempt to span that divide.

In our study of American history, the importance of freedom and independence is the cornerstone of every conversation. In the second division, "Individual Liberty" is promoted and cherished, for through the people alone does the government have the authority to act. "This is," wrote Thomas Paine, "the only *mode* in which governments have a right to *arise*, and the only *principle* on which they have a right to *exist*."[3] Individual liberty is thus central to a free and prosperous people.

Next, we will progress through each branch of the federal government in the same order the Constitution created them, thus beginning with "The

Legislature." The Constitution explicitly enumerates the powers of Congress, and overextensions of those authorities threaten not only the nature of governance but also the sovereignty of the people. James Madison quoted Thomas Jefferson in 1788 when writing, "All the powers of the government (legislative, executive, and judiciary) . . . in the same hands is precisely the definition of despotic government. An *elective despotism* was not the government we fought for."[4]

Thereafter, "The Executive" becomes the focus of our attention, during which time we scrutinize his role as the commander-in-chief and articulate his civilian powers. Further discussed is the balance of his authorities and the intentions of the founders as contrasted with the modern scope of the presidency.

Last of the three federal branches of power discussed is "The Judiciary," where we focus heavily on its assumed role as the "Chief Arbitrator" of the constitutionality of congressional and presidential actions. Moreover, we discuss the troubles with lifetime tenure and examine the relationship between the federal courts and state sovereignty. As we will see, nowhere else in the world is freedom so honored and power so divided than here in America.

The next three partitions of *The Conservative Collection* spotlight different areas of American strength. As with most issues in the political spectrum, these strengths are not entirely exclusive to one another and very often are, to some degree, dependent on the strength of the others. We begin by studying "Economic Strength"—the pistons that turn the American engine. Elaborated are the troubles associated with redistributive schemes and the rights and obligations of the worker, along with those of the employer as well. We critique the present American welfare state and the inefficient and overburdening tax structure.

Our concentration next turns to "Educational Strength." Here, we consider the general inadequacy of modern education in the United States and press the need to instill American values and exceptionalism. Moreover, we encourage the education of the citizen *outside* formal schooling institutions, for, as Thomas Jefferson wrote, "Whenever the people are well-informed, they can be trusted with their own government."[5] We will further give thought to the influence parents have on the educational upbringing of their children and the value of a family.

We then focus on that which makes all other American freedoms possible: "Military Strength." The requisite recognition of evil is raised, as well as international military force and soft power. As one of American history's leading and most heroic generals, George Washington, argued, "To be prepared for war is one of the most effectual means of preserving peace."[6] Let us always hope for that peace but be ever-ready to protect American interests.

Next, our attention turns to "Personal Responsibility," wherein we discuss the profits of accountability and explore the troubles plaguing those first to blame others. Without an understanding of our histories, an emphasis on individual responsibility, and a jealous guarding of our liberties, we ordain ourselves to "live in a culture of Peter Pans, flying free in Neverland with no past and no future, only the ever-present game, the mock battle against pirates and Indians."[7] We can do better, and we owe it to our country to try.

Subsequently, our focus becomes international relations and their impacts on domestic concerns. In "International Leadership," we undertake a lengthy debate over globalization and its influence on the Constitution's supremacy and summarize the international roles of government.

In ending *The Conservative Collection*, we highlight a variety of further matters, all with the intention of "Moving America Forward." This includes the choosing of leaders who can foresee trouble and provide feasible alternatives while nonetheless maintaining their conservative principles. Discussed are religion, God, and purpose, all the while promoting the criticality of marriage. Morality is so imperative to a country and its people's health that "history fails to record a single precedent," said Douglas MacArthur, "in which nations subject to moral decay have not passed into political and economic decline."[8] To truly move the United States forward, we Conservatives must look to our history for guidance and trust our sound judgment in applying the principles of our purpose.

The Conservative Collection, although extensive, does not incorporate every corner of American living. It omits certain aspects of life for various reasons, and so it is not intended to act as an encyclopedic resource. Nonetheless, the format that follows aims to provide easy access to the general holdings of conservatism. Further, this book does not speak for all Conservatives. Indeed, there are matters discussed here that other Conservatives will find differing from their own opinions. Even so, this is the beauty of conservatism. We accept diversity and individualism and appreciate the fruits of competing thoughts. We do not see the individual as a disposable number nor do we see him as expendable. Rather, the individual *is* America. We promote self-restraint and traditionalism while simultaneously embracing progress. We as a nation cannot move forward without applying the conservative roots of our past. America must succeed with each generation and repel the threats of tyranny and oppression, those both foreign and domestic.

There are several misconceptions about conservatism this book will attempt to correct. Because it would be false to pretend that an individual comes to understand and appreciate conservatism on his own fully, I have relied heavily throughout this work on the writings and teachings of other Conservatives, making numerous cites to political and philosophical thinkers from antiquity through the present day. I have striven to duly give credit to each source from which I have directly borrowed, whether in the chapters themselves, in the notes section at the end, or both. To make conservatism attractive and successful in the eyes of the electorate, we Conservatives must work in conjunction with one another to achieve these ends.

One of the misconceptions regarding conservatism is a belief that the further to the Right on the political spectrum one goes, the closer to *tyranny* one becomes. And, conversely, the further to the Left one moves, the nearer to *anarchy* he is. But how can this be? Being a Conservative is to cherish individual liberty and limited government. It is to keep an ever-watchful and -skeptical eye on governments of every field, ensuring they remain within their authorized bounds. The Conservative is in persistent pursuit of personal responsibility and demands that true sovereignty is in the people alone, not the government. Thus, rather than moving toward tyranny the further Right one travels, he instead enters the realm of anarchy, where any form of government is virtually non-existent or severely minimized. Alternatively, to be a Liberal is to seek larger and more involved governments, and such governments should serve as the mediators in local concerns. Dependence and collective thought are esteemed, and a significant reliance on the government is not to be feared. Thus, the government grows and consequently (as history has proven inevitable at such times) encroaches upon the people to the extent that individual liberty is but a phrase. Eventually, if far-Left ideologies were given unadulterated reign, "The republic [would become] nothing but a name, without substance or reality."[9] Accordingly, as Thomas Paine wrote, "though we have been wise enough to shut and lock a door against absolute Monarchy, we at the same time have been foolish enough to put the Crown in possession of the key."[10] Therefore, rather than the far-Left embracing anarchism, it is instead a standard-bearer toward tyranny.

In writing *The Conservative Collection*, my chief sources and filters of conservative political thought rested on two documents alone: the Declaration of Independence and the Constitution. Regrettably, these two founding works have been, through centuries of jurisprudence, thwarted, misconstrued, and misinterpreted, resulting in a web of congressional overextensions, presidential fiats, and judicial political activism. But we Conservatives are Originalists, seeking to uphold the original meaning and context of the founding documents and to avoid modern variations and interpretations. If the Constitution is fluid and adaptable for subjective circumstances, then we in practicality have no constitution at all. Accordingly, when modern legal doctrines do not align with originalist and conservative principles, I take the liberty to discount those modern interpretations, or to raise them and then denounce them, for they act contrary to the Constitution and harm long-term American interests. In the legal world, this would be considered an affirmative defense, for while you needn't deny that actuality of a certain occurrence (such as the passing of a particular bill), you can deny its validity for being in violation of something else (such as Congress reaching beyond its enumerated powers to pass the bill). For that reason, many concerns and propositions raised in this work may contradict years of legal understanding but are nonetheless in line with the founding documents of America.

Furthermore, in the absence of commonly accepted gender-neutral pronouns when referring individuals, and to avoid the sometimes confusing or awkward alternations between sexes as some authors do, I have written *The Conservative Collection* using the traditional masculine tense, although, in such places, interchanging either masculine or feminine pronouns will often not alter the context of the statement.

Representative government is not a preordained destiny—it must be earned and retained. Before an American can represent his countrymen, he must first know his countrymen. Even the earliest of our founding fathers struggled to maintain the republic they created, and governmental encroachments began almost as soon as they enacted the new government. Centuries later, Ronald Reagan saw the real risks of losing our way, of unhinging from our past, and the importance of instilling conservative values and American patriotism in each successive generation. Addressing the Phoenix Chamber of Commerce in March of 1961, he concisely and passionately argued the case of conservatism:

> Our founding fathers, here in this country, brought about the only true revolution that has ever taken place in man's history. Every other revolution simply exchanged one set of rulers for another set of rulers. But only here did that little band of men so advanced beyond their time that the world has never seen their like since, evolve the idea that you and I have within ourselves the God-given right and the ability to determine our own destiny. But freedom is never more than one generation away from extinction. We didn't pass it on to our children in the bloodstream. The only way they can inherit the freedom we have known is if we fight for it, protect it, defend it, and then hand it to them with the well-taught lessons of how they in their lifetime must do the same. And if you and I don't do this, then you and I may well spend our sunset years telling our children and our children's children what it once was like in America when men were free.[11]

This is the purpose of conservatism, these are the stakes at hand, and this is what all Americans must recognize to maintain the liberties we have long-labored to secure.

CONSERVATIVE HISTORY

Our History Roots Us

WE CONSERVATIVES BELIEVE that to ignore the past is to deny the spring of our liberty. It strips our grasp from those fundamental principles that cemented our early bonds in self-governance, and it regressively ensures the eventual captivity of a once freedom-loving people. To ignore the past is to minimize the foundation from upon which we root our collective notions of civil society. To withdraw from history is to lift the anchor holding steady the nation as it rolls through continual storms.

There is an often-held belief that history repeats itself. An individual sees events from one period (usually the present) that in some manner strongly represent and reflect another. According to the observer, these comparisons may be about recurring wars, declining economies, similar leaders, religious powers, or, most commonly, a society's rise of and fall from global influence. Regardless of which comparison, they are nearly never conducted in a positive light. They unanimously fret an impending doom from which the alleged "pattern of history" has proven no escape. They point to the unfortunate fates of those in a parallel past and recognize similar fortunes as likely to be imminently present once again.

The modern understanding of historic recurrence stems itself from a comparative history approach. When looking at history, the person is unable to remove himself and his story (even partially) from that of the past, a time before his existence and comprehensions of society. This type of anachronism leads to, by default, supposed links to history in the person's mind, using standards of today's social order to consider and evaluate the world of yesterday. That is, "Since we can never completely escape, even imaginatively, from our present, some degree of anachronism is inevitable in all history writing. But any good historian needs constantly to worry about the problem of injecting his or her contemporary consciousness back into the past."[1]

History is not simply names and dates, nor is it merely a chronological chain of events predetermined and always comforting to the actors in it. Just as in our world today, no certainty existed in the past, where we see conscious efforts to overcome adversity, determine the best course forward, and stay focused on the overall goals of a society. Consequently, history should not be looked upon as a simple narrative of tedious doings by shadowy figures from long ago; it should instead be studied and appreciated for its teachings on the motivations of mankind and society. In other words, history is not the *what* and *when*; it is the *why* and *how*.

Ignorance of the past not only causes an unraveling of the stitches that secure the nation's fabric but also *creates* the recurring patterns perceived by many. Each new generation of children, for instance, in America and abroad, has the natural inclination to establish a groundwork built by their own experiences and understandings; often, they resist and minimize learned truths from previous generations. This inevitably, from time-to-time, results in mishaps and misfortune which members of that newest generation could easily have avoided had they taken to heart the cautions provided by the older generations. Even more, had they truly valued such instruction, they may have advanced further and faster than naturally inclined. So, too, might our nation at large gain from the lessons learned by our ancestors if only we would heed the depth of insight they are willing to offer through history and its outcome. Instead of dismissing our collective past (and in turn ignoring its teachings), the value of history ought to be embraced, for the more one understands the past, the more equipped he is for the future. Must a society or nation, with each new generation, just like a child, insist on learning anew on its own while disregarding the truths of history? And if so, at what expense to the individual and nation?

History, therefore, does not repeat itself. Rather, it is the failure of those who refuse to learn from history who repeat the mistakes of history. WE CONSERVATIVES BELIEVE that through our history we are infinitely wiser in our progression.

That Which Governs Least

WE CONSERVATIVES BELIEVE the greatest societies throughout history share the common belief in limited government. This observation was key in the founding of America and was upheld until the early twentieth century, at which point government expansions grew exponentially and individual freedoms became evermore encroached.

The framers and those who positively influenced them were intent on maintaining a government of limited scope. They distrusted overly large and powerful institutions of men and recognized man's inclination toward the abuse of power. In all their studies of history, the founders learned of expansive governments that inevitably became oppressive. Thus, to serve as precautions, they set out to create abundant checks and balances on each branch of government and between the federal and state governments. What resulted was an enumeration of powers resting between three divisions of a federal government, with the remaining powers left to the states and people. Further, federal officials were to be elected by differing ways to serve as yet another check on superfluous government.

"Society in every state is a blessing, but government, even in its best state, is but a necessary evil; in its worst state an intolerable one," wrote Thomas Paine in his 1776 *Common Sense*.[2] No institution created by man has a greater ability—or potential—to inflict the intolerable sufferings that accompany oppression than does government. Yet unfortunate for man (and as governments well understand), "mankind are more disposed to suffer, while evils are sufferable, than to right themselves by abolishing the forms to which they are accustomed."[3] This reality (from the Declaration of Independence) serves as but another purpose for preventing such distresses from commencing in the first place. Once begun, they grow cancerous, and the cure is all the more elusive.

In 1791, Thomas Jefferson wrote about the importance of limited and defined government: "To take a single step beyond the boundaries thus specially drawn around the powers of Congress, is to take possession of a boundless field of power, no longer susceptible of any definition."[4] It is to be naïve and ignorant of history to hope that powerful bureaucrats will, by themselves, stay within the bounds of their defined powers. Therefore, the best and most effective check on government derives from a learned citizenry. Those acting in representative roles ought to fear the wrath of those they represent, for "when the people fear their government, there is tyranny; when the government fears the people, there is liberty."[5] Consequently, "freedom is lost gradually from an uninterested, uninformed, and uninvolved people."[6]

Losing liberty most frequently occurs over a long and gradual course, yet the tide is just as difficult to stop as is a wall of water once begun. "There are more instances of the abridgment of the freedom of the people by gradual and silent encroachments of those in power than by violent and sudden usurpations."[7] Thus, for the citizens, education on the proper role of government is only one half of the equation; the citizen body must also be willing to enforce its freedom against the governmental body seeking to encroach its natural rights. WE CONSERVATIVES BELIEVE government's warranted role is constrained to those enumerated powers granted to it by the people, thus reaffirming the historical truth that the best governments are those which govern least.[8]

ORIGINALISM

Natural Law

WE CONSERVATIVES BELIEVE man does not confer the unalienable rights (natural law) enshrined in the Constitution, but instead they are endowed by our collective creator. This belief weaves throughout the founding documents and the writings of those who helped craft them. It acts as a limit on the reach and extent of governmental power—divinely ordered, not self-imposed.

But what does it mean to have unalienable rights? The Declaration of Independence tells us that "all men are created equal," and "that they are endowed by their Creator with certain unalienable Rights."[9] These rights are *secured* by the governments men create, the actions of which become illegitimate should it exceed its purpose of providing such guarantees of protection. This belief was at the core of the founders' philosophies, suggesting government's role is to promote "Life, Liberty and the pursuit of Happiness."

The Conservative understands that "the Creator makes truth and other moral absolutes evident to us; we do not create them."[10] It matters not what religion or faith a man holds, nor concerned are we from where he hails; natural law applies to *all* mankind. In America, the framers created a government intent on safeguarding these moral absolutes from ambitious actors' suppressions and the tyrannical desires of elites. The government, as crafted by the Constitution, was designed first to protect the people's natural rights and then to protect the people from the government. Never before has there been a republic that has not slipped into the restraint of its citizens' liberties—a very real threat in today's America. WE CONSERVATIVES BELIEVE in the importance of recognizing natural rights and the limitations they impose on governmental authority.

An Objective Standard

WE CONSERVATIVES BELIEVE in interpreting the Constitution through the moral lens of an objective standard—unchanging and immovable. God (the maker of truths and absolutes) provides this objectivity; through it, we can recognize the existence of immorality and evil. The Constitution as written coexists with this reality and encompasses the traditional wisdom of our ancestors.

This understanding of the Constitution is sometimes referred to as an "originalist" perspective—or originalism—for it takes the Constitution at its word and rejects modern variations and manipulations of the framers' intents. The Constitution serves as the foundation upon which the nation was (and continues to be) built. In its unwavering stance, the Constitution provides stability and consistency and connects each generation to the last. An Originalist recognizes human dignity, not because man maintains it but because God dictates it.

Further, the Originalist looks to history and sees the threats that faced nations when no objective standard was acknowledged. He sees evil as more than a simplistic dismissal of ideological differences and knows "good government is not immoral or amoral. Good government is moral."[11] This morality comes from the steadiness found in the rule of legitimate law, as seen in John Adams's insistence on remaining a "government of laws and not of men."[12]

The Originalist does not trust man alone to protect the natural rights of other men. WE CONSERVATIVES BELIEVE a free America must maintain an objective post against which to measure governmental actions (other than the standards of contemporary officials), and the good of our creator provides this sought-after standard.

The Modernist Opposition

WE CONSERVATIVES BELIEVE a subjective, human-centered moral standard—one that is fluid and susceptible to modern evolutions—is flawed and dangerous. Ethics based on human interpretation is certain to be as flawed and imperfect as mankind itself. The very principle of natural rights—that man does not give liberties but is born into them—relies upon the recognition of an objective and fixed standard, not prone to political agendas or fad-like schemes.

Opposing originalist understandings of God-given liberty are the "Modernists." The Modernist rejects natural law, choosing instead to depend on man's alleged moral compass. He holds to no objective measure of good or bad and believes in the adaptation of our founding governing principles only to the extent they suit his present needs; he identifies morality as subject to change. In other words, "*individuals* determine whether liberty exists based on circumstance and personal convenience or autonomy . . .; the human subject is the source of all rights and laws."[13] Unlike the Originalist, there is no objective filter through which he must first pass potential governance to ensure its conformity with natural rights; if the Modernist believes an action to be proper, it is.

The Conservative—as an Originalist—sees the Modernist's approach to morality as dangerous and wrong. The Modernist places himself in the role of God and thus "enables those in power to define law and liberty according to their own morally relative evolving views of 'neutrality.' "[14] Man, when unrestrained and on his own, has never shown the ability to act within the bounds of natural law. WE CONSERVATIVES BELIEVE the Modernist's understanding of liberty (that man crafts liberty) threatens both man and liberty.

The Modernist Influence

WE CONSERVATIVES BELIEVE the Constitution, while not perfect, is the best governing doctrine man has yet ratified and that its imperfections are in fact adjustable, so long as done through the processes permitted by the Constitution itself. The Modernist, on the other hand, believes flaws in the Constitution can (and should) be corrected through other means (for instance, through the judiciary, the executive, or the administrative agencies) and views the Constitution not as a protector of natural law and liberties but as a hindrance to his agenda-driven purpose.

Great nations only become so after periods of stability and consistency. Their people depend upon regularity and the avoidance of large swings in the balance of power. The American Constitution provides just such a foundation and was written to guarantee no single branch, tier, or person of government could gain too much control. This acceptance of steadiness is how the Constitution was *written*, but when the Modernist uses the Constitution as he *wishes it were written*, he undermines the very reliance on stability the Constitution gives.

If ambitious politicians and lobbyists can use the Constitution when suiting their ends and disregard it when not, what reassurances do the American people have that their government will maintain constancy? What is left to restrain governmental action if overlooking the very document limiting it? And, further, if the Modernist is willing to overlook yesterday's tried-and-tested truisms in return for political expediency today, why then should tomorrow's Modernists continue enforcing *today's* policies? The threat is real and happening. WE CONSERVATIVES BELIEVE in a steadfast application of the founding principles as first ratified by the states, not what is merely fitting and expedient today.

The Modernist Threat

WE CONSERVATIVES BELIEVE the threat of the Modernist's philosophy is present in every branch of government and perhaps most dangerously so in the judiciary. The now-accepted ability of unelected judges and justices to evolve the meaning and scope of the Constitution has transformed the role of the judiciary. It no longer zealously protects absolute objectivity but rather searches for progressive change, emphasizing manmade morality.

Members of all three branches of the federal government must first, before taking office, swear an oath to uphold and defend the Constitution. This means that all their public actions, decisions, and initiatives must satisfy the spirit of the Constitution and must fit within its reach. So what is left of this oath when, in the course of their terms, judges adopt a Darwinist interpretation of the Constitution they swore to uphold? How can they legitimately work within the limits of the Constitution when they allow themselves to be both the judge and jury?

Modernist judges see their roles as unique insofar as they can craft the Constitution in a way no other branch can, all the while suggesting their motives are evolutionary and progressive. Yet in reality, rather than *uphold* the Constitution as they so swore, they *remold* the Constitution as it was never intended to be. They abuse the Commerce Clause, pretending that *not* participating in commerce is, in fact, commerce; they usurp the legislature's authority by supporting oppressive administrative agencies' regulations; and they ignore the principle of federalism and states' rights when exploiting the Supremacy Clause. WE CONSERVATIVES BELIEVE the inundation of Modernists in the judiciary limits individual liberty by gradually and systematically diminishing natural law's influence.

Following Blindly

WE CONSERVATIVES BELIEVE it is far better to be ignorant and of no opinion than to maintain one without knowing why. Those who blindly follow will just as soon blindly run from the truth when confronted by it. This is a real threat to the future prosperity of the individual and our nation.

Unfortunately, this blind following is not new to our existence. Further, the hazards accompanying such feelings largely prevent any justified considerations of public matters. These followers enter the debate process with their verdict already determined, unaware or uncaring of opposing arguments; the adoption process of the Constitution in the late 1780s provides such an example. Writing in the *Federalist*, James Madison argued in favor of the Constitution and showed his frustration with those predisposed to striking it. Because of mankind's inclination to regularly prejudge, he lamented how "it is a misfortune, inseparable from human affairs, that public measures are rarely investigated with that spirit of moderation which is essential to a just estimate of their real tendency to advance or obstruct the public good."[15] Madison, who had played a critical role in authoring the Constitution, knew harsh criticism was certain to escort his finished work: "it could not appear surprising, that the act of the convention, which recommends so many important changes and innovations, which may be viewed in so many lights and relations, and which touches the springs of so many passions and interests, should find or excite dispositions unfriendly, both on one side and on the other, to a fair discussion and accurate judgment of its merits." However, the "fair discussion and accurate judgment" he longed for instead confronted, among others, these two predetermined holdings either for or against the newly written Constitution.

It was clear to Madison that many rejected the document without ever subjecting it to a balanced consideration, discarding it without regard to its content. "In some, it has been too evident from their own publications, that they have scanned the proposed Constitution, not only with a predisposition to censure, but with a predetermination to condemn."[16] For others, they were prone to support the proposed Constitution without thought of its substance: "the language held by others betrays an opposite predetermination or bias, which must render their opinions also of little moment in the question." Madison viewed these two followings similarly, even though one appeared to be in agreeance with Madison's Constitution, yet was in such an agreeance without a material understanding of why. Both sides fell in line to where they were predisposed.

In *Federalist 37*, Madison continued to elaborate slight differences in these two conclusions but realized that true discussions would not arise from either group. Rather, the debates found in the *Federalist* and others over the Constitution "are not addressed to persons falling under either of these characters. They solicit the attention of those only, who add to a sincere zeal for the happiness of their country, a temper favorable to a just estimate of the means of promoting it."[17] Couldn't the same circumstances apply today? Don't today's politicians regularly rely on prejudgments when faced with debates? WE CONSERVATIVES BELIEVE it falls to the citizens to openly and civilly discuss America's central issues, interests, and values, and, with the fruits of those conversations, elect statesmen who best represent their beliefs and who are best able to continue the discussion once in office.

The Order of the Amendments

WE CONSERVATIVES BELIEVE an amendment's importance is not dependant on its placement within the Constitution. We believe the Tenth is as significant as the Third and the Third as much as the Seventeenth. We understand this with perhaps one exception: the First, for without the First the viability of the others is undermined.

Calls for the original amendments (the Bill of Rights) came after fears that the federal government might grow too powerful, thus enabling it to encroach upon the rights of the citizenry. The Bill of Rights's ratification enshrined certain liberties in a national document of protection. Yet with the passage of the amendments, the government did not *grant* these freedoms; instead, it *guaranteed* them.

Throughout our history, politicians have postured themselves and their parties through manipulation and misinterpretation of the Constitution, habitually adopting a blasé acceptance of the amendments (particularly when they prevent political objectives). Suffocating limitations on gun ownership, for instance, pass without consideration of the Second Amendment; inappropriate seizures of personal and real property occur without regard to the Fourth; and misconstructions of the Fourteenth continue without thought of its original intent.

As with a speech or play, the most memorable sections are often those at the beginning and end, with the middle (although the bulk) muddled. This realism has unfortunately befallen the citizenry, who are regularly unaware of the precise limitations imposed by the amendments outside the First and Second. WE CONSERVATIVES BELIEVE every amendment restrains governmental action and encroachment regardless of whether the First or Twenty-Seventh.

The Tenth Amendment

WE CONSERVATIVES BELIEVE one of the most conveniently overlooked constitutional amendments is also one that greatly limits the scope of the federal government: the Tenth. All three branches of government are guilty of its infringement and violation and, with time, have rendered it virtually extinct. Its roots lie deep in American originalist thought and are at the core of what distinguishes the United States from other nations.

In America, a political model known as federalism balances the relationship between the state and the federal governments. It stems from the history of the American states, which were born as sovereign and independent entities. The generally weak central body created by America's first constitution (the Articles of Confederation) was not sufficient enough to undertake the wide-scale needs of the several states as a whole, and a reworking and reorganization of central powers became necessary. However, the founders also needed to solidify the federal government while not encroaching on the states' autonomy. To accomplish this task, they set out to ensure "that only in limited areas—including national defense, immigration, issuing currency, raising revenue to operate national government, foreign relations, resolving conflicts between the states, and certain other specific, enumerated circumstances—could the federal government have primary if not exclusive power. In all other respects, the states retained their authority."[18]

To make certain these distinctions were unambiguous, the framers amended the Constitution with the first ten amendments, known collectively as the Bill of Rights. The last of these original amendments (the Tenth) expressly laid out how to accomplish this division: "The powers not delegated to the United States by the Constitution, nor prohibited by it to the States, are reserved to the States respectively, or to the people."[19] This surely does not ring as the most complex and convoluted amendment, especially when considering other amendments that read in a much heavier tone. But through centuries of ambitious politicians and unanchored judges, the amendment, as read today, rings hollow. The federal government is now able to sidestep this restraint through perverse interpretations of other articles and provisions in the Constitution. The government forces a great deal of its legislation through misconstrued viewings of the Commerce Clause, the Necessary and Proper Clause, and the General Welfare provision in the Taxing and Spending Clause. Further, while not always able to compel the states to act on behalf of the federal government, it now effectively "blackmails the states to implement its policies by threatening to deny them 'their fair share' of federal tax dollars should they object."[20]

Worse yet, the courts have done little to impede the attack on states' rights. For example, in 1992, the US Supreme Court struck down a case on the grounds of violating the Tenth Amendment for the first time in *fifty-five years.*[21] And what is to be made of states that attempt to fulfill duties of the federal government that the latter refuses to perform, thus threatening the welfare of a state's people? Must this always be followed by federal prosecution of the state?

What powers, then, *do* the states still retain? Regrettably, this is becoming more and more difficult to discern. In a nation where it has grown acceptable for the federal government to compel all Americans to purchase and retain health insurance—a power not in the articles of the Constitution and prohibited by the Tenth Amendment thereto—we can only begin to turn the tide through a general and widespread understanding of the Constitution's guaranteed protections. No matter where in the amendments lies a safeguard, it falls upon the citizenry to ensure its continuation. WE CONSERVATIVES BELIEVE in the authority of the states and thereby in the limitations of the federal government to act generally only in matters of national consequence—a principle underlined by the Tenth Amendment.

And to the Republic

WE CONSERVATIVES BELIEVE that among America's greatest assets is our built-in republic, not a presumed democracy. This distinction is very often confused but fundamental if we are to preserve our strong heritage and continued prosperity truly.

Our founders, through their studies of history and mankind, witnessed the inherent dangers associated with true democracy. Generally, a democracy is the "control of a group by the majority of its members."[22] While at first glance this notion appears rather fair, a more in-depth look reveals some apparent flaws. Democracies look for popular consensus when determining the fate of the group or individuals within that group but disregard the *rights* of those who find themselves in the minority. A democracy's concern rests wholly on the will of the majority at any given moment—it can overlook the rights and liberties of the minority when it pleases. The rights of the accused, in effect, do not exist, as they are at the whim of the majority's wishes.

Alternatively, in a republic, "power is held by the people and their elected officials," with certain immovable rights and guarantees protecting both the present majority and minority.[23] The people can still act but do so through the mechanisms their elected officials (chosen from among the same body of people) have created. Grievances, rather than being settled with the majority opinion, are resolved through a custom of laws, and an indifferent jury of peers may assign fault. And even in the jury room, rule by majority/democracy does not exist—unanimity generally is required.

The framers of the Constitution did not lose sight of these understandings, and they used the Constitution to protect many enshrined rights from governmental or individual intrusion. James Madison, on the matter of minority safety, noted that "it is of great importance in a republic not only to guard the society against the oppression of its rulers, but to guard one part of the society against the injustice of the other part. Different interests necessarily exist in different classes of citizens. If a majority be united by a common interest, the rights of the minority will be insecure."[24] Put another way, "Democracy is not freedom. Democracy is two wolves and a lamb voting on what to eat for lunch. Freedom comes from the recognition of certain rights which may not be taken, not even by a ninety-nine percent vote."[25] Why then do Americans frequently view the United States as a democracy when so clearly it is a republic? Is it that democracies ring of Democrats and republics ring of Republicans? Regardless the reason, and whatever one calls it, may we forever know that America's designation as the "land of the free" rests on certain protections for all—protections for more than the present majority, such as even the Pledge of Allegiance underscores. WE CONSERVATIVES BELIEVE a republic acts to ensure the safeguards of liberty and protect the privileges of those finding themselves in the minority—in essence, it is the bedrock of civilized society.

Trusting the Founders

WE CONSERVATIVES BELIEVE faith in history's time-tested truths is key to the continued success of our great nation and the endurance of limited government. The revolution through which America's founders excelled was an illumination of mankind's natural tendencies and governments' repeated shortcomings. As a consequence, the founders undertook the creation of a new government, one to which the sovereign people delegated certain powers of authority and retained others. Never before had such an entrustment been successfully achieved, yet for centuries it has largely remained intact, producing a society of prosperity and individual liberty. Only since the early twentieth century has the very *idea* of America come under relentless attack and the founders' experiences continually minimized.

But why should we care what the founders had to say or what their writings teach? How is their wisdom relevant in today's United States? The study of history is, by its nature, the acquisition of knowledge. Just as an expert in any other field must first learn his craft before excelling, so, too, must the citizenry learn its past to understand its present. Without such an effort, every successive generation begins anew, blind and adrift, leaving the country groundless and guessing—something further agitated in a republic such as ours. An individual, born innocent yet selfish, matures from a child to an adult after a collection of experiences influence his worldview. The individual learns to consider those outside his sphere and recognizes the existence of time before and after that of his own. Like the timeline of an individual, a country develops as well through its maturity. The hardships of history cement our common pursuits, while past sins steer us toward more noble convictions. The founding fathers lived through a moment of incredible political change and philosophical enlightenment. Their shared experiences, along with in-depth understandings of history, coupled to design the shared powers of government we continue to use today. For hundreds of years, they served as the bases of American political action and the groundwork upon which American exceptionalism swelled. They have dutifully served as the anchor in the turbulent sea of republican governance. Without history as our backbone, others who *do* grasp their pasts will overshadow us as America inevitably diminishes.

It is not always easy to trust the founders, especially in a new world of technology and internationalism. But such factors are all the more reason to remain vigilant against attacks from detractors and pessimists. If the Constitution is subject to informal dismissal, then in practice we have no Constitution at all. What will protect the rights of political minorities if legality is subjective? What will ensure the innocence of the accused until conviction? What will preserve the right of *all* to speak without censure? What will permit the people to protect themselves against their government by taking up arms if necessary? What will preserve power in the states or keep armed soldiers and police out of our homes? What will protect the citizenry from cruel and unusual punishments? These questions, and thousands more, have already been confronted by ancestors before us and enumerated as protections in the founding documents. Must we always begin again with each generation, living in an endless cycle of rebirth? Or can we finally learn to trust our founders to serve us once more, as they have time and again proven so effective at throughout the ages? Can we finally mature as a nation?

The founding fathers, just as all mankind, were imperfect beings. All were sinners, and all were contemplating things yet unknown. But what they left for us, most notably the Constitution, is firm but not unchangeable. If we, in modern America, wish to alter the Constitution, we can, as it has been successfully done twenty-seven times before. Yet it *should* be difficult to amend, for the stability of the Constitution depends on it. WE CONSERVATIVES BELIEVE, just as did James Madison in his dying days, "The advice nearest to [our hearts] and deepest in [our] convictions is that the Union of the States be cherished and perpetuated."[26]

INDIVIDUAL LIBERTY

Protect Freedom, Ensure Security

WE CONSERVATIVES BELIEVE government is intended to do two fundamental things: protect freedom and ensure security. An overly weak government will prove insufficient to guarantee either purpose, and an overly powerful government will certainly violate both intentions. That is, regarding the latter, an overly dominant central control will invariably become the very enemy against which government was intended to defend.

Prior to the enactment of the Constitution, the nation's central governing body was defined and run by the Articles of Confederation, yet the government created thereby was paralyzingly weak from the start. It had no power of taxation, so in turn no way to fund a military or repay debts; it maintained a unicameral Congress with no national court system or executive, thus no separation of powers; it had members who voted together as one state, not as individuals; it allowed states to coin individual currencies, minimizing the value of any attempted central currency; and it had no direct origin in itself, recognizing only the sovereignty of the states. While the founders created this body to avoid an overbearing central authority that might threaten their liberties, it proved insufficient even to protect those same rights, thus minimizing its primary purpose.

As such, the call for a new approach became apparent. By the late 1780s, a version of the Constitution we know today was circulating among the many states for proposed ratification. The document incorporated various remedies to the problems of the Articles and further protected the rights of citizens. After ratification, a wave of support to amend the Constitution dominated the political scene, with the intention being to include more specific provisions protecting the people from governmental intrusions. On June 8, 1789, James Madison made a speech in Congress proposing the first rough draft of what would become the Bill of Rights. In introducing such legislation, Madison reaffirmed the need to protect the citizenry from an overly large government: "If all power is subject to abuse, . . . it is possible the abuse of the powers of the general government may be guarded against in a more secure manner than is now done."[1] The Bill of Rights is unique in that it does not tell the citizenry what they *can* do; rather it tells the government what it *cannot* do.

Another example of the function and role of government can be found through Alexander Hamilton's writings in the *Federalist*, noting that "the principle purposes to be answered by union are these—the common defense of the members; the preservation of the public peace, as well against internal convulsions as external attacks."[2] *Limited government* is just that: limited. The extent of government in the lives of constituents should first run through a thick filter. That is, does this intrusion of government, in a fairly clear way, further protect freedom and ensure security? Absent an affirmative answer to this question, the action is by itself an abuse of governmental authority and naturally invalid.

The first founding document of our union shows the government as the protector of rights: the Declaration of Independence. WE CONSERVATIVES BELIEVE government's role is limited to extensions of its primary purposes of protecting freedom and ensuring security, and "That to secure these rights, Governments are instituted among Men, deriving their just powers from the consent of the governed."[3]

The Source of Individual Rights

Born at Liberty

WE CONSERVATIVES BELIEVE individual liberty is not a government-granted entitlement but rather an unalienable natural right. We believe governments are purposefully created to protect such rights, not to erode. Legitimate governments are established only with the consent of society and only to the effect that the formed government can advance the wellbeing of the governed at large. Therefore, it is not the citizenry who obtains their rights from a government; it is a government that obtains its rights from the people.

Growing throughout America in the eighteenth century was a defense of the rights inherent to all men and the realization that governmental intrusions of those rights were divergent from the fundamental purpose of government. The framers agreed that certain rights were so essential in the maintenance of a free people that virtually no government intrusion of those liberties could be justified. (Chief among these "untouchables" are the "1) freedom of conscience, (2) freedom of communication, (3) the right to be free from arbitrary laws, (4) the rights of assembly and petition, (5) the property right, [and] (6) the right of self-government."[4]

The founders' steady affirmation of natural rights is rooted in works composed by contemporary political thinkers before and during the American Revolution. John Locke, one of the most influential theorists studied by the framers, argued that men (in both private and public spheres) are required to obey the order of nature: "The law of nature stands as an eternal rule to all men, legislators as well as others. The rules that they make for other men's actions must, as well as their own and other men's actions, be conformable to the law of nature, *i.e.*, to the will of God, of which that is a declaration, and the fundamental law of nature being the preservation of mankind, no human sanction can be good, or valid against it."[5]

We Conservatives realize if a government is deemed to be the granter of rights, it can just as easily revoke those rights. Thomas Paine, in his 1791 *Rights of Man*, illustrated how "it is a perversion of terms to say, that a charter gives rights. It operates by a contrary effect, that of taking rights away. Rights are inherently in all the inhabitants; but charters, by annulling those rights, in the majority, leave the right by exclusion in the hands of a few."[6] More directly, "Man did not enter into society to become worse than he was before, nor to have fewer rights than he had before, but to have those rights better secured. His natural rights are the foundation of all his civil rights."[7] When the granting of rights is vested in the hands of governmental officials, the certainty for abuse of that authority is absolute.

A most powerful and noteworthy example showcasing the natural rights of individuals as vested in the people themselves is within the Declaration of Independence itself, which continually repeats the fundamentals of natural law and its coupled natural rights. Arguing for an "equal station to which the Laws of Nature and of Nature's God entitle them," it holds true "that all men are created equal, that they are endowed by their Creator with certain unalienable Rights, that among these are Life, Liberty and the pursuit of Happiness."[8] What's more, instead of a government being formed to impose individual rights upon its people, "Governments are instituted among Men, deriving their just powers from the consent of the governed." WE CONSERVATIVES BELIEVE a righteous society is not one that impresses selected and qualified "freedoms" onto its people; a just society communes in an effort to protect the very freedoms "endowed by their Creator"—a government is not only *unauthorized* to act as the source of liberty, but it is also by nature *unable.*

Two Societal Compacts

WE CONSERVATIVES BELIEVE the American people maintain their sovereignty over their government as ordained by the natural order of life. By nature, no one man has the legitimate right to rule over another man unilaterally. Achieving this can only occur if, by entering into a compact with others, those to be governed consent to be so ruled. This then becomes the only form of a just government.

To have a government of valid purpose, the people who are to be disposed to that government must first enter into two separate social compacts. The first of these compacts creates the body of people to be governed. It defines the extent of those people and the purpose for which they have so distinguished themselves. For Americans, this first compact is the Declaration of Independence, which stipulates that only from "the Consent of the Governed" can governments derive their "just Powers."[9] Further, "the only legitimate reason for consent is for the 'Safety and Happiness' of those who agree to be ruled."[10] By entering into this social body, each constituent "accepts the obligation to protect the rights of fellow citizens in return for protection of his own rights. The 'just Powers' of government are thus directed to the equal protection of the equal rights of those who consent to be governed."

The second compact under which this now-defined body enters is one that determines *how* they will govern. This compact establishes the precise form of government to be enacted and its interactions with the people. In essence, the second compact puts the first compact into practice. In the United States, this second compact is now the Constitution, under which the federal branches of government were created and are defined. With the consent of the governed, the Constitution was produced to "establish Justice, insure domestic Tranquility, provide for the common defence, promote the general Welfare, and secure the Blessings of Liberty."[11] Yet even though the citizenry have agreed to form a government to meet these ends, the ultimate sovereignty of those same people is not waived. Hence, to assure the protection of their natural rights, the populace retains their right to revise or abolish its current government, returning once more to the basis that no man can unjustly rule over another. As so, "when a long Train of Abuses and Usurpations, pursuing invariably the same Object, evinces a Design to reduce them under absolute Despotism, it is their Right, it is their Duty, to throw off such Government, and to provide new Guards for their future Security."[12] These two compacts, which are fundamental to any legitimate society, remain interlinked with each other—neither one becomes obsolete or irrelevant since government must continue to fit within their defined bounds. In a worthy and noble social order, there cannot be one compact without the other.

These compacts further articulate how the government is not the source of individual rights, as "Governments are instituted among Men" by the people.[13] The government is only suitable when within the restraints those people place upon it. In America's second compact, the framers attached an amendment that further evinced the natural quality of the rights held by the citizenry. While the Constitution does specify several rights of the people, the Ninth Amendment makes clear that the Constitution does not list all the rights of the people: "The enumeration in the Constitution, of certain rights, shall not be construed to deny or disparage others retained by the people."[14] If the Constitution granted rights to the people, then why would the Ninth Amendment exist? If the people only enjoyed liberties specifically identified, there would be no mention of other rights "retained by the people." Instead, as our founding fathers knew, the rights of the people do not come from a fluid body of men; their rights exist *because they are people.* WE CONSERVATIVES BELIEVE THE government is only just insofar as it propels the natural rights of the citizenry—rights with which the people are born.

The Rights to Property

WE CONSERVATIVES BELIEVE the right of every man to own and control his property is central to the themes of natural law and one of the principal purposes for which governments are instituted to protect. Although the defense of property is chief among the roles of governments and citizens alike, how to define and protect that property is an increasingly difficult undertaking to accomplish, particularly when the government and citizenry are so often at odds.

The entitlement to property, most fundamentally, can be defined as "the right to possess, use, and enjoy a determinate thing."[15] Alternatively, "This term in its particular application means 'that dominion which one man claims and exercises over the external things of the world, in exclusion of every other individual.' "[16] In property's grander understandings, "it embraces every thing to which a man may attach a value and have a right; and *which leaves to every one else the like advantage*." Thus, "a man's land, or merchandize, or money is called his property," as are "his opinions and the free communication of them. He has a property . . . in his religious opinions, . . . and in the safety and liberty of his person." For what greater purpose—if not at least equally so—can governments be created than to defend these natural and just rights? If not for the mutual protection of one's interests, as well as one's neighbors' interests, under the rule of law, on what substitute grounds can government exist? When a government thus exceeds its guardianship duties over individual property rights and embarks on confiscatory quests, few legitimate purposes are remaining for that particular government's existence to continue.

As illustrated in "The Source of Individual Rights—Born at Liberty," "Man did not enter into society to become worse than he was before, nor to have fewer rights than he had before, but to have those rights better secured."[17] Further, "Where an excess of power prevails, property of no sort is duly respected. No man is safe in his opinions, his person, his faculties, or his possessions."[18] Instead, "Government is instituted to protect property of every sort; as well as that which lies in the various rights of individuals . . . . This being the end of government, that alone is a *just* government, which *impartially* secures to every man, whatever is his *own*." Government is not just, nor is property secure, "where the property which a man has in his personal safety and liberty, is violated by arbitrary seizures of one class of citizens for the service of the rest. . . . If the United States mean to obtain or deserve the full praise due to wise and just governments, they will equally respect the rights of property, and property in rights." WE CONSERVATIVES BELIEVE that among the chief roles of every government is the protection of its constituents' property, both that which is material and that which is intangible, for without such guarantees the very purpose of sound governance is undermined.

THE SECOND AMENDMENT

A History of Purpose

WE CONSERVATIVES BELIEVE in the promotion of firearm rights and their protection as guaranteed by the Second Amendment to the Constitution. We encourage the safe use of weaponry in self- and home-defense, hunting, sport, and marksmanship. Further, understanding the history surrounding the right to bear arms, we maintain weaponry as a deterrent to tyrannical governments and the oppressive state and to defend our homeland from foreign invasion.

Before the American Revolution, the colonies formed individual militias with allegiance to British rule. As sentiment for the dissolution of British ties grew, some members of these militias sought to develop their own armed forces independent of the earlier, British-subjected militias. These new American militias moved to arm themselves with ammunition, firearms, and other weaponry to give their new organizations legitimacy and influence. Upon learning of the attempted arms build-up, the British Parliament launched an arms embargo on the American colonies, severely restricting the colonists' access to firearms and impeding the development of the new militias. These British motives were, of course, opposed by American colonists who cited natural law, common law, the laws of the individual colonies, and their militia laws to support claims of governmental overreach.[19]

For the Americans, the War for Independence was fought by a collaboration of these newly split militias, along with the Continental Army created by Congress. Following the war, the perceived historical threat of standing armies was so dangerous that the American army was virtually eliminated, leaving the union's defense largely to the states themselves—that is, to the militias. When, later, the Constitution was under consideration for ratification, many realized that in the event of any significant military threat to the United States, this patchwork of militias might not be a sufficient enough force to ensure success over the enemy. Thus, arguments arose that would allow the federal government (through the new Constitution) "To raise and support armies; . . . To provide and maintain a navy; . . . To provide for calling forth the militia to execute the laws of the union, suppress insurrections and repel invasions; . . . [and] To provide for organizing, arming, and disciplining, the militia."[20] Yet to ease the states' concerns that an overly powerful central body might strip the original militias of their standing (just as the British had tried to do through their arms embargo), James Madison penned what would become the Second Amendment: "A well regulated Militia, being necessary to the security of a free State, the right of the people to keep and bear Arms, shall not be infringed."[21] This text, the final and thus ratified version of the Second Amendment, in fact, protects two liberties: the right of a militia to exist through regulation and the right of individuals to own and use firearms. To ensure the militias were both well prepared and armed, Alexander Hamilton argued that the arms must remain in the hands of the people. In the event of a crisis, the states would experience great hindrances if they first needed to assemble the militiamen, equip them, train them, and only then send them into the field. "A tolerable expertness in military movements is a business that requires time and practice," and "to oblige the great body of the yeomanry and of the other classes of the citizens to be under arms for the purpose of going through military exercises and evolutions . . . would be a real grievance to the people and a serious public inconvenience and loss."[22] Hamilton concluded that to meet the demands of national defense, "little more can reasonably be aimed at with respect to *the people at large* than to have them properly armed and equipped."[23] WE CONSERVATIVES BELIEVE the Second Amendment enumerates two truths: to have a free state, we need a defense force, and to have a free people, we need an armed citizenry.

Misplaced Fear

WE CONSERVATIVES BELIEVE continued restrictions on the ownership and usage of personal weaponry do little to reduce the occurrence of crime and often increase illegal activity. Guns and other weaponry do not by themselves commit crime, and greater respect for, and understandings of, the proper uses of arms is our first step in minimizing violent crimes that include such armaments.

Violent crime did not commence with the advent of guns; instead, it has been a relentless thorn in humanity's side since the dawn of man. Yet what is it about gun ownership that draws such particularly negative attention? Why does a broad swath of the country find guns both menacing and inappropriate? Cannot a crime be committed with either a gun or a knife? A baton, an arrow, or an ax? And what would be the effect of removing the protections guaranteed by the Second Amendment?

Recall the Eighteenth Amendment that prohibited "the manufacture, sale, or transportation of intoxicating liquors."[24] The impact of this outright ban resulted in an immediate increase in demand for the now-illegal alcohol, turning many Americans into overnight criminals for their participation in the trade. Courts and justice departments grew overwhelmed with associated cases while gangs and organized crime found a greatly profitable business. We can expect more of the same should even larger prohibitions on gun ownership continue, thus turning Americans into criminals, flooding our courts, encouraging secretive dealings, and deeper organized crime. WE CONSERVATIVES BELIEVE the implications of further restrictions on gun ownership are not just bad for the courts and American people—it violates the natural law that governs the government.

Punishing the Innocent

WE CONSERVATIVES BELIEVE excessive restrictions on firearms harm the innocent far more than they do the guilty. Revoking the citizenry's ability to defend itself does not reduce crime nor does it weaken the power of the wicked. Instead, those immersed in evil will relentlessly and successfully obtain the very weapons the ruling class would rather the citizens not acquire, leaving the innocent little more than helpless against evermore sophisticated and violent crimes.

Every time there is a violent use of guns in the commission of a crime, we readily hear public cries against the gun. But who is actually to blame in each case? Should culpability be attached to the gun that acted as a medium between the offender and the victim? Is it the gun that is the source of evil? Or is it the offender who perpetrated the crime? Repeating an argument for the argument's sake (that firearms are the problem) does not necessarily make the argument any more powerful.

On the same day in December 2012, two similar and wretched acts of evil occurred on opposite ends of the planet. In Chengping, China, a knife-wielding, thirty-six-year-old male entered an elementary school where he attacked and slashed twenty-two schoolchildren and one adult.[25] Meanwhile, in Newtown, Connecticut, a twenty-year-old gunman also entered an elementary school and killed twenty children and six adults.[26] Exceptionally similar crimes on remarkably similar victims committed under the same underlying standard: evil.

If evil in its most basic form does not exist on Earth—that is, that most bad acts are simply the outcome of circumstances—there remains no other reasonable explanation for such atrocious conflicts with life's natural order. Further restrictions on the mediums through which crimes can be committed will do little to reduce the likelihood of such crimes occurring. The wicked man who seeks to hunt innocent children will pursue his sinful cause regardless of the weapon he can obtain.

Other Western countries have, indeed, proposed and passed strict gun laws in attempts to minimize ownership and crime, but the results of such bans were not as their proponents had hoped. Consider the United Kingdom, where "within a decade of the handgun ban and the confiscation of handguns from registered owners, crime with handguns had *doubled*.... Gun crime, not a serious problem in the past, now is."[27] In Australia, a prospective gun owner required a "genuine reason" to purchase a firearm. "Hunting and protecting crops from feral animals were genuine reasons—personal protection wasn't.... The government also launched a forced buyback scheme to remove thousands of firearms from private hands." The result: a sharp rise in the use of *unregistered* handguns during the commission of crimes, a 40 percent increase in assaults and a 20 percent increase in sexual assaults. These "cautionary tales of gun control" should act as further evidence against continued and deepening restrictions on firearm ownership in the United States. WE CONSERVATIVES BELIEVE unremitting attempts to restrict firearm ownership among upstanding citizens serve to harm those very citizens and further expose them to the dangers of evil.

Crime Correlations

WE CONSERVATIVES BELIEVE the citizen must first equip himself with sound information regarding violent crimes committed with firearms prior to asserting that evil sprouts from guns. It is easy to lodge an argument not based in fact and even easier to ignore the truth when so confronted.

Consider, for example, the Commonwealth of Virginia. A recent analysis of the association between gun ownership and violent crimes involving guns tells a story most often silenced in the press. Since 2006, gun sales in Virginia have risen 73 percent while at the same time it has seen a 27 percent drop in violent crimes involving guns.[28] But "for years, we've heard the shrill voices of those who hate your guns. 'More guns on the street means more crime!' 'More guns equals more murder!' and so on. And yet, clearly that's not the case."

Or consider another example of the alleged expansion of mass murders in the United States. The reality is that "mass shootings are no more common [today] than they have been in past decades, despite the impression given by the media. In fact, the high point for mass killings in the U.S. was *1929*."[29]

In response to mass shootings, knee-jerk reactions have frequently called for the implementation of more "gun-free zones," wherein it is a crime to be in possession of a firearm within the zone's boundaries. These areas, rather than protecting the intended people, create "helpless-victim zone[s] . . .. Preventing any adult [in a gun-free-zone] from having access to a firearm eliminates any chance the killer can be stopped in time to prevent a rampage."[30] In 2012, a shooter entered a movie theater and killed twelve people during the showing of *Batman*. The shooter had the choice of seven nearby cinemas at which he might unleash his evil plot. "The [theater] the killer ultimately chose wasn't the closest, but it was the only one that posted signs saying it banned concealed handguns carried by law-abiding individuals. All of the other theaters allowed the approximately 4 percent of Colorado adults who have a concealed-handgun permit to enter with their weapons." The reality of evil shows that the possibility of being charged with carrying a firearm in a gun-free zone will not sway a person intent on committing mass murder—in fact, it will encourage the commission of his offense.

Indeed, gun-free zones are so counterproductive that "with just one single exception (the 2011 Tucson attack on Congresswoman Gabrielle Giffords) every public shooting since at least 1950 in the U.S. in which more than three people have been killed has taken place where citizens are not allowed to carry guns." WE CONSERVATIVES BELIEVE a nation cannot rid itself of evil through legislation, and a well-armed citizenry is one of the best counterforces we can utilize in its opposition.

Counterforce Against Evil

WE CONSERVATIVES BELIEVE evil comes in many forms and on many faces and, most regrettably, can hide extraordinarily well. But well-armed and innocent citizens universally act as the greatest first barrier to untethered deviltry.

Consider this observation from eighteenth-century political theorist Thomas Paine on the proper usage and ownership of firearms:

> The supposed quietude of a good man allures the ruffian; while on the other hand, arms like laws discourage and keep the invader and the plunderer in awe, and preserve order in the world as well as property. The balance of power is the scale of peace. The same balance would be preserved were all the world destitute of arms, for all would be alike; but since some *will not*, others *dare not* lay them aside. . . . Horrid mischief would ensue were one half the world deprived of the use of them; for while avarice and ambition have a place in the heart of man, the weak will become a prey to the strong.[31]

Just as timid men invite those who oppress, armed men of conviction dishearten potential oppressors.

It is of further importance—far more than continual quasi-prohibitions of firearms—that there be proper enforcement of gun laws. The restrictions on gun ownership, their sale, license renewal, carrying, and storing are already burdensome. But the execution of those laws can be unsuitably and inconsistently applied, and for those who consider deterrence when developing the commission of a crime, this inconsistency regularly acts like an escape hatch through which they slip after committing the offense. As the Bible notices, "Because the sentence against an evil deed is not executed speedily, the heart of the children of man is fully set to do evil."[32] WE CONSERVATIVES BELIEVE gun ownership is a serious and solemn right that serves as a protector for the innocent; we demand reliable enforcement of pertinent laws and regulations against those who offend and abuse the privileges and liberties of the guiltless.

A History of Oppression

WE CONSERVATIVES BELIEVE the Second Amendment's purpose extends beyond protecting citizens from other citizens—it also protects citizens from their government. Consistent and extensive gun control laws throughout history have shown a governmental propensity to consequently oppress and control its populace, frequently in utterly horrendous manners.

In the 1920s, the Soviet Union passed severe restrictions on gun ownership with the intended targets being political opponents and farming communities.[33] From 1929 to 1949, nearly twenty million civilians were rounded up and executed.

In the 1930s, Nazi Germany banned the possession of firearms and required licensing measures for those already in custody of handguns. Thereafter, from 1933 to 1945, the Nazis exterminated twenty million political opponents and those deemed "enemies of the state."

During the 1950s, Red China imposed gun bans and promised the death or imprisonment of anyone resisting government schemes, and it pledged the death penalty to anyone supplying weaponry to such "criminals." Between 1949 and 1976, twenty to thirty-five million civilians were killed, mostly suspected political opponents.

From 1960 to 1981, Guatemala enforced bans on guns and sharp tools, and the government bestowed itself with confiscation powers. Over 200,000

Guatemalans were executed during the period, mostly all at the hands of government-sanctioned designs.

In Uganda from 1970 to 1979, 300,000 Christians and political enemies were murdered after the government restricted the rights of gun owners and granted itself the powers of warrantless searches and speculative confiscation.

From 1975 to 1979, Cambodia enacted various policies that made the possession of firearms and ammunition exceptionally difficult. Its government then systematically seized, tortured, and killed suspected offenders of various "crimes," including academics, professionals, and certain ethnic minorities. By 1979, two million were dead.

In 1994, Rwandan citizens were living under strict gun controls and were required to justify any need for weapons to their government. Concealed weapons were banned, and the government held confiscatory powers. In that same year, 800,000 Tutsi people were slaughtered—nearly 20 percent of the country's entire population.

The argument over proper gun control often rests solely on relations between citizen and citizen, but we give so little attention to the threat of governmental encroachments that evolve into governmental crimes against humanity. Just as a victim in a gun-free zone is defenseless against a shooter on a rampage, so too is the citizen defenseless in a gun-free country. James Madison wrote that America's Constitution preserves a unique advantage of being armed, something "which Americans possess over the people of almost every other nation, . . . [where] the governments are afraid to trust the people with arms."[34] And to ensure the government remains thus fearful of the people and continues to preserve freedoms, Thomas Jefferson asked, "What country can preserve its liberties if its rulers are not warned, from time to time, that the people preserve the spirit of resistance? Let them take arms."[35] "To disarm the people," Founder George Mason argued, is "the best and most effectual way to enslave them."[36] Chillingly, one of recent history's most notorious and evil government leaders thoroughly feared an armed citizenry when he, Adolph Hitler, argued, "The most foolish mistake we could possibly make would be to allow the subjected races to possess arms. History shows that all conquerors who have allowed their subject races to carry arms have prepared their own downfall by so doing."[37] WE CONSERVATIVES

BELIEVE every great nation is dependent on a strong, free people who do not fear their government but whose government maintains a healthy fear of its people—something best accomplished with an armed citizenry.

A Free Press

WE CONSERVATIVES BELIEVE overt and evident assaults against a citizenry's liberty, as well as—and perhaps far more dangerously so—by slow and continual degrees to the contrary of the people's will by representative bodies under the pretense of enshrining their freedoms, endangers that very liberty.

To have a truly free people, a genuinely free press is required. Retaining a free press is not necessarily defined by its extent of objectivity nor by any given outlet's encompassment of countering views. Instead, measure a free press by its *independence*. Independence of thought, independence of influence, and, most critically, independence from government. For nearly all Americans, the press serves as the source of information and news regarding the proceedings and intentions of their government, and what greater role can the press hold than that of watchdog over the doings of those who represent the people? For a country birthed in liberty, it is vital to have a press independent of governmental influence and its associated pressure, for when the latter body assumes the role of the employer over the former, what amount of uninfluenced reporting can we expect? A press subordinated to its government is a press that will do the bidding of that government without due care for fact or reality. A *dependent* press is dangerous to liberty; it minimizes the independence of thought and influence and seeks to eliminate perspectives counter to that of the government's—and now the press's—interests.

Of even more significant threat to liberty than a dependent press pandering to its parental government is a press sanctioning governmental encroachments. Little-by-little, in collaboration with each other, they erode the blessings of liberty under the veil of some greater good long in the distance, requiring regrettable sacrifices of freedom today:

> Where utopianism is advanced through gradualism rather than revolution, albeit steady and persistent as in democratic

> societies, it can deceive and disarm an unsuspecting population, which is largely content and passive. It is sold as reforming and improving the existing society's imperfections and weaknesses without imperiling its basic nature. Under these conditions, it is mostly ignored, dismissed, or tolerated by much of the citizenry and celebrated by some. Transformation is deemed innocuous, well-intentioned, and perhaps constructive but not a dangerous trespass on fundamental liberties.[38]

WE CONSERVATIVES BELIEVE American civil discourse is reliant, in part, on a press that adequately and accurately (though not necessarily objectively) distributes the doings of the people's government for their consumption and analysis independent of governmental influence, whether directly or indirectly through the press.

THE LEGISLATURE

A Government, With and For

WE CONSERVATIVES BELIEVE the original states, when forming into a union under the Constitution, were not subjecting themselves to the boundless enterprises of a central government; instead, they delegated *some* of their sovereign authority for the betterment of their interests and the union at large. A federal government was not designed by the states to act *above* the states but instead *with* and *for* the states.

Barely a decade after the Constitution's ratification, President John Adams and his Federalist Party enacted a set of laws (known as the Alien and Sedition Acts) which criminalized certain conduct of private citizens and aliens who opposed the Federalists' initiatives. So alarming was the overt interference with fundamental rights that some of America's most prominent statesmen came forward to object to the proposed expansion of governmental power, although they did so in secret to avoid the penalties under the very law itself. Adams's own vice president, Thomas Jefferson, composed what became known as the Kentucky Resolutions, in which he blasted the acts' unconstitutional authority and deemed them "unauthoritative, void, and of no force."[1] And when in the context of the union's interplay with the states' rights over themselves, he remained very clear as to the proper relationship between the two:

> *Resolved*, That the several States composing the United States of America, are not united on the principle of unlimited submission to their General Government; but that, by compact under the style and title of a Constitution for the United States, and of Amendments thereto, they constituted a General Government for special purposes,—delegated to that Government certain definite powers, reserving, each State to itself, the residuary mass of right to their own self-government.

Jefferson further articulated (as later discussed in "States, Congress, and the Veto—Nullification") that states retained the power to judge over the constitutionality of federal law: "that to this compact each State acceded as a State, and is an integral party, its co-States forming, as to itself, the other party: that the Government created by this compact was not made the exclusive or final judge of the extent of the powers delegated to itself; since that would have made its discretion, and not the Constitution, the measure of its powers."[2] Jefferson believed a government—particularly regarding those powers delegated to the legislature—ought to be well defined and limited, and any powers not so defined by the Constitution did not exist under the federal government's control but instead remained in the states and the people. WE CONSERVATIVES BELIEVE permitting a central government the ability to interfere with the rights of the states (and, by consequence, those of the people) is destructive to the American style of federalism—a style that has proven most effectual in protecting the individual liberties of a free people.

Enumerated Powers

Defining the Scope

WE CONSERVATIVES BELIEVE in a Constitution of enumerated powers through which Congress is only permitted to act under one of these specified authorities. All proposed legislation must first be attached to one of the enumerated powers or else face a striking from the checks performed by other areas of government; absent such a balance, we easily discount the authority of the Constitution.

The Constitution, along with its amendments, provides for the express authorities of the federal legislative body. "The powers of the federal government are enumerated," argued James Madison. "It can only operate in certain cases: it has legislative powers on defined and limited objects, beyond which it cannot extend its jurisdiction."[3] These definitions of power were intended to limit the scope of a central government and to ensure that the states retained most of the lawmaking authority. In fact, two Amendments directly attempt to further the protections of individual liberty and states' rights. With the Ninth, the framers addressed rights of the people not specifically discussed in the Constitution: "The enumeration in the Constitution, of certain rights, shall not be construed to deny or disparage others retained by the people."[4] And the Tenth Amendment underlines the foundation of federalism: "The powers not delegated to the United States by the Constitution, nor prohibited by it to the States, are reserved to the States respectively, or to the people."[5]

Modern constitutional interpretations by governmental activists have moved the meaning of enumeration away from that of a specific list and instead toward a list of implications. WE CONSERVATIVES BELIEVE Congress, as realistically the most powerful branch, is best controlled when forced to remain within the bounds of its articulated authority.

The Overlooked Constitution

WE CONSERVATIVES BELIEVE legislation enacted outside the Constitution's scope of enumerated authorities is inappropriate and illegitimate. Congress does not retain plenary power in all corners of American living, and it is this reality that was meant to create a government of limited means.

The modern, mainstream interpretation of the Constitution is radically different from that of our founders. Congress has granted itself (and the judiciary has reaffirmed) virtually uninhibited powers—if Congress has the will to pass a law that restrains liberty, then it now, by default, has the way. The judiciary (which has also assumed new roles) will rarely strike down a law because it expands beyond Congress's enumerated powers and instead will endorse perverse skewings of constitutional law. Now, for example, the judiciary has permitted Congress to tax Americans for their failure to purchase health insurance under the legal fiction that by taxing a non-action (rather than mandating a purchase), Congress is within its legal boundaries (the power to tax). Only through a blind and ignorant reading of the Constitution can one come to this understanding of it and suggest that inaction may create taxation. Taxing inaction is effectively synonymous with mandating an action, for either way the citizen is losing capital. This is not liberty. The lack of a prohibition does not equate to a license to prescribe.

A government set on expanding its control requires it to overlook limits set upon it by the Constitution. WE CONSERVATIVES BELIEVE, as did

James Madison, "the powers delegated by the . . . Constitution to the federal government are few and defined. Those which are to remain in the State governments are numerous and indefinite."[6]

Secondary Sources

WE CONSERVATIVES BELIEVE other sources of power also found in the Constitution may aid the implementation of the Constitution's enumerated powers, yet these supplemental sources are only proper if used to make an enumerated power more workable. That is, Congress may only craft laws using a supplemental power if the failure to do so would otherwise prevent Congress from employing an enumerated power.

Of the few secondary sources of power Congress has in the Constitution, the Necessary and Proper Clause of Article. I. is among the most cited. Through it, "The Congress shall have Power . . . To make all Laws which shall be necessary and proper for carrying into Execution the foregoing Powers, and all other Powers vested by this Constitution in the Government of the United States, or in any Department or Officer thereof."[7] This clause follows a list of specific powers delineated for Congress that the founders considered numerous enough for that body, leaving any remainders to the states and people. The enumerated powers and the Necessary and Proper Clause are coupled together and uniquely tied to one another. Yet this clause, as with so many others in the Constitution, is rarely taken at face value. The text alone makes the original intent obvious, permitting the government to extend to itself other legislative controls only necessary for the execution of the enumerated powers. This was not meant to indicate (as people who view the Constitution as "living and breathing" believe) Congress may act in any realm remotely related to a listed power. Rather, Congress must act within the bounds of the enumerations and can, from time-to-time when proper, use other means to make certain those enumerations are practically satisfied. Only then can Congress reach to other means of legislation, with the end purpose always being the fulfillment of an enumerated power.

For ambitious politicians who seek a continually larger government, the Constitution's enumerated powers should act as a barrier for many of their proposed projects since often they will not fit into a specific power source. But instead, these politicians turn to provisions like the Necessary and

Proper Clause to presuppose that it grants broad powers of ambiguous bounds and argue that seemingly anything can be considered necessary if done for the general welfare of the people. This unilateral grab of power pushes some to believe that clauses like the Necessary and Proper Clause are too vague and open-ended, and they raise comparable arguments made during the Constitutional Convention and the push for the Constitution's ratification.

In countering similar concerns over this very clause, the "Father of the Constitution," James Madison, argued that without the Necessary and Proper Clause "the whole Constitution would be a dead letter."[8] Madison noted that without the clause, it would become impossible for Congress to utilize its enumerated powers, and it would consistently face governmental checks on even the most fundamental legislation. He grasped the impossibility of listing all the potential circumstances present and future Congresses would face along with the corresponding legal remedies to confront those challenges: "Had the Convention attempted a positive enumeration of the powers necessary and proper for carrying their other powers into effect, the attempt would have involved a complete digest of laws on every subject to which the Constitution relates; accommodated too not only to the existing state of things, but to all the possible changes which futurity may produce."[9] Thus, Madison alternatively believed that those who rejected the proposed Necessary and Proper Clause did not actually oppose the "*substance*" of the clause but rather its "*form*," for, without the substance, the remainder of the Constitution would be ineffective. WE CONSERVATIVES BELIEVE that present-day Modernists have materialized the very threats feared by those who originally opposed broad powers and now overlook the powers granted in the Constitution by improperly applying supplemental authorities.

Health Insurance

An Attack on Liberty

WE CONSERVATIVES BELIEVE the federal legislature does not have the authority to require individuals to purchase services or products, and the

Constitution explicitly prohibits any such exercise of power. Most recently and of most deliberate violation of this principle is the Patient Protection and Affordable Care Act, or, as more commonly called, Obamacare.

Under Obamacare, every citizen is required to obtain health insurance either privately, through an employer, Medicare, Medicaid, or another government-sponsored program. If an individual chooses not to purchase insurance, he receives a tax penalty—an arbitrary monetary amount determined by Congress. The alleged purpose behind this tax penalty is to cover the gap in the insurance pool's funding by those who opt-out of the insurance mandate. Obamacare intends to fund itself, generally, through the collection of mandated insurance premiums and taxes on those who decide not to participate.

The primary ground upon which proponents of Obamacare rest their arguments is in the Commerce Clause of the Constitution, which states, "Congress shall have Power . . . To regulate Commerce with foreign Nations, and among the several States, and with the Indian tribes."[10] In the last hundred years, the Commerce Clause has grown into Congress's most abused source of power, and consecutive Congresses have consistently expanded the clause into distortions for which the clause was never intended.

One particular misrepresentation that eventually aided the implementation of Obamacare was upheld by the Supreme Court in 1942 and has become precedent for numerous legal questions. In 1938, the Agricultural Adjustment Act was enacted to replace earlier New Deal legislation that had been found unconstitutional. The 1938 act restricted the amount of wheat a farmer could grow in an attempt to control the supply of wheat in the market and the price thereof. The general source of power Congress used to create this law was that found in the Commerce Clause, arguing that wheat farming is a matter that concerns interstate economic activity. When an Ohio farmer was found to be growing wheat in excess of this limit, he received a fine in accordance with the law. The farmer's surplus wheat had never been used for market sale and instead remained within his family for their personal consumption. Nevertheless, when a lawsuit ensued, the Supreme Court held that because the farmer had grown wheat he chose not to sell, his choosing *not to sell* nonetheless had an impact on interstate commerce (that is, through a lower supply of wheat in the market than had he entered the wheat into the steam of commerce, no matter how negligible his participation would have been).[11] If all the farmers who grew wheat retained some for personal consumption, the Court argued, that retention would have a substantial impact on interstate commerce. This "aggregation theory" thus allowed Congress to regulate farmers who did not participate in the marketplace under the pretense that their absence from the market affected interstate commerce—in effect, Congress could now regulate *inactivity.*

This same perverse argument is the basis for Obamacare. Since there is nowhere in the Constitution that authorizes Congress to require the purchase of health insurance, the 111th Congress voted on party lines to create that power through the Commerce Clause, just as was upheld in the 1942 wheat farmer case. The effects of health insurance and the medical industry are ones that cross state lines, argued Democrats, and are consequently susceptible to regulation under the interstate Commerce Clause. Furthermore, if an individual chooses not to purchase health insurance (that is, chooses to be inactive), he is presumably affecting those who *are* participating in insurance schemes. Thus, when that person remains insurance-free, he can be fined with a tax-penalty for his inactivity. WE CONSERVATIVES BELIEVE this attack on individual liberty is an extraordinary distortion of the true intent of the Commerce Clause and unquestionably unconstitutional.

The Lack of Avoidance

WE CONSERVATIVES BELIEVE the unconstitutionality of the mandated insurance program was further compressed with its upholding by the Supreme Court in 2012, and the nature of the law sets a perilous course for republican-styled governance.

Supporters of Obamacare will suggest that the requirement to purchase health insurance is actually not a requirement at all. Indeed the law does not explicitly order Americans to purchase insurance but instead punishes those who do not buy the service. Is that not in reality the exact same thing? Does this not erode the individual liberty upon which America was so deeply founded? Never before has the federal government required (with the added threat of severe penalty) the purchase of anything for merely being alive. In all previous regulations and laws passed through the Commerce Clause, the citizen had a choice. Even the wheat farmer, with his excess levels of wheat, could decide congressional rules pertaining to his farming were too restrictive, and so pursue other crops or lifestyles. But with Obamacare, there is no escape until death. There is no alternative path for the individual if he decides, for whatever reason, not to buy health insurance.

Proponents of Obamacare will also try to lure the undecided by presenting monetary figures of alleged deficit savings and debt reductions. But these deflective matters are subject to the most extreme manipulations and are nevertheless immaterial. Whether or not Obamacare affects the nation's bottom-line does not, therefore, make it appropriate. Simply because one policy or another would help or hinder the economy does not, by its own accord, make it suitable. Would it be legitimate to unilaterally confiscate every millionaire's assets simply because it would affect America's financial situation? Of course not, for this, too, would not overcome constitutional scrutiny.

But if Congress does not have the enumerated authority to enact measures such as Obamacare, where precisely in the Constitution is it prohibited? This very dangerous idea (that without an explicity Constitutional ban Congress might act as it pleases) is central to the need for the Bill of Rights. The Tenth Amendment greatly limits the power of the federal government and leaves to the states and people all remaining "powers not delegated to the United States by the Constitution."[12] Therefore, because the Constitution did not delegate such powers to it, the federal legislature cannot enact legislation like Obamacare—the silence of the Constitution is the ban.

The Tenth Amendment does not mean, however, that the states themselves may not enact laws that require health insurance, such as Massachusetts did. That the states may indeed try different policies is the beauty of the relationship between the states, for it allows them to act as "laboratories of democracy."[13] If a citizen of Massachusetts, for example, decides he is unsatisfied with that state's insurance scheme, not only is it easier for him to lobby elected officials in his state rather than the US capital, but the citizen can also move to another state if he so chooses and avoid the mandate altogether. This same notion is how states (not the federal government) can require car insurance, for not only is the citizen able to move about the states in avoidance, but he can also choose not to drive at all if so wished and thus circumvent the legislation. With Obamacare, not only can Americans not move to other states to escape the unconstitutional law, they cannot even change their routines, for as long as they are alive, they are bound to it. And once the precedent is locked in, what will stop the government from requiring Americans to purchase anything else? WE CONSERVATIVES BELIEVE Obamacare is unconstitutional, a violation of the Tenth Amendment, and an unparalleled interference with personal liberty.

The Entitlement State

Missing a Definition

WE CONSERVATIVES BELIEVE a fundamental difference between us on the Right and Liberals on the Left is our approach to welfare and entitlement programs. For Conservatives, the welfare state is dangerously and inappropriately broad and demanding. For Liberals, its size can never be large enough.

When a Conservative is asked precisely what conservatism stands for, there are basic and generally universal understandings of its positions. For example, "We believe in freedom and liberty, and we're for low taxes, less government, traditional values, and a strong national defense."[14] But regarding liberalism, what precisely does *it* stand for? The trouble for the Left in answering this question (beyond broad and feel-good initiatives) is that Liberals simply cannot answer it and still maintain their liberalism. At the core of liberalism is an ideology that believes "everything works on a case-by-case basis."[15] If a Liberal were to propose a definition of his sect's beliefs—that is, to promote an overarching and collective principle—he could not, therefore, approach circumstances individually and would instead be bound by an objective standard. Thus, for Liberals, there forever remains an internal struggle between steadfast holdings and the flexibility that comes with subjectivity.

This same struggle is at the core of the liberal welfare state. Just as the Left will not (cannot) articulate its central premises, neither can it define the scope and breadth of any of its entitlement longings. "Liberal rhetoric never engages this issue: what would be the size and nature of a welfare state that was not contemptibly austere, that did not urgently need a larger budget and a broader agenda?"[16] Nor does it provide "instructive examples of social programs that are too expensive, too intrusive, or demand too much of government and too little of their beneficiaries."[17] And so, being in accordance with how Liberals will not define their primary holdings, they also will not identify a welfare state that is indeed adequate and in no need of further expansion.

For the Left to supply an elaboration of any "big ideas," those same ideas would "have the unintended but unavoidable consequence of making clear what [those ideas are] *not* supposed to do."[18] Providing immovable and principle-based foundational holdings would just as well define where liberalism should not venture and the limits of where government (from their perspective) belongs. By evading any such clarity, Liberals can avoid inadvertently "restraining" themselves to their own "beliefs." Instead, they can argue that every potential difficulty that arises requires individual attention not otherwise provided through alternative fashions. Just as much, neither should the range of welfare entitlements be definitively labeled, for "every problem deserves a program." Absent any hardline standards and beliefs (analogous to those we Conservatives endorse), "liberalism has no authoritative way to tell anyone who's dissatisfied, either with the contours of his own life or the condition of society, that his grievance does not deserve to be taken seriously and alleviated through a program of its own." Consequently, the Left cradles the welfare state, and the entitlement nation has a flag-bearer around which it can rally. WE CONSERVATIVES BELIEVE the Left's lack of precise and clear positions has allowed it to foster calls for larger welfare initiatives and concurrently expand the power of the federal government.

Fiscally Infeasible

WE CONSERVATIVES BELIEVE the general inability of the Left to articulate its chief holdings, as well as the absence of specific barriers beyond which government must not reach, enables an erosion of the constitutional role of government and the promotion of ever-decreasing personal responsibility.

The explosion of governmental interference into the lives of private citizens primarily began during the Great Depression under the administration of President Franklin D. Roosevelt. The dire economic circumstances created an opportunity for overly ambitious politicians and bureaucrats to craft rules and legislation that allegedly promoted the general welfare of the nation and which have proved difficult to roll back:

> [Under FDR,] an array of federal projects, entitlements, taxes, and regulations known as the New Deal, breached the Constitution's firewalls. At first, the Supreme Court fought back, striking down New Deal programs as exceeding the limits of federal constitutional authority, violating state sovereignty, and trampling on private property rights. But rather than seek an expansion of federal power through the amendment process, which would likely have blunted Roosevelt's ambitions, Roosevelt threatened the very makeup of the Court by proposing to pack it with sympathetic justices who would go along with his counterrevolution.[19]

Yet contrary to broad belief, the policies of FDR's New Deal did little to minimize the effects and duration of the Great Depression. Rather, it was "industrial expansion resulting from World War II [that] eventually ended the Great Depression, not the New Deal. Indeed, the enormous tax and regulatory burden imposed on the private sector by the New Deal prolonged the economic recovery."[20] But regardless of what indeed ended the Great Depression, one other certainty is known: "the New Deal changed America's Constitution from one where the powers of government were enumerated into one where they were innumerable."[21] Its foremost success, rather than remedying widespread economic hardship, was "the evisceration of the principle that government, especially the federal government, has no rightful business undertaking a whole range of social improvements, no matter how gratifying the beneficiaries might find them."[22] Having removed such a barrier, "Liberals could frame the politics of the welfare state as a contest between the compassionate party that wants the government to give things to people and do things for them, and the mean-spirited party that wants to deprive people of all those indispensable and beneficial things."

With the demonization of Conservatives underway, Liberals could promote their welfare programs without having to discuss their inability of paying for them openly. Instead, a fiscal delusion was and is candidly embraced which holds that "the welfare state programs will pay for themselves," or that simply the "very, very, very rich people and giant corporations will pick up the tab; the rest of us only have to chip in to cover the tip."[23] Thus, the Left has successfully imposed in many minds (including those who preach it) an unattainable and unrealistic belief that "every household can be a net importer of the wealth redistributed by the government." WE CONSERVATIVES BELIEVE the lack of definitive and consistent principles among the Left have, with time, transformed it into a sect which embraces larger government intervention, less personal responsibility, and more redistributive schemes.

IMMIGRATION AND LEGALITY

Not a Birthright

WE CONSERVATIVES BELIEVE immigration is a prime factor in any nation seeking continued prosperity, yet the extent and methodology to achieve effective immigration adds to Conservative division amongst ourselves and we Conservatives against Liberals. Even with these partitions, there are several principle-based holdings we Conservatives must insist upon in any proposed immigration policy, each promoting legal immigration and American superiority.

Many of those who oppose conservatism's belief in orderly and regulated immigration structures also believe that "all seven billion people in the world are born with a God-given right to immigrate to the United States."[24] Thus, when such challengers—almost exclusively Democrats and those on the Left—argue about the brokenness of America's immigration system, "they are not bemoaning our policies that are biased towards low-skilled immigration; they are complaining that our generous acceptance of over 1 million new immigrants every year, predominantly from the third world, is not enough." Conservatives' reluctance to award some form of legal forgiveness (or amnesty) upon the estimated twelve million illegal immigrants in the United States is then manufactured by the Left to be an unintended exposure "of our sinister bigotry towards others," a characteristic strategy of the Democratic Party (as later discussed in "Race, Sex, and Class"). Consequently, in any negotiations over the crafting of new immigration policies, Conservatives must hold firm to certain principles that ensure safety, consistency, and structure. WE CONSERVATIVES BELIEVE the expansion of a diverse citizenry through immigration procedures is critical to a country's longevity so long as coupled with *bona fide* implementation schemes.

Enforcement and Criteria

WE CONSERVATIVES BELIEVE the intents behind some who anguish over the alleged need for substantial immigration alterations—rather than the mere enforcement of existing immigration laws—are self-interested, worrisome for the nation at large, and divisive by their nature. Accordingly, to counterbalance these troubling aims, Conservatives must stand together in promoting upright ideologies to make certain any immigration modifications are worthwhile, in furtherance of American prosperity, and independent from the political aspirations of an ambitious ruling class.

Current estimates of the number of aliens who have come to America and remain illegally are around twelve million. These twelve million aliens, rather than being pursued under the rule of law for their violations of American jurisprudence, are classified by the Left not as lawbreakers but as heroic countrymen to be given thanks. The illegal immigrant is considered "universally more virtuous than the citizen. He is said to aspire to and, indeed, achieve a higher position of worthiness than the citizen, for he is doing 'the jobs Americans won't do,' 'is a person of faith,' and 'a strong family man.' The citizen is said to owe his sustenance to the immigrant."[25] To thank the supposed universal merit of these illegal immigrants, they ought to be collectively rewarded with citizenship, argues the Left. Only through citizenship, they propose, can violations of illegal immigrants' natural rights be rectified.

But we Conservatives see a different picture. The idea that immigration holds a leading role in America's continued strength is one that Conservatives value, but we also recognize the need for restraining unbridled mass-migration. Overly large numbers of immigrants resulting from Democrat initiatives do "not allow the nation time to try to absorb the aliens who are already here before encouraging more to follow. Federal and state laws and policies that grant *de facto* citizenship to illegal aliens . . . send a signal to aliens around the world that America is not serious about immigration enforcement."[26] Moreover, the great majority of illegal aliens in the United States came from third-world countries who originally sought refuge in America but did not intend to do so through the proper legal means. For most, it was far easier and more efficient to secretly cross the border (or remain after the expiration of a visa) than to apply for permanent residence. For those in this third-world working class, "Being without work [in the United States] is still far better for most people than being employed in Central America."[27]

We Conservatives, therefore, must be certain to set several foundations during any immigration reformation that are consistent with our holdings and that are for the betterment of the United States. First, we must insist that modifications of immigration and citizenship pathways are not direct routes for immigrants to join the welfare state. This means a return to, or at minimum enforcement of, means-based immigration policies. Immigrating to America is not a natural right, and America must insist on accepting those with the most to offer, with the most peaceful demeanor, and who have the best work ethic among the applicants. Also, because low-income earners tend to fill mass-immigration rolls presently, and thus are frequently state-dependent, the pursuance of immigration reform must not be to boost the voting bloc of the Democratic Party. If, as Rush Limbaugh questioned, illegal immigrants were granted citizenship but barred from voting for twenty-five years, would Democrats still support amnesty?[28] And "before any amnesty is implemented, there [must be] a complete establishment of visa tracking, border control, and mandatory E-verify to ensure that this won't create another . . . scenario of more waves of illegal immigration."[29] WE CONSERVATIVES BELIEVE arguments over the proper avenues necessary to tackle illegal immigration will persist so long as immigrants seek to bypass the legal means to enter the United States, but throughout the debate, we must hold true to our primary principles and always put the country's interests first.

Means and Ends

WE CONSERVATIVES BELIEVE the legislative power of Congress is defined by the Constitution and further restrained by the power of the states. Nevertheless, congressional attempts at overextensions, coupled with judicial approvals, constitute a plague that has burdened the United States since its founding and one which the founders themselves troubled over.

In 1819, Chief Justice of the Supreme Court John Marshall heard a case over the legality of a national bank (the second one of its kind at the time).[30] The State of Maryland, in an attempt to curtail the power of the new national bank, "passed a tax on the transactions of out-of-state banks. James McCulloch," clerk of the national bank's Baltimore branch, "had conducted business without paying the tax, whereupon Maryland sued him," and the appeal ultimately rose to the Supreme Court.[31]

In the handed-down opinion of the Court, Marshall sided with the federal bank, and revisited arguments "over ends and means which had pitted Madison and Hamilton against each other in 1791 when the first Bank of the United States was proposed and taking Hamilton's side."[32] Once again stirring up the debate of the Necessary and Proper Clause of the Constitution, Marshall wrote, "If the end be legitimate, and within the scope of the constitution, all the means which are appropriate, which are plainly adapted to that end, and which are not prohibited, may constitutionally be employed to carry it into effect."[33] In essence, "Establishing a Bank of the United States was a legitimate end, branch banks were a means, and neither Maryland nor any other state could hobble them with taxation."[34]

Writing from retirement after having served as America's fourth president, James Madison responded to the Court's opinion in a private letter. Greatly concerned about the potential increase in legislative authority now held by Congress under the guise of expanded Necessary and Proper powers, Madison argued, "everything is related immediately or remotely to every other thing; and consequently a Power over any one thing, if not limited by some obvious and precise affinity, may amount to a Power over every other."[35] That is, to interpret the Constitution's Necessary and Proper Clause as one permitting any action so long as somehow related to an end-goal of Congress was a dangerous notion. "Ends & means may shift their character at will & according to the ingenuity of the Legislative Body," Madison continued. "What is an end in one case may be a means in another; nay in the same case, may be either an end or a means of the Legislative option."

The threats associated with these kinds of unleashed authorities further evidenced the need for structured enumerations of congressional powers. Otherwise, "Is there a Legislative power in fact, not expressly prohibited by the Constitution, which might not, according to the doctrine of the Court, be exercised as a means of carrying into effect some specified power?"[36] And does not such approval of authority relinquish a great amount of the check and balance powers of the other branches and states, for if Congress is permitted unbridled means to reach an end, where is it ever restrained? WE CONSERVATIVES BELIEVE the specific powers of Congress, as enumerated in the Constitution, may not simply be expanded by a collaboration with judicial players and the mistreatment of states' rights—to do so is to "break down the landmarks intended by the specification of the Powers of Congress, and to substitute for a definite connection between means and ends, a Legislative discretion as . . . to which no practical limit can be assigned."

The European America

WE CONSERVATIVES BELIEVE the more extensive a government grows and the more intrusive it becomes, the more minimized our founding principles shrink. European-style taxation and its crippling welfare state have no place in America, yet they are precisely what the modern Democratic Party and the Left are now clung to, resulting in an evermore encroaching central government, an attack on wealth creation, less personal freedom, and a perversion of American values.

In most European countries, "the individual is heavily taxed, but receives back from the state the approved form of medical care, vacation money, money for having children, and other such goods, services, and subsidies that the state, in its wisdom, decides he or she should have."[37] When converted to modern American politics, this same vision is the one assumed by the Left, with persistent calls for greater wealth redistributions and higher taxes to fund their social program initiatives—in effect, a "trickle-down government," wherein one should leave life's tough decisions to the brilliance of those in Congress and the presidency.

Yet we Conservatives retain a considerably different ideology. Our forefathers founded the United States upon the belief that every man will be the best judge of how to apply his energies and assets, and that a government must not interfere with those decisions absent a clear necessity. Through this eighteenth-century belief, the United States not only threw off a European monarch, but it also prospered into the world's most wealthy nation. WE CONSERVATIVES BELIEVE individual liberty, not excessive control through governmental decision-makers, is the most effectual means by which to guarantee the prosperity of a free people—it is also the vision most in line with every man's natural rights.

THE EXECUTIVE

Limits of the Presidency

We Conservatives believe the presidency is not an office of infinite and continually expansive powers; it is instead one that must act through channels of specified powers and (on remote occasions) through certain implied powers.

The executive branch has several enumerated authorities granted to it by the Constitution, and the president is vested with all executive power—that is, "he shall take care that the laws be faithfully executed."[1] Of these powers, he "shall be Commander in Chief of the Army and Navy of the United States . . .;[2] He shall have Power, by and with the Advice and Consent of the Senate, to make Treaties . . .;"[3] he may nominate "Ambassadors, other public Ministers and Consuls, Judges of the supreme Court, and all other Officers of the United States" not otherwise provided for in the Constitution;[4] he may veto congressional enactments;[5] and "shall have Power to grant Reprieves and Pardons for Offenses against the United States, except in Cases of Impeachment."[6]

This list of specific controls of the president is within the Constitution, and there is no debate as to the authenticity of such powers when executed appropriately by the executive. But what is to be made of a president who moves beyond this scope and of a Congress that is complicit in rebuking those expansions?

We Conservatives recognize that the presidency of today is a far cry from the presidency created by the framers. Since America's beginning, the presidency has carried with it the potential to grow into an overly powerful entity. In fact, the executive powers were not even predestined to reside in a single person, and the Constitutional Convention had to determine (among many other aspects) "whether the president would be a 'he' or a 'they.' Indeed, when James Wilson of Pennsylvania moved that the executive should consist of a single person, the room lapsed into an uncomfortable silence."[7]

And to those who believed the powers of the president ought to be "strictly divided as a bar to future tyranny, . . . a single executive was, in Virginia Governor Edmund Randolph's phrase, 'the [fetus] of monarchy.' "

Simply because either the legislature or the courts do not reproach a president's acts does not imply his actions are necessarily proper. If a president acts but does not utilize the powers granted to him in the Constitution, we Conservatives presume he has stepped beyond the reach of his office. The burden then falls upon the president to justify his proceedings and elaborate from where he garnished the authority to act. If he cannot do both, he must not perform. Furthermore, even if the legislature, courts, or both approve his expansive measures, they are still not altogether appropriate. The limits on presidential power are quite extensive, and as once remarked, "No man would want to be President of the United States in strict accordance with the Constitution."[8] But guarding against over-extensions of executive power—beyond that "in strict accordance with the Constitution"—is precisely what the other branches and levels of government are duty-bound to do. Yet as a consequence of human nature, it is most usually a duty overlooked.

In a letter written by George Washington to "The People of the United States" at the end of his public duty, he encouraged elected officials and the electorate alike to sternly check—in fact, suspect—those holding public office: "It is important, likewise, that the habits of thinking in a free country should inspire caution in those entrusted with its administration, to confine themselves within their respective constitutional spheres, avoiding in the exercise of the powers of one department to encroach upon another. The spirit of encroachment tends to consolidate the powers of all the departments in one, and thus to create, whatever the form of government, a real despotism."[9] WE CONSERVATIVES BELIEVE, to preserve liberty, presidential powers are to remain limited, defined, and under the incessant scrutiny of the American people and their elected leaders.

A Vague Executive

WE CONSERVATIVES BELIEVE the United States Constitution is, in many respects, vague so as to allow for unforeseeable contingencies the founders could not have anticipated. This vagueness, however, was not intended as an opportunity to apply modernist and evolving interpretations of the Constitution. Furthermore, the certain ambiguities in Article. II. (pertaining to the executive) and the silences therein do not license the president to act simply because he is not explicitly prohibited. Rather, the president remains significantly hemmed in (intentionally so) and bound by the terms of the Constitution he swears to abide by.

One of the ambiguities in Article. II. is that of the first sentence: "The executive power shall be vested in a President of the United States of America."[10] Contrast this grant of authority to that of Article. I., which "adds a key qualifier, that 'all legislative powers *herein granted* shall be vested in Congress.' This might imply that 'the executive power' goes beyond the list of powers delineated in the rest of the article."[11] Yet this distinction, very often capitalized upon by presidents seeking expansive powers, is rooted in a deeper realization of the two branches' roles; the lacking words in Article. II. was not a mistake.

Generally speaking, the president is only permitted to act when working to enforce the laws of Congress. As the executive, he *executes* laws, not creates them. He is, for that reason, largely "subordinate" to the legislative powers as he must work within the constraints of Congress's reach. Put another way by James Madison, "The natural province of the executive magistrate is to execute laws, as that of the legislature is to make laws. All his acts therefore, properly executed, must pre-suppose the existence of the laws to be executed."[12] Consequently, all the powers of the president needn't be defined because the powers of the legislature, which *are* specifically enumerated, bind him already.

The order of the Constitution's articles themselves gives further weight to the subordination of the executive, placing congressional powers in Article. I., the executive in Article. II., and the judiciary in Article. III. Even "the ultimate power of removal" is granted to the legislature "since Congress can get rid of the president but not vice versa . . .. In short, the president is necessary" for Congress to see its laws enforced, but Congress is not reliant on the president to create those laws.[13] WE CONSERVATIVES BELIEVE the vagueness of the Constitution does not expand the powers of the executive—they are already limited in scope by its fundamental role in executing the laws of Congress.

Presidential Enforcement of the Law

WE CONSERVATIVES BELIEVE a chief responsibility of the president is to enforce the laws passed by Congress, regardless of whether he agrees with them. Article. II. of the Constitution, more specifically the Take Care Clause, names the powers and assigns the duty to fulfill this task. A president who fails to execute congressional legislation both violates the separation of powers and undermines a primary purpose of the office he holds.

Article. II., Section. 3. of the Constitution dictates the president to "take Care that the Laws be faithfully executed," and as the elected head of the executive branch, he has enormous prosecutorial power in the enforcement of federal law. But just as city prosecutors enjoy a certain level of discretion in their enforcement of laws against alleged offenders, so too does the president. For example, we know that the Constitution also provides the president with pardon power over federal crimes (Article. II., Section. 2.). This, on its face, suggests the framers intended to give the president a large degree of discretion in some matters, "for, notwithstanding his faithful-execution duty, the President may pardon an offense even before a trial or conviction."[14]

But there are limits to this discretion. What is the effect of a law that the president decides not to enforce on an entire class of people? What happens to a law that the president overlooks regarding regulation of government agencies? The result becomes, in truth, a president who legislates from the Oval Office. If a president, rather than taking care to execute federal law faithfully, refuses outright to act upon it toward all people, does this not virtually repeal the law? Does this not reach far beyond prosecutorial discretion? By such inaction, the president is not considering discretionary variables case-by-case but is instead determining the fate of an entire class of alleged offenders. Not only does he then legislate from the Oval Office, but he also judges. He determines the effective innocence of the very people Congress was intent on having prosecuted. By abuses of the Take Care Clause, the president simultaneously acts as the executive, the legislature, and the judiciary.

Through presidentially interpreted extensions of Article. II., Section. 3., the executive branch gains broad domestic authority not granted by the Constitution. The more expansive these self-imposed powers grow, the more minimized the other branches become. In a paper published by two law professors on this issue, the authors raise concerns over what this means for the weight of congressional legislation:

> Can a President decline to enforce federal laws barring [a] class from voting in federal elections? Can a President decline to enforce the deportation statute against all illegal immigrants because of a belief in an "open borders" policy? Can a President who wants tax cuts that a recalcitrant Congress will not enact decline to enforce the income tax laws? Can a President effectively repeal the environmental laws by refusing to sue polluters, or workplace and labor laws by refusing to fine violators?[15]

These threats may seem improbable, but gradual encroachments on the other governmental branches are sometimes not only unnoticed, they are accepted. WE CONSERVATIVES BELIEVE in the separation of powers, in the duty of the president to enforce the laws and findings of the other branches and to maintain civil order through equal justice under the law.

A LIMITED COMMANDER-IN-CHIEF

Reliance on Congress

WE CONSERVATIVES BELIEVE the founders did not intend the authority of the president to act as the commander-in-chief of the armed forces as an arbitrary and plenary power. The extensive command utilized today by presidents far exceeds the executive's scope as envisioned by the framers, and, with each president's continued wartime expansions, the threats (and realities) of an overly powerful official also grow.

Certainly when in war, a centralized authority of sorts can be most efficient. Alexander Hamilton, writing in the *Federalist*, noted, "Of all the cares or concerns of government, the direction of war most peculiarly demands those qualities which distinguish the exercise of power by a single hand. The direction of war implies the direction of the common strength; and the power of directing and employing the common strength, forms a usual and essential part in the definition of the executive authority."[16] History has shown that the concentration of wartime power into a singular person or small group is generally the most efficient approach to tackling the tasks of war. It allows for rapid decision-making and strategic developments and avoids a great deal of political interference. It also minimizes the risk of leaked intelligence when confined to a limited body. Yet this small group of military leaders must not go unchecked, for history has also shown the real dangers of unbridled military ambitions when left in the hands of a few.

To confront this challenge (that is, minimizing the number of wartime leaders but keeping those leaders under watch), the Constitution provides a balanced approach. First, Congress is provided with the authority "to declare War, grant Letters of Marque and Reprisal, and make Rules concerning Captures on Land and Water," as well as "to raise and support Armies" and "provide and maintain a Navy."[17] Simultaneously, the Constitution also provides that "the President shall be Commander in Chief of the Army and Navy of the United States, and of the Militia of the several States, when called into the actual Service of the United States."[18] Thus, both branches of government are dependent upon the other in war—the president is dependent on Congress to authorize war, and the legislature is dependent on the president to execute the war. The Constitution does not grant presidential power to start a war, and it does not authorize Congress the power to direct it. "Those who are to *conduct a war*," wrote James Madison, "cannot in the nature of things, be proper or safe judges, whether *a war ought* to be *commenced, continued*, or *concluded*."[19] WE CONSERVATIVES BELIEVE the framers attempted to limit the scope of the commander-in-chief when engaged in that role but still allowed him to operate largely independent of peacetime constraints on the military—during a declared war, the president may exercise the power to direct the forces as the most superior ranking official.

Called into Service

WE CONSERVATIVES BELIEVE that although the Constitution does give the president the ability to serve as the commander-in-chief, he is only permitted to do so when the armed forces are "called into the actual Service of the United States."[20]—this distinction is at the root of the proper employment of the president's military powers.

For modern Americans, the calling of our military personnel into service may seem triggered when a citizen enlists and serves under any of the five military branches. But to fully grasp the "called into actual Service" requirement of the Constitution, we are obligated to look to America's history at the time and circumstances during the writing of the Constitution.

Throughout much of history, and especially following the Revolutionary War, populations widely viewed standing armies in times of peace as dangerous to individual liberty. A large body of armed men under the direction of a governmental organization had historically and regularly proven fatal to the protection of natural and legal rights. This actuality was even more liable to realization when the citizenry had little-to-no means of resistance against such a force (hence part of the significance behind the right to bear arms). Accordingly, when the founders debated and wrote the new American Constitution, a large army and navy were presupposed to be needed only in war, with Congress being the authority under which any remaining military force was to act during peacetime. Not until Congress made an affirmative intent to engage an enemy in war would the president serve as the commander-in-chief.

The context under which the founders wrote the Constitution (and thus the commander-in-chief power) was wholly different than the modern-day reality of a considerable standing military during both peace and war. Subsequently, when speculating about precisely when the president is permitted to function in a military capacity, look not to whether there is a military but instead to whether that military is engaged. If Congress has authorized the military to be engaged, the president can serve as the commander-in-chief. In all other occurrences, except where Congress has spoken otherwise, the president is exceeding his military authority and is liable to sanction. Thus, it falls upon the legislature to carefully watch the actions of the president to ensure he remains within the bounds of his office, and it is incumbent upon the people at each election to hold accountable their president for constitutional violations. WE CONSERVATIVES BELIEVE the president's commander-in-chief powers are limited to the scope of engagements authorized by Congress and only within the timeframe of such military commitments.

The War Powers Resolution

WE CONSERVATIVES BELIEVE the power of the president to act in the capacity of the commander-in-chief is both limited by the Constitution and checks by the federal legislature. As seen in "A Limited Commander-in-Chief," the president was not intended to be the leader of the armed forces at all times, and the legislature has the ability to define his now-assumed commanding ability during peacetime. The most significant legislation created by Congress to confront this issue is the War Powers Resolution of 1973, a law frequently overlooked by presidents without any resulting sanction.

The resolution fashions several requirements the president must satisfy if unilaterally deploying American troops abroad. It first specifies:

> *In the absence of a declaration of war*, in any case in which United States Armed Forces are introduced into hostilities or into situations where imminent involvement in hostilities is clearly indicated by the circumstances . . . the President shall submit within forty-eight hours to the Speaker of the House of Representatives and to the President pro tempore of the Senate a report, in writing, setting forth: (a) the circumstances necessitating the introduction of United States Armed Forces; (b) the constitutional and legislative authority under which such introduction took place; and (c) the estimated scope and duration of the hostilities or involvement.[21]

This maximum forty-eight-hour reporting requirement shall continue at least "once every six months . . . so long as such armed forces continue to be engaged in such hostilities or situation."

After the president has submitted the report to Congress, he has sixty days to utilize the military before he must "terminate any use of United States Armed Forces with respect to which such report was submitted *unless Congress* (1) has declared war or has enacted a specific authorization for such use of United States Armed Forces; (2) has extended by law such sixty-day period; or (3) is physically unable to meet as a result of an armed attack upon the United States."[22] If none of these three conditions are triggered, the president thereafter has a maximum of thirty days to withdraw the troops he originally engaged.

The War Powers Resolution came about after continued violent conflicts persisted in the Korean and Vietnam wars, all without a formal declaration of war from Congress as the Constitution specifies. While presidents engaged troops without congressional authorization, Congress worried its war-determination powers might become minimized if presidents were allowed to continue unchecked. Yet because of the changing nature of war, Congress also recognized the need for quick and hostile commitments of the military that might otherwise be encumbered if formal declarations were required. Thus, through the War Powers Resolution, the president could now act unilaterally within a limited timeframe while still consulting with and requiring the consent of Congress if the hostilities were to continue.

Not surprisingly, since the law greatly limits the powers presidents have accumulated over centuries, every president since its enactment has expressed beliefs that the law is unconstitutional. Even when first introduced, Congress overcame the veto of President Richard Nixon, who also considered it an invalid use of congressional power. Yet the law is appropriate, and it serves as a suitable check on the president's ability to act unilaterally with the world's most powerful military. If a military conflict is so central to American safety, "The facts & proofs themselves," wrote James Madison, "are to sway the judgment of Congress in declaring war."[23] WE CONSERVATIVES BELIEVE the powers of the president are large and expansive, and with regard to his singular uses of the military, his powers ought not to be infinite—precisely what the resolution prevents.

The Electoral College

WE CONSERVATIVES BELIEVE in the value of the Electoral College and its protection of both large and small states' interests in the election of American presidents. The Electoral College ensures candidates devote attention and time to all states, not just those with large populations and popular influence.

The Offices of the President and Vice President are the only ones for which the entire nation votes. As such, the founders deemed it necessary to devise a method under which no one state could become overly significant while others became disposable. Through Article. II. and Amendment

Twelve of the Constitution, the electorate does not in fact vote for the president or vice president; Americans vote for electors who then vote on their behalf. Each state is designated a number of electors based on their representation in Congress, totaling 538 (435 in the House of Representatives, 100 in the Senate, and 3 additional electors for the District of Columbia). Each state and the District of Columbia receives a minimum of three electors.

When a candidate wins a state's popular vote, the party to whom that candidate belongs sends its pre-selected electors to vote on behalf of the people and party. For example, if a state has fifteen electors assigned to it, the candidate who wins that state's popular vote will also win its electoral votes. There is generally no splitting of the electoral vote since the candidate's party has previously determined the electors.[24] This means that the winner of the popular vote in that state receives all fifteen of those electoral votes. The first candidate to obtain a majority of the electoral votes across the country—270—wins (excluding the provisions for potential ties).

To some, this process at first seems contrary to the republican principles of our country. After all, the voters do not directly vote for their president. But a more extensive look at the likely implications of not having the Electoral College underscores its importance. Imagine an America in which the popular vote alone elected the president. This would permit a presidential candidate to simply pander to a few states that house the vast majority of the country's population. If he could gain those votes, he would win the election. Never would he need to travel to states of less population, and he could ignore the wills and troubles of those smaller states. No longer would America be a body of states united, and the political wishes of the large states alone could direct the agenda of all the states. This would be destructive to the cohesiveness of the states, for no longer would each state carry potentially crucial electoral votes.

The Electoral College does give states with higher populations a greater share of the electoral votes (just as in the House of Representatives), but it forces candidates to move beyond merely the largest of states. WE CONSERVATIVES BELIEVE the mechanism that our framers created for the election of presidents—such that ensures each state's significance—is fair, comprehensive, and necessary for the legitimacy of our federal government.

Ending Term Limits

WE CONSERVATIVES BELIEVE presidential term limits are contrary to the founders' intents, are dangerous to a free people, were created as a politically imposed doctrine, and enable passiveness amongst the electorate.

Not until 1951, with the ratification of the Twenty-Second Amendment, were presidents limited to two terms. The amendment reads, in part, "No person shall be elected to the office of the President more than twice, and no person who has held the office of President, or acted as President, for more than two years of a term to which some other person was elected President shall be elected to the office of President more than once."[25] Yet what are the benefits of such an amendment? Surely proponents suggest it diminishes the likelihood of a monarchial president usurping the powers of the legislature under pretenses of republican leadership, and that it allows for "fresh thoughts" to stir up the office. But this belief is short-sighted, for the Constitution already provides the remedy to such a threat: Election Day. By automatically disqualifying individuals from the office after a period of time, the voting populace is not only permitted to be passive in their watchfulness of the president (for he will be removed within two terms regardless), it also requires Americans to uncertainly place their faith in another person even if they were pleased with the performance of the preceding president. If, by analogy, you hired an employee who provided satisfactory work for eight consecutive years, would you impose a forced retirement on that employee soley as a result of his consistency? This is precisely the reality of presidential term limits since all elected and appointed officials are subordinate to the general electorate and serve at their pleasure.

While supporters of term limits argue that they prevent tyrannical tendencies, the prohibitions, in fact, promote such propensities. In 1788, during the ratification debates over the then-proposed Constitution, term limits were considered and thereafter excluded from the original draft of the document. "The ineligibility [of a past president]," wrote James Madison, "though not perhaps without advantages, is also liable to a variety of strong objections. It takes away one powerful motive to a faithful & useful administration, the desire of acquiring that title to a re-appointment."[26] Requiring the regular and repeated changes, Madison continued, "discourages beneficial undertakings which require perseverance and system.... It may inspire desperate enterprizes for the attainment of what is not attainable by legitimate means. . . . It would tempt him to neglect the constitutional rights of his department, and to connive at usurpations by the Legislative department." Allowing presidents to serve a second term, yet be barred from a third, both "fetters the judgment and inclination of the Community" and encourages presidents to act in ways that may have otherwise poised significant reelection concerns. Without the threat of losing an election, the president is considerably more free to act unilaterally and contrary to the textual restraints of the Constitution.

If averting monarchial inclinations was truly the intent of term limits, why did Congress, when proposing the Twenty-Second Amendment, not also impose boundaries on its own members' terms in Congress? Does not Congress retain a significant power to threaten the liberty of the American people if not properly restrained? Or what of the federal judiciary, whose judges can virtually serve for life? The president, whose office has grown into one of considerable power and expanse, ought to be tempered by the prospect of another term—not largely unchained and disconnected from the judgment of the voting population. WE CONSERVATIVES BELIEVE limiting the president's ability to seek reelection is hazardous to the safety of the Constitution, politically toned, and dismissive of voting Americans' intellect.

The Administrative State

Independent Agencies

WE CONSERVATIVES BELIEVE reductions in the size and scope of the executive branch is both conducive to efficiency and more appropriate for the role of the president. The presidency, limited by the powers of the Constitution, has expanded into a bureaucracy of unbridled capacity, utilizing executive departments to bypass the legislature and courts and to trump the rights of states.

The departments and agencies attached to the federal executive are numerous and broadly inclusive. Among those directly answerable to the president include the Departments of State, the Treasury, Justice, the Interior, Agriculture, Commerce, Labor, Defense, Health and Human Services,

Housing and Urban Development, Transportation, Energy, Education, Veterans Affairs, and Homeland Security. Those within these departments serve under the authority of the president and work to enforce the mandates of the executive branch and statutory requirements of Congress, all the while representing the federal government in certain affairs. The Department of State, for instance, is charged with administering international relations on behalf of the president and embodying the wishes of the United States generally. And the Department of Justice oversees compliance with federal laws and regulations and prosecutes those it suspects are acting contrary to societal guidelines.

But these executive departments are not nearly the entirety of the executive's reach. Countless "independent agencies" also fill the ranks of the federal government. An independent agency is one that, while having its leadership nominated by the president, "is not under the direction of the executive" because the president is not able to remove independent agencies' leaders except under extraordinary circumstances.[27] Even more, these agencies very often have independent rulemaking power by which they can set regulations and decrees pertaining to their particular field of focus. These rules, generally having the same weight as congressionally passed federal law, may also be enforced on the unsuspecting public, and inter-agency courts (presided over by administrative law judges) may determine the fate of violators. In effect, independent agencies may have the power to create their own laws, enforce their own laws, and judge their own laws—precisely what the Constitution was designed to avoid. Examples of independent agencies include the Federal Trade Commission (FTC), the Federal Communications Commission (FCC), the National Labor Relations Board (NLRB), the Social Security Administration (SSA), and the Securities and Exchange Commission (SEC).

Congress establishes independent agencies and each has a specific grant of authority highlighting its scope and purpose. But while Congress may create the agencies and the president is authorized to nominate their leaders, they act largely on their own—except, that is, when the president and an agency are both pursuing the same ends. Then, an unashamed disregard for the legislative authority of Congress is exposed, and they undertake political agendas with virtually no threat of recourse—after all, the agencies and the president are considered independent of each other. WE CONSERVATIVES BELIEVE the present extent of executive departments and independent agencies is perilous to the proper execution of laws and serves as an arm with which the president can extend into the realms of the other branches of government seemingly unchecked.

Buried in Complexity

WE CONSERVATIVES BELIEVE the extent of the executive branch's scope both impedes the powers of the other governmental branches and the states and aids executive players in the avoidance of responsibility for misfortunes caused by their decisions.

The Constitution, as designed, was not created to grant the executive overwhelming power and influence over the lives of the American people. Rather, the president and his administration were meant to remain limited and narrowly focused, with specific roles and duties. For the founders, the threat of an overly dominant executive was real, with great concern given to avoid the establishment of another monarchy, such as the one they just overthrew. Consequently, aside from the president's role as the commander-in-chief during wartime, the task of being the American president was intended to be rather uncomplicated. So restrained by the enumerated powers of the Constitution (and by its silences), the president can rarely perform constitutionally when not in response to congressional action (such as the signing of a bill passed by both chambers). But why, then, does the power of American presidents seem so expansive and encompassing, especially when furthered by the vast array of executive departments and independent agencies?

Concerns over a large executive branch began as soon as constitutional debates were underway in the 1780s. Writing in defense of the Constitution, Alexander Hamilton argued that the threat of a powerful presidential administration, one with numerous partitions and divisions, was troubling not only for the up-keeping of the separation of powers but also for the attachment of accountability:

> One of the weightiest objections to a plurality in the executive . . . is that it tends to conceal faults and destroy responsibility. . . . It often becomes impossible, amidst mutual accusations, to determine on whom the blame or the punishment of

> a pernicious measure, or series of measures, ought really to fall. It is shifted from one to another with so much dexterity, and under such plausible appearances, that the public opinion is left in suspense about the real author. The circumstances which may have led to any national miscarriage or misfortune are sometimes so complicated that where there are a number of actors who may have had different degrees and kinds of agency, though we may clearly see upon the whole that there has been mismanagement, yet it may be impracticable to pronounce to whose account the evil which may have been incurred is truly chargeable.[28]

The very concerns of an extensive executive raised by Hamilton and others in the 1780s have unequivocally come to fruition in modern America, one in which presidents and their collaborators can "clothe the circumstances with so much ambiguity as to render it uncertain what was the precise conduct of any of those parties."[29] Instead, when restraining the limited powers of the president in as few as possible, the threat of an unchecked execution of laws is, in fact, reduced. A circumstance of a confined executive results in one who "will be more narrowly watched and more readily suspected, and who cannot unite so great a mass of influence as when he is associated with others."[30] WE CONSERVATIVES BELIEVE the presidency, intended to be refined and restrained, is most closely and carefully monitored for abuses of authority when limited in scope, power, and numbers—a principle continually denounced with each new expanse of the administrative state.

The Fourth Branch

WE CONSERVATIVES BELIEVE the present-day administrative state, created through a collaboration of Congress and the president, regularly acts in clear violation of the Constitution and erodes away the distinct roles of the different branches of government and the states. And when they cannot accomplish legitimate legislation, it further serves as an alternative route to the legislative process, whether as a reality of altering political philosophies or impatient legislators and executives.

The president, being the head of the executive branch, has great influence over the doings of the various departments and cabinets therein, even those purportedly qualified as independent. Thus, when the president thinks of an initiative of interest to him or his party (a responsibility not even within the authentic purpose of his position), he can either seek legislative action or order his administrative state to regulate activity according to his wishes, thus bypassing Congress altogether. Recent examples under President Barack Obama stress the undermining effect the administrative state has on the constitutional governance of the nation:

> Even though the Democrat-controlled Senate rejected the President's cap-and-trade plan, his Environmental Protection Agency classified carbon dioxide, the compound that sustains vegetative life, as a pollutant so that it could regulate it under the Clean Air Act.
>
> After the Employee Free Choice Act—designed to bolster labor unions' dwindling membership rolls—was defeated by Congress, the National Labor Relations Board announced a rule that would implement "snap elections" for union representation, limiting employers' abilities to make their case to workers and virtually guaranteeing a higher rate of unionization at the expense of workplace democracy.
>
> After an Internet regulation proposal failed to make it through Congress, the Federal Communications Commission announced that it would regulate the Web anyway, even despite a federal court's ruling that it had no authority to do so.
>
> Although Congress consistently has barred the Department of Education from getting involved in curriculum matters, the Administration has offered waivers for the No Child Left Behind law in exchange for states adopting national education standards, all without congressional authorization.[31]

Do these examples ring of balanced governance consistent with the Constitution's requirements? It remains remarkably ironic how presidents lament over alleged usurpations of executive authority when Congress retrains their war powers, but they make no such grievances when that same

Congress authorizes executive agencies to legislate, execute, and judge on matters of ever-increasing expanse. WE CONSERVATIVES BELIEVE the administrative state in America is fundamentally flawed and depreciating the value of the constitutional authority of governmental actors—a toxin of considerable damage in republics such as ours.

THE PRESIDENTIAL PERSON

WE CONSERVATIVES BELIEVE the presidency, designed by imperfect men, is to be temporarily occupied by fallible citizens among us and is an office that ought to remain under the greatest scrutiny for attempts of authoritative abuses. The time one spends in the executive office should humble him to serve the wishes of the electorate, not elevate him to demigod-stature.

Presidents and presidential contenders have come to rely on the cult-like followings of respective bases in the voting bloc. A politician thus upheld is one who commits no wrong in the minds of his followers. Followers perceive him as the only resistance against the evil intentions of his opposition, and they lambast any divergence or disagreement regarding his designs. Those who are of countering opinions are labeled un-American and as pursuing anti-equality.

But is this a safe reality under which to live? One where an inherently flawed human, acting at the helm of a nation, is considered to live without erring? Is this not akin to monarchial perspectives (such as the one early Americans overthrew) in which a king is not only the source of law but above the law as well? Instead, we Conservatives see true patriotism through a different focus and definition, one deftly articulated by President Theodore Roosevelt in the early twentieth century: "Patriotism means to stand by the country. It does not mean to stand by the President or any other public official save exactly to the degree in which he himself stands by the country. It is patriotic to support him in so far as he efficiently serves the country. It is unpatriotic not to oppose him to the exact extent that by inefficiency or otherwise he fails in his duty to stand by the country."[32]

Being the president is being a leader, one who works to convince the American people through reasoned argument and debate, not emotional warfare and deceit. Or, as John Quincy Adams was quoted, "If your actions inspire others to dream more, learn more, do more, and become more, you are a leader."[33] To hold the Office of the President is a tremendous opportunity to do either good for the entire country or good for just one half of it. It takes great humility to stow personal ambitions not aligned with the nation's best interests—something very few presidents have achieved. The unassuming but solidly Conservative Ronald Reagan was "a man who understood instinctively that he did not 'become' president, but was given 'temporary custody' of an office that ultimately belongs to the people."[34] In his diaries, he wrote continually about his concern for the welfare of the population and the gravity of the great influence he wielded—"I pray constantly that I won't let them down" is a common theme throughout.[35] WE CONSERVATIVES BELIEVE the president should be subjected to the jealous guarding of liberty by a populous of freedom-loving people, one that does not attach more admiration to the person in the office than is due by his actions therein.

THE JUDICIARY

Bound by the Oath

WE CONSERVATIVES BELIEVE judges and justices of the federal judiciary are bound to, and limited by, the Constitution they swore to defend when first taking office. The Constitution dramatically limits the reach of the judiciary, and further conversations regarding the founders exhibit great concern for an overly powerful third branch.

Prior to exercising judicial authority in federal courts, a judge or justice must first take an oath or affirmation vowing to perform his responsibilities properly:

> I, ________ ________, do solemnly swear (or affirm) that I will administer justice without respect to persons, and do equal right to the poor and to the rich, and that I will faithfully and impartially discharge and perform all the duties incumbent upon me as ________ under the Constitution and laws of the United States. So help me God.[1]

Within this oath rests the symbolic spirit of Lady Justice, who, with blindfolded eyes, determines objective rulings without regard to identity or power, holding legal scales in one hand and a sword with the other. The oath further requires judges and justices to work under the Constitution—not outside or beyond its limits, where judges' inclinations may often take them. This consequently requires an originalist interpretation of the Constitution, for one cannot work under the Constitution while simultaneously interpreting it as one wishes.

The oath for judges and justices is so very different from that of legislators or the executive for two reasons: first, federal judges are not elected, and second, judges are not meant to be politicians. Because they are not elected, the citizenry does not have direct recourse against a rogue judge or justice, such as can be accomplished in the voting booth for elected officials. Instead, the people must work through their legislature to impose sanctions or attempt removal. And because judges are not politicians, "Judicial decisions should not be based on the personal beliefs and policy preferences of a particular judge. Judges are appointed for life *because* they're not politicians."[2] Therefore, a judge or justice who is not making decisions through the original and actual intent of the Constitution is acting beyond the frame of his position. When judges perform as though the Constitution does not bind them, the people are thus bound to lobby their elected officials for due redress. WE CONSERVATIVES BELIEVE the powers of the judiciary are intended to be limited and narrowly defined within the bounds of an originalist worldview, and the oath each judge and justice must first take underscores that truth.

Judicial Review

Proper Jurisdiction

WE CONSERVATIVES BELIEVE the judiciary frequently exercises its power in manners not suiting the branch nor the intentions of its creators. Greatest among these violations is an overly wide application of a legal principle known as "judicial review," an authority the founders did not grant to the courts in the Constitution.

Judicial review, most fundamentally, is "a court's power to review the actions of other branches or levels of government; [especially] the court's power to invalidate legislative and executive actions as being unconstitutional."[3] The idea of judicial review powers as held in the federal judiciary has grown so ingrained in American society that rarely is it considered if it is even appropriate. The power "is founded on the principle that courts will be unbiased guardians of the clear meaning of the Constitution," and that they will serve as referees over potential overexpansions of power.[4] Yet this lofty hope has been nearly universally thwarted by the activism and lawmaking roles judges and justices have assumed throughout most of American history.

Article. III. of the Constitution established the federal judiciary, and (just as with Congress) it enumerates the powers and scope of the courts:

> The judicial Power shall extend to all Cases, in Law and Equity, arising under this Constitution, the Laws of the United States, and Treaties made, or which shall be made, under their Authority;
> —to all Cases affecting Ambassadors, other public Ministers and Consuls;
> —to all Cases of admiralty and maritime Jurisdiction;
> —to Controversies to which the United States shall be a Party;
> —to Controversies between two or more States;
> —between a State and Citizens of another State,
> —between Citizens of different States,
> —between Citizens of the same State claiming Lands under Grants of different States, and between a State, or the Citizens thereof, and foreign States, Citizens or Subjects.
>
> In all Cases affecting Ambassadors, other public Ministers and Consuls, and those in which a State shall be Party, the supreme Court shall have original Jurisdiction. In all the other Cases before mentioned, the supreme Court shall have appellate Jurisdiction, both as to Law and Fact, with such Exceptions, and under such Regulations as the Congress shall make.[5]

Nowhere in the above text or anywhere else in Article. III. does the Constitution provide the judiciary with the power to review congressional laws and executive orders for their constitutionality. Yet although this is true, shouldn't some branch have the authority to examine the federal government to ensure it remains limited to the Constitution? Yes, but *not* the Supreme Court. "Judicial Review—A Conflict of Interest" discusses several rationales as to why the power ought not to rest with the federal courts and the end-effect the legal doctrine has on federal and state governance. WE CONSERVATIVES BELIEVE the power of the federal courts to judicially review the constitutionality of legislative and executive actions not only elevates them to a superior vantage point but is also in itself unconstitutional.

A Conflict of Interest

WE CONSERVATIVES BELIEVE there are several grounds upon which to show judicial review as unconstitutional and beyond the scope of the federal government's power. At the core of these bases is the text of the Constitution itself (and its lack of text at various points).

There are numerous reasons why judicial review is, in fact, lacking from the authority of the federal courts. Most importantly, the Constitution, the supreme law that binds them to its text, does not provide for it, .[6] Secondly, judicial review allows the federal government to determine, through the federal judiciary, the constitutionality of its actions. Rather than promoting a separation of powers as designed by the founders, judicial review allows the branches to couple together and undermine the contraints of the Constitution. If Congress writes an encroaching law and the president signs it, followed by a judicial stamp of approval, there is no immediate redress available to the states for encroachments on their sovereignty. In determining the constitutionality of its laws, the federal government acts as "the fox guarding the hen house"—federal judicial review serves not as a check on the federal government but rather as an enormous conflict of interest.

Furthermore and unrealistically, if the judiciary were indeed able to watch over the other branches for constitutional violations perfectly, there is no one watching over the courts to prohibit them from acting unconstitutionally. Not only are its holdings generally deemed final and supreme, but the federal judges and justices are also themselves virtually appointed for life (they "hold their offices during good Behaviour").[7] If the people wish to remove a judge, they must petition their members of Congress to impeach him. And even if so impeached, judicial holdings they made are still final. Thus, for instance, if wishing to change a decision made by the Supreme Court, the Supreme Court itself would have to rule again in a different way or the people would have to pass an amendment to the Constitution.

On the conflict of interest created by the acquisition of judicial review, and on the troubles associated with life tenure for federal judges, Thomas Jefferson wrote in 1823:

> At the establishment of our constitutions, the judiciary bodies were supposed to be the most helpless and harmless members

> of the government. Experience, however, soon showed in what way they were to become the most dangerous; that the insufficiency of the means provided for their removal gave them a freehold and irresponsibility in office; that their decisions, seeming to concern individual suitors only, pass silent and unheeded by the public at large; that these decisions, nevertheless, become law by precedent, sapping, by little and little, the foundations of the constitution, and working its change by construction, before any one has perceived that [the] invisible and helpless worm has been busily employed in consuming its substance.[8]

Still today, holdings of the courts handed down by unelected and lifelong judges "pass silent and unheeded by the public at large," yet, just the same, sap little-by-little "the foundations of the constitution."[9] This is the consequence of a judiciary that has amassed for itself the power to largely control the doings of the legislature and executive under the pretense of constitutional guardians. WE CONSERVATIVES BELIEVE the Constitution's silence on federal judicial review is not a license to assume that power—it is a prohibition.

The Sovereign States

WE CONSERVATIVES BELIEVE the history of the Constitution's creation sheds further light on the fallacy that judicial review is within reach of the federal judiciary. It was the states that created the Constitution, but, under today's structure, those same states have no real ability to deem what is or is not constitutional.

Prior to the Constitution's ratification and enactment, there was virtually no centralized judicial body. Under the Articles of Confederation (the predecessor to the present constitution), state courts confronted matters of legal concern. Until "the time of the Constitutional Convention in 1787, there were only a handful of instances in which state courts overruled legislation for violating state constitutions. . . . They ruled on criminal law, matters of equity between individuals and businesses, and other legal matters."[10] Problems arose, however, on how to tackle legal disputes that occurred in more than one state. When, therefore, the framers determined the need for a new Constitution, they sought to remedy this judicial absence with a federal court system, one that could hear "Controversies between two or more States;—between a State and Citizens of another State,—[and] between Citizens of different States."[11] Additionally, the judiciary was to have jurisdiction "to all Cases, in Law and Equity, arising under this Constitution." That the federal courts would have jurisdiction over matters "arising under this Constitution" did not imply that the courts also could strike or uphold laws based on their constitutionality. Instead, as intended by the framers, the courts would maintain the ability to hear disputes on matters *affected by* the Constitution, not on matters *about* the Constitution. For example, the federal judiciary is appropriately authorized to hear cases on whether a citizen was justly compensated for a governmental taking of his property for public use, as protected by the Takings Clause of the Fifth Amendment.[12]

Understanding that the Constitution was created and adopted by the states and that it requires their approval to amend it further, begs the question of why the states have no say in whether a federal action violates the Constitution. The states created "the supreme Law of the Land," but, once having fashioned it, apparently lost all influence over what is constitutional.[13] As one writer put it, "When you make rules for your children, do you permit your children to interpret your rules in any manner they like? Of course not. Yet the states are permitting the federal government—the 'child' of the states—to do exactly that."[14]

One of the greatest threats to the value of the Constitution is an overly large presumption of implied powers—those powers not specifically enumerated in the Constitution but which have been deemed present for various reasons. Certainly, some implied powers do exist, such as the president's prosecutorial discretion. But great limits on the potential for implied powers must be enforced, and every exercise of it should meet the scrutiny of liberty-loving people. Even more, the Constitution is not silent on how to interpret its silences. The framers originally amended the Constitution with ten amendments, known collectively as the Bill of Rights. As discussed in "The Tenth Amendment," the Tenth Amendment prohibits the federal government from interfering in matters that are not central to its purpose, opting instead to reserve governance of those concerns "to the States respectively, or to the people."[15] In other words, since judicial review is not within in the authority of the federal government, it would require a constitutional amendment, passed by the states, to provide it with such powers. Instead, the states retain the power to, collectively, invalidate federal violations of the Constitution. Exactly how this can be accomplished, along with other proposals, is discussed later in "States, Congress, and the Veto." WE CONSERVATIVES BELIEVE the states, as the creators of the Constitution and originally sovereign entities, are the true judges of whether federal law violates the Constitution.

A Veto Power

WE CONSERVATIVES BELIEVE the end-effect of judicial review is, in practice, a veto power on the laws of the legislative branch—something rejected by the framers. The power to veto legislation (as permitted by the Constitution) rests solely with the executive, as he is elected and political by nature.

To allow judges to intervene in the political process, the framers presumed, would taint their decisions with underlying bias and inevitably draw them further away from properly performing their duties "under the Constitution."[16] A judge or justice cannot be expected to legitimately and sincerely hear and give an opinion on a case or controversy if he is simultaneously being swayed by the power to veto almost any legislation. That authority, as the Constitution requires, rests only with the president.

Not until 1803 did the judiciary assume for itself the power to strike down the actions of the other two branches. With the decision in *Marbury v. Madison*, the courts unilaterally bestowed upon themselves "the power to review and, when appropriate, invalidate acts of Congress, as well as the power to issue mandatory writs . . . to members of the Executive branch."[17] Chief Justice John Marshall ruled in his opinion that "it is emphatically the province and duty of the judicial department to say *what the law is*."[18] With one stroke of a pen, the unelected judiciary had amassed a virtually limitless ability to intervene in the political workings of the American republic.

A year after the *Marbury* decision and the new roles assumed by judges, Thomas Jefferson would write that the Constitution was "meant that its coordinate branches should be checks on each other. But the opinion which gives to the Judges the right to decide what laws are constitutional, and what not, not only for themselves in their own sphere of action, but for the Legislature and Executive also, in their spheres, would make the Judiciary a despotic branch."[19] More than a decade later, he was still maintaining the same argument: "To consider the judges as the ultimate arbiters of all constitutional questions [is] a very dangerous doctrine indeed, and one which would place us under the despotism of an oligarchy. Our judges . . . have, with others, the same passions for party, for power, and the privilege of their corps. . . . The Constitution has erected no such single tribunal, knowing that to whatever hands confided, with the corruptions of time and party, its members would become despots."[20] In effect, the assumed role to judicially review the other branches transforms the judiciary from a co-equal branch to a quasi-parental branch, determining what is and is not proper behavior for the legislature and executive. WE CONSERVATIVES BELIEVE unchecked judicial review is a dangerous and unbalanced "separation" of powers, for it dramatically elevates the powers of the judiciary over those of the elected branches and steers an oligarchy of judges generally undeterred by the text of the Constitution to which they are bound.

Activism and Abuse

WE CONSERVATIVES BELIEVE that through a pretense of properly interpreting legislative laws, the judiciary has grown inexorably in size and capacity, now exercising powers that, at times, far exceed those of the other branches. The great benefit of hindsight has given us a unique ability to capture the forward-thinking talents of the American founders but, on occasion, has just as much shown their misleadings. The ability of the judiciary to strike down various laws and actions as being unconstitutional carries with it a superiority over the legislature and executive.

Fears of judicial supremacy were genuine in the drafting of the Constitution, leading many to argue that "The authority of the proposed Supreme Court of the United States, which is to be a separate and independent body, will be superior to that of the legislature. The power of construing the laws according to the *spirit* of the Constitution will enable that court to mould them into whatever shape it may think proper; especially as its decisions will not be in any manner subject to the revision or correction of the legislative body."[21] Alexander Hamilton, on the contrary, suggested this fear was unfounded, for "there is not a syllable in the [Constitution] under consideration which *directly* empowers the national courts to construe the laws according to the spirit of the Constitution." True as this may be, the court *did* soon amass such abilities by judicial decree (as seen previously in the 1803 case, *Marbury v. Madison*, for example).

Hamilton further relied upon "the standard of good behavior" as "the best expedient which can be devised in any government to secure a steady, upright, and impartial administration of the laws."[22] But this attempt at ensuring the independence of the judiciary also rested upon the active role of the legislature in monitoring the excesses of the courts. The potential dangers of governmental encroachment from the judiciary were then—and generally still today—considered the least worrisome of all three branches. Yet this trust in the watchful eye of others is largely to blame for the occurrence of the exact opposite, transforming the courts into a branch powerful enough to act as judge, jury, and lawmaker. Robert Yates, a delegate at the Constitutional Convention, rightly predicted that the courts "will be able to extend the limits of the general government gradually, and by insensible degrees, and to accommodate themselves to the temper of the people."[23] And once the judiciary extended its constitutional authority and obtained supremacy over the other branches, "This power in the judicial, will enable them to mould the government, into almost any shape they please."[24]

The judiciary has now, by Yates's "insensible degrees," brought itself into nearly every corner of American living. "Activist judges have taken over school systems, prisons, private-sector hiring and firing practices, and farm quotas; they have ordered local governments to raise property taxes and states to grant benefits to illegal immigrants; . . . and they've protected . . . the seizure of private property without just compensation, and partial-birth abortion."[25] They have further upheld the power to force Americans to purchase services through the façade of affordable healthcare.[26]

This incredible turn of position for the judiciary is exceedingly difficult to overcome. On reigning-in the courts, Thomas Jefferson offered this advice: "[How] to check these unconstitutional invasions of State rights by the Federal Judiciary. How? Not by impeachment, in the first instance, but by a strong protestation of both houses of Congress that such and such doctrines, advanced by the Supreme Court, are contrary to the Constitution; and if afterwards they relapse into the same heresies, impeach and set the whole adrift. For what was the government divided into three branches, but that each should watch over the others and oppose their usurpations?"[27] WE CONSERVATIVES BELIEVE, contrary to some early anticipations, the judiciary has grown into perhaps the most dangerous branch and in need of the closest watch.

STATES, CONGRESS, AND THE VETO

Appropriate Review

WE CONSERVATIVES BELIEVE there are times when a constitutional review of federal legislation is appropriate, for, as Alexander Hamilton argued, "it [cannot] be said that the legislative body are themselves the constitutional judges of their own powers."[28] If this were entirely the reality, the United States would not be a republic in which all are guaranteed equal justice under the law; rather, those in the legislature would be the law. This threat is specifically why the Constitution's framers enumerated the powers of Congress and limited it within those bounds. And "by a limited Constitution," Hamilton continued, "I understand one which contains certain specified exceptions to the legislative authority; such, for instance, as that it shall pass no bills of attainder, no *ex post facto* laws, and the like."[29]

Although we Conservatives recognize the need for occasional constitutional review, from where it comes is the point of contention. As discussed in "Judicial Review," the authority does not constitutionally rest in the federal courts. Yet history has made clear that the Constitution's silence toward federal judicial review has not impeded federal judges from overcoming the Tenth Amendment's obstructions. Even during the original debates on the Constitution's ratification, many founders recognized the unlikelihood that judges would be swayed by either lacking or present text—as long as man seats courts, forever will their predispositions and vices tempt them. Robert Yates, a particular opponent of the proposed Constitution, greatly feared the opportunity judges might take to craft the then-proposed Constitution in any manner they wished:

> They will give the sense of every article of the constitution, that may from time to time come before them. And in their decisions they will not confine themselves to any fixed or established rules, but will determine, according to what appears before them, the reason and spirit of the constitution. The opinions of the supreme court, whatever they may be, will have the force of law; because there is no power provided in the constitution, that can correct their errors, or controul their adjudications. From this court there is no appeal.[30]

The reality of this and the foresight of Yates are stunning. The federal judiciary, contrary to its intent and the proper purposes for which the founders created it, has spent most of its existence silently and maliciously fashioning itself as though it is all three branches combined. Yet remarkably, the federal judiciary has the potential of serving as the noblest of the branches—it can be (or, instead, ought to be) the body that best preserves individual liberty and that which is least threatening. "States, Congress, and the Veto—Nullification" examines some potential options (some practical, others hopeful) on how to correct the inappropriate course of the present judiciary and bring back the true and safest interpretation of America's most sacred document. WE CONSERVATIVES BELIEVE the federal judiciary, being originally roped-in by the textuality of the Constitution, has, by steady degrees, expanded its scope and purpose and consequently mislead and failed the American people for centuries.

Nullification

WE CONSERVATIVES BELIEVE continued judicial activism and encroachments on states' rights endanger the foundations of authentic liberty and threaten to minimize the underpinnings of American federalism.

Several individuals and think-tanks have proposed suggestions that would clarify the relationship between the federal judiciary and the other federal branches and between the judiciary and the states. Because the power to judicially review the constitutionality of laws does not rest with the federal judiciary, many have argued for the creation of a mechanism through which the states would be able to scrutinize and, if necessary, strike down congressional and executive actions. For example, crafting a constitutional amendment that provides the following possibility has been offered by some: if Congress and the president enact a law the states believe reaches beyond the scope provided for those branches, the legislatures of each state may, among themselves, vote as to the constitutionality of the act. If a minimal percentage of the total states (50 percent, for instance) vote against it, the law's force is nullified. This scheme would allow for constitutional review of the federal government while avoiding the built-in conflict of interest that arises when federal judiciaries make those determinations.

For the states to nullify federal law by a resolution was an issue of disputation even for the founders and marked a clear distinction between two of the most prominent: James Madison and Thomas Jefferson. Madison argued that if the states obtained this ability, they would expose themselves to "the charge of usurpation in the very act of protesting against usurpations of Congress."[31] That is, if the states raised objections stating that federal actions had extended their proper reach and consequently attempted to void such extensions, the states, Madison suggested, might just as much be impeding on the federal government. Conversely, Jefferson held "where powers are assumed which have not been delegated, a nullification of the act is the rightful remedy: that every State has a natural right in cases not within the [Constitution] . . . to nullify of their own authority all assumptions of power by others within their limits: that without this right, they would be under the dominion, absolute and unlimited, of whosoever might exercise this right of judgment for them."[32] Congress, he argued, is "not a party [among the states], but merely the creature of the [Constitution], and subject as to its assumptions of power to the final judgment of those by whom, and for whose use itself and its powers were all created and modified."

Yet with centuries of precedent and misunderstandings of the Constitution deeply stitched into the American fabric, the practicality of crafting, passing, and practicing a state-led constitutional review amendment is marginally likely. Another option, also considered by the framers, is that of a legislative veto over the judiciary, analogous to the executive veto the president enjoys over Congress. In this option, Congress can act after the judiciary has ruled legislation to be unconstitutional and thereby has vetoed efficiently congressional law. Now, however, Congress would hold power to override "judicial vetoes" by a bicameral vote requiring a two-thirds majority in each house (just as is necessary for the override of a presidential veto). While this may be a tempting remedy against judicial activism (and perhaps even effective), it still raises the same conflict-of-interest concern presented when the federal courts rule on constitutionality. In reality, the best manner in which to once again control the federal judicial system and to restore a limited government is to elevate the roles of the states and their influence over Washington expansions. Only then, with a collaboration of the "parent" states, will individual liberty once more grow and the threat of soft-tyranny diminish. WE CONSERVATIVES BELIEVE the federal judiciary, as the home of unelected and life-tenured officials, has steadily and consistently developed into an organization rewarding activism and providing no present appeal—a perilous combination.

LIFETIME TENURE

Three Consequences

WE CONSERVATIVES BELIEVE a judiciary virtually untethered by its lifelong tenure is dangerous to the true representation of American morals and "reduces the efficacy of the democratic check that the appointment process provides on the Court's membership."[33] Americans continue to live longer, in part due to medical advances and lifestyle choices, thereby minimizing the role of the president and Senate in appointing justices to the Supreme Court. Thus, the infrequency of Court vacancies translates into significantly more intense confirmation battles, as "there is so much at stake." Also, and of most perilous consequence, the ever-increasing length of sitting justices permits them to influence American politics and manners of living incessantly for decades, all the while unaffected by the presumed checks of the other branches.

Since the founding of the United States and the creation of the Supreme Court, the average length of sitting justices has radically changed. For the nearly two-hundred years from 1789 through 1970, the average tenure of a justice was 14.9 years.[34] Yet for justices "who have retired since 1970, the average tenure has jumped to 26.1 years." Authors in the *Harvard Journal of*

Law & Public Policy suggest three principal consequences of this expanded Supreme Court tenure.[35] First, it reduces the democratic accountability of the Court. Under the Constitution, only three "channels of democratic accountability" are in place: the selection of justices when vacancies arise, the impeachment of justices who no longer serve with "good Behaviour," and the ratification of constitutional amendments to overturn Court decisions.[36] Yet in reality, utilization of the latter two checks is practically unforeseeable. Constitutional amendments in response to Court rulings are unlikely, and in all the history of American constitutional law, "not a single justice has ever been successfully impeached and removed from office by the Senate."[37] Therefore, the only practical check on the Court is through the appointment process, but with the swelling length of justices' tenures, this check occurs less and less.

The second result of life tenure is an "increased politicization of the confirmation process."[38] Because of the rarity of Supreme Court vacancies and the spontaneous nature of their occurrences, "the president and the Senate (especially when controlled by the party opposite the president) inevitably get drawn into a political fight that hurts the Court both directly and indirectly," so much so that the appointment process will likely "grind to a halt."

The third of these consequences is "a rise in 'mental decrepitude' on the Court."[39] Although advances in medicine have allowed justices to serve on the bench for longer periods, it has also allowed them to do so at much older ages, with or without their full mental capacities. Mental inadequacies from aging have been a persistent issue with the Court throughout all its history, but its frequency has lately increased. "The illnesses have on occasion been so severe as to deprive justices of the ability to handle their duties competently without substantial help and influence from their law clerks and other staff." The effect and impact of this actuality can be outright detrimental to parties before the Court, fellow justices on the Court, the stature of the judiciary, and the lives of the American people.

It is clear that the growing length of time served on the Supreme Court has a direct correlation to presumed federal checks upon the Court, the politicization of the appointment process, and the mental integrity of sitting justices. WE CONSERVATIVES BELIEVE that, as history has shown, simply relying on justices to serve "during good Behaviour" is insufficient to ensure they remain a co-equal branch of government and answerable to the American people through their elected representatives.[40]

Subject to the People

WE CONSERVATIVES BELIEVE limits on the length of judicial tenure enable a careful watch of the Supreme Court as intended by the framers and the Constitution. The imposition of staggered terms which lapse following a defined period of time promotes constitutional ideals, limits the potential for erroneous judgments and rouge justices, and enshrines proper checks by the other co-equal branches of government.

The founders struggled themselves with whether to provide lifetime tenure or limited terms. Among the most vocal in favor of lifetime appointments was Alexander Hamilton, who worried the Court would otherwise be overly susceptible to political winds and aspirations. Complete independence of the judiciary could be best accomplished, Hamilton argued, through term-free justices. Hamilton furthered believed "the judiciary, from the nature of its functions, will always be the least dangerous to the political rights of the Constitution; because it will be least in a capacity to annoy or injure them."[41] Alas, "Hamilton's argument has not stood the test of time."[42] Instead of an independent judiciary not prone to political persuasion, the "Supreme Court has become, if anything, too insulated from public opinion, because justices stay on the Court for an average of twenty-six years and because vacancies have opened up only once every three years or so."[43] This reversal of expectations has often enabled Court justices to disregard the reality that they serve as arbitrators of the law, not Washington policymakers.

Contrary to Hamilton, Thomas Jefferson promoted a standardized limit on judicial tenure. In response to a submission that the Senate act as the "Supreme Appellate Court," Jefferson turned instead to crafting "a Constitutional Amendment abolishing the present judicial tenure. 'A better remedy,' " suggested Jefferson, " '. . . would be to give future commissions to Judges for six years (the Senatorial term) with a reappointmentability by the President, with the approbation of both Houses.' "[44] Other, more contemporary suggestions have been advocated, including a constitutional amendment that would limit justices to one eighteen-year term.[45] Each term for the individual justices would be staggered against others so that on every second year ("the first and third year of a president's four-year term") a new justice would need to be appointed. Under this plan, a justice could only serve one term, thus helping to "guarantee the independence of the justices by removing any incentive for them to curry favor with politicians in order to win a second term on the high Court."

The creation of term limits on the Supreme Court would tackle all the consequences of lifelong tenure addressed in "Lifetime Tenure—Three Consequences." First, more frequent turnover of justices would increase the Court's accountability. It would further retain its independence as a co-equal branch through the eighteen-year term proposition (longer than any other limited term in the federal government). Second, regularity of Court appointments would considerably lower the stakes during the confirmation process while nonetheless carrying the weight of the Supreme Court's legal importance. Thus, with two-year intervals, a president would be guaranteed at least two appointments, and each senator (serving six-year terms) could participate in the confirmation process at least thrice. And third, the fixed term "would likely lead in practice to a younger average retirement age for justices than the current age of 78.7 years."[46] As a result, the mental capacities of justices would not likely be of concern, and an arbitrary maximum age for retirement (as often suggested) would not be necessary.

Many have long recognized the need for restrictions of the Supreme Court's scope and political influence. WE CONSERVATIVES BELIEVE judicial term limits, along with other impositions, is a workable and fair solution that promotes accountability and continued legal capabilities—all which we expect from our Supreme Court.

ECONOMIC STRENGTH

The Immorality of Redistribution

WE CONSERVATIVES BELIEVE wealth redistribution cannot produce economic liberty. It kills innovation, breeds inactivity, stifles competition, broadens corruption, and, worse yet, is immoral. One cannot rightfully defend the taking of one man's lawfully obtained property without just compensation.

Redistribution—that is, the taking of one's treasure, property, or income and transferring it to another, usually through the means of a tax or other legal policy—universally presents a two-fold problem. First, it penalizes the successful. The very principle of redistribution requires deductions from the more wealthy in society and imposes arbitrary caps on how much wealth someone can justifiably maintain and on what they can obtain. This, in turn, breeds divisiveness among the citizenry between those who want the other's wealth and those who either have it or defend it. The once positive longings of envy turn into the negative aggressions of anger. Secondly, wealth redistribution creates an overall idleness in the general population. It encourages class distinctions and attitudes of entitlement. Through its villainization of the successful and enabling of dependence, it stalls a nation's productivity and creativity in both present and future endeavors.

But in America, redistribution is more than the two-fold problem it universally presents; it is also unconstitutional. Numerous indications from the framers, both direct and indirect, make this quite clear. James Madison, known as the author of the Constitution, was troubled by the beginnings of socialist undertakings and the "dangerous precedent" that may be perceived thereby: "He could not undertake to lay his finger on that article in the Federal Constitution which granted a right to Congress of expending, on objects of benevolence, the money of their constituents. And if once they broke the fine line laid down before them, for the direction of their conduct, it was impossible to say to what lengths they might go, or to what extremities this practice might be carried."[1] That is, "Charity is no part of the legislative duty of the government."[2] Founder Samuel Adams emphasized that "the utopian schemes of [redistribution], and a community of goods, are as visionary and impracticable, as those that vest all property in the Crown, are arbitrary, despotic, and in our government unconstitutional."[3] Thomas Jefferson argued, "To take from one, because it is thought that his own industry and that of his fathers has acquired too much, in order to spare to others, who, or whose fathers, have not exercised equal industry and skill, is to violate arbitrarily the first principle of association, the guarantee to every one of a free exercise of his industry, and the fruits acquired by it."[4]

We needn't only rely on the founders' understanding of the dangers associated with redistribution; we can see in our time how these ideals never measure up to the implementers' aims. Examples of distributive governments' falls from power in the twentieth century include those in Poland, Hungary, East Germany, Bulgaria, Czechoslovakia, Romania, and the Soviet Union.[5] Time and again, we have seen the failure of redistributive philosophies.

Wealth redistribution is, as Adrian Rogers argued, a theft:

> You cannot legislate the poor into freedom by legislating the wealthy out of freedom.[6] What one person receives without working for, another person must work for without receiving. . . . When half of the people get the idea that they do not have to work because the other half is going to take care of them, and when the other half gets the idea that it does no good to work because somebody else is going to get what they work for, that is about the end of any nation. *You cannot multiply wealth by dividing it.*[7]

WE CONSERVATIVES BELIEVE the fruits of one's own labor, without the injection of redistributive ideologies, is the most justifiable way to obtain economic freedom.

The Morality of a Free Market

WE CONSERVATIVES BELIEVE free market engagements are the most moral and just form of economic enterprise. The free market is centered on voluntary actions between producers and consumers and on the value of the services one provides for another. Only in free markets do consumers and producers fairly retain or expend their capital, and only in free markets do the greatest number of people have the largest chance of economic success.

A purely free market system is largely absent of government intrusion. Most basically, it is "a private and consensual system of production and distribution, [usually] conducted for profit in a competitive environment that is relatively free of governmental interference."[8] In free enterprise, the only role of government is "to outlaw and prosecute fraud and coercion."[9] Certainly, in today's America, our economy is a far cry from this economic scheme. We possess vast agencies and laws that place great hindrances on the marketplace and penalize those who, notwithstanding these obstructions, still achieve economic independence. Instead, the United States now rests on a "mixed economy, one with both free market and socialistic attributes." The results of these mixtures are inequitable and inconsistent policies that provide little-to-no stability upon which economic growth can occur and ones that propel the immorality of redistribution.

Consider this example given by economist Walter Williams on the integrity associated with free enterprise and how it reflects upon the individual and the larger society:

> Let's say I mow your lawn and you pay me twenty dollars. What does that twenty dollars really mean? When I go to the grocer and say, "I would like to have four pounds of steak" He, in effect, says to me, "You want a lot of people to serve you -- ranchers, truckers, butchers, and packagers. All these people have to be paid. What did you do to serve your fellow man?"
>
> "Well," I say, "I mowed my fellow man's lawn." And the grocer says, "Prove it." Then I offer him the twenty dollars. Think of the money that you've earned as a certificate of performance. It's proof that you've served your fellow man.[10]

Opponents of free enterprise are quick to argue that only at the expense of another is an individual's success accomplished. This "zero-sum game" relies on the notion that for every winner there must also be a loser. Yet the underlying problem with this premise is that in free markets, every trade (being voluntary) benefits both parties. The producer receives cash or another asset, and the consumer receives the product or service the producer offered. This win-win situation is in stark contrast with the actual zero-sum game of government-imposed wealth redistribution. Under that ideology, government takes wealth from those who have earned it and reallocates it to others who have not. Thus, while the receiving party benefits from the transfer, the party who legitimately earned it suffers. Here, there is truly one winner and one loser. WE CONSERVATIVES BELIEVE the practice of free enterprise, even with its turbulence and exceptions, is vastly more moral than a misled belief in wealth redistribution.

The Zero-Sum Deception

WE CONSERVATIVES BELIEVE policies of economic trade are infinitely more profitable than those of pillage, the latter being at the core of contemporary redistributive schemes. The notion that a country's economy affixes to a particular sum of wealth is both erroneous and deceitful yet is nonetheless a platform increasingly embraced by the political Left in America.

Advancing the perception that the total wealth of a nation (or the world) is flat allows for several political agendas to be promoted while disregarding the economic truth. Its persuasion is so compelling not because of its accuracy but because of its ability to erupt emotions of reprisal. When "there is a fixed amount of good things," life is like a pizza.[11] "If some people have too many slices, other people have to eat the box." Yet zero-sum advocates have no answer to arguments "for more pizza parlors baking more pizzas. The solution to our problems," they say, "is redistribution of the pizzas we've got—with low-cost, government-subsidized pepperoni somehow materializing as a result of higher taxes on pizza-parlor owners." This economic attitude not only demonizes those making the pizza and those owning more pizza than others, but it also encourages victimhood. When there is only limited wealth, there can only be (allegedly by consequence) so much happiness.

It is the idea "that if we wipe the smile off the faces of people with prosperous businesses and successful careers," their lost smiles will somehow transfer and "make the rest of us grin."

By creating an illusion of stagnant wealth, one in which rigid barriers are intrinsic, individuals with greater portions are deemed to have an unfair share. Thus, for proponents of this belief, the most economically fair recourse is achieved through the acquisition of gluttonous countrymen's property; more specifically, their finances. And what better and more powerful (and unavoidable) institution to see this through than that of the government? Politicians who then refuse or remain hesitant to impose such takings are somehow "letting [their] citizens down."[12] But who, exactly, should be eligible for politically thieving distributions? If only the truly poor were entitled, the mass majority of constituents would be in no different condition, for most Americans are not truly poor. Therefore, the government must allocate funds to the "middle class, something most well-off [and voting] Americans consider themselves to be members of." Their plan is then "to take from the more rich and the more-or-less rich, and give to the less rich, more-or-less. It is as if Robin Hood stole treasure from the Sheriff of Nottingham and bestowed it on the Deputy Sherriff." Or in other words, "a political policy of sneaking in America's back door, swiping a laptop, going around to the front door, ringing the bell, and announcing, 'Free computer equipment for all school children!' "

Generally, redistribution through zero-sum ideologies is to politics just as plagiarism is to writing—that is, to "take the work or idea [or finances] of someone else and pass it off as one's own."[13] Moreover, merely taking ever-larger sums from someone who has more than oneself does not make either party any better off, other than a momentary satisfaction often associated with victimhood's anger toward others. We as a people, and as a country, can do better. WE CONSERVATIVES BELIEVE the best and most affluent economies are those that embrace voluntary trade, competition in the marketplace, and unburdened wealth creation.

Income Tax, Growth, and Wealth

WE CONSERVATIVES BELIEVE lower taxation over a wider swath of people is fundamentally more effective in amassing governmental revenue than the high taxation of a wealthy few, and it is necessarily more equitable for the citizens. Moreover, it undeniably excels economic growth and propels American ingenuity.

The secret to financial prosperity for the states, and thus for the country, is, in fact, no secret at all but is instead a principle very often ignored or denounced. A state's income tax, which levies tariffs on those working within a state's borders, has a clear and direct impact on that same state's economic stability. For states imposing no income tax, coupled with lower state spending, growth is significantly faster, stronger, and longer-lasting than those penalizing citizens' labors. For instance, over the last ten years in no-income-tax states, growth in private-sector gross domestic product increased 17 percentage points more than those with such a tax (59 percent versus 42 percent).[14] They have also collectively "increased the number of jobs by 4.9 percent while jobs in the rest of the states decreased by 2.6 percent. States without an income tax gained population (+5.5 percent) from domestic migration (U.S. residents moving in and out of states) while other states as a whole lost 1.3 percent of population between 2000 and 2009."[15]

As an alternative to the income tax, some governors have proposed (and some states enacted) replacing "it with a broader sales tax."[16] Under this initiative, the tax burden shifts away from income collection and instead toward that from consumption while still "exempting food, medicine, and utilities." This tends to avoid the "direct penalty on saving, investment, and labor that create[s] new wealth." Nine states with no income tax evidence the effectiveness of similar proposals: "from 2002 to 2012, 62 percent of the three million net new jobs in America were created in nine states without an income tax, though these states account for only about 20 percent of the national population. The no-income-tax states have had more stable revenue growth while states like New York, New Jersey, and California that depend on the top 1 percent of earners for nearly half of their income-tax revenue suffer wide and destabilizing swings in their tax collections."[17] Even more, a revenue study in North Carolina unveiled "that a tax reform that shifts more of the burden to consumption from income would increase average annual personal income growth by 0.38 percent to 0.66 percent," something that "would lead to much higher state tax revenues" than opting for ever-increasing income levies. In all, "the path to superior economic growth and job creation is clear," and widespread and continued attacks on the income earners of America has never been, nor ever will be, the solution.[18] WE CONSERVATIVES BELIEVE states can boost their tax revenues through reductions and shifts of their taxation schemes—something the evidence clearly portrays.

Flat Taxation

WE CONSERVATIVES BELIEVE fundamental tax reform is necessary to achieve financial solvency and reduce the politics of envy and resentment. To best achieve these goals, we must begin by moving away from one of America's most discriminating and unsettling economic schemes: the progressive tax.

The current tax code in the United States regularly serves as the bridle and bit in restraining economic growth. "High marginal tax rates and a battalion of tax distortions discourage productivity, slowing the rise in wages and economic growth and making it difficult for businesses to compete globally."[19] Further, the tax code is far too complex, inflicting "a multitude of rules and exceptions that lack transparency and fairness." Presently, the federal government (in addition to state-imposed levies) compels the American worker into an income tax, payroll tax, death tax, and a plethora of excises. The required rate for each is variable, contingent on the level of income a worker earns. For many who make "too little" under the Internal Revenue Code, it requires no income tax at all, yet for those who make substantially more, it appropriates great sums of their earnings.

This sliding scale taxation design is harmful in several ways, but two key points stand out. First, it unfairly penalizes those of greater success and ebbs away at the pursuit of financial accomplishments. The added reward for those obtaining economic stability is a government evermore thirsty to share in their achievements and thereafter redistribute collected earnings to others who have not been as successful. And second, sliding scale taxation inevitably produces the class warfare and envy brought on by inequitable justice under the law. Both those who are required to relinquish the greatest portion of earnings and those required to give over nothing at all inevitably resent the other's alleged greed. Thus, any conversations over an extinction of our progressive tax structure begin with attacks that assert bigotry and gluttony. The rich (who in today's America can be labeled so when earning $200,000) are held not to pay their fair share of taxes. Since no level of taxation—regardless of how extreme—on only the rich can adequately solve America's fiscal disorder, the case for more taxes on the wealthy can forever be argued, even after tax increases on those very individuals occur. But ultimately, of these two "classes" of Americans, who hasn't done their fair share more: those earning the most money and consequently paying the greatest level of tax or those paying no tax at all and receiving redistributions of money they did not earn?

Instead, the argument for a flat tax over all American workers is more strongly rooted in fiscal solvency and ethical honesty. The Heritage Foundation has proposed a flat tax scheme that would remove the harmful progressive tax of today yet retain some of its advantageous distinctions. The New Flat Tax (as they have dubbed it, or the NFT) replaces all current tax variations with one flat rate, applicable equally to every American consumer.[20] That is, the NFT taxes both the worker earning $1,000,000 and the worker earning $20,000 at the same percentage; neither pays more or less than the other proportionally. Next, the NFT "retains the Earned Income Credit [(a tax credit for low-income workers)] to preserve the level of income support for low-wage workers. And low- and middle-income families also receive a tax credit of $3,000 ($2,500 for singles) toward the purchase of health insurance." Moreover, the NFT maintains three potential deductions for each filing year: "higher education, gifts and charitable contributions, and an optional home mortgage interest deduction." Lastly, the NFT would allow for deductions of personal savings and business investment, promoting individual planning and industrial venturing—something necessary in every strong economy. WE CONSERVATIVES BELIEVE a flat tax would be equitable in its applicability, be effective in its economic strengthening, and would produce higher wages and stronger companies.

THE LAFFER CURVE

An Economic Principle

WE CONSERVATIVES BELIEVE the Laffer Curve, one of the most fundamental realities of economics, is key to understanding the effects of high taxation in a national economy and should serve as the basis for taxation policies.

Named after American economist Arthur Laffer, the Laffer Curve "illustrates the two most important things we need to know about taxes: [(1)] how much money the government can raise from taxes, and [(2)] at what level of taxation the government might start getting less, not more, revenue."[21] To begin, picture a graph upon which the horizontal axis represents the tax rate imposed by the government, and the vertical axis symbolizes the level of revenue the government receives from those collected taxes. That is, the further to the right on the horizontal axis we tread, the greater the tax burden becomes on the citizenry. Just the same, the higher we look on the vertical axis, the more tax money the government collects.

First, because a taxation rate of 0 percent will undoubtedly accumulate no government revenue, the initial point on the graph should be at the zero marker for both axes (entirely to the left and bottom, respectively). However, if the government requires a small tax rate of, say, 1 or 2 percent, government revenue will then, accordingly, begin to rise. Our graphing point will both trend to the right and upwards, equaling a higher tax rate and higher government intake. This principle can continue for a time (that is, more taxes equals more money), but as the Laffer Curve will show, it cannot continue indefinitely.

Now consider a tax rate of 100 percent. Under this scenario, our graph point is fully to the right of the horizontal axis, representing maximum taxation. If the government retained everything a worker earned, it is self-evident that no one would work. Without any financial benefit attached to one's labor, virtually all economic activity would cease. And so, because of the lacking workforce from which to collect taxes, the government will, again, bring in no revenue under a tax scheme of 100 percent. Thus, the first point and the last point on the vertical axis will remain at the zero marker.

The uniqueness of the Laffer Curve, however, is its attempt to determine when increased taxation eventually leads to decreased revenue. In other words, at what point are taxes so high that economic output begins to decline? If, as in the preceding example, we began the graph at the double-zero marker and slowly rose governmental takings with higher taxation but eventually ended again with zero revenue coupled with a 100 percent tax rate, where exactly did the graph begin to decline? Where does taxation become so burdensome that governmental revenues actually decline with higher taxes? "All economists—even the most Left-wing ones—agree that the true Laffer Curve . . . has a downward sloping part, meaning at some point tax revenues start going down."[22] The controversy arises, however, over when the downward slope begins. In "The Laffer Curve—A High-Tax Threshold," variations of interpretations over this dilemma are discussed, and historical examples are provided to illuminate the realities of this economic principle. WE CONSERVATIVES BELIEVE the Laffer Curve delivers a platform for economic policy that demonstrates how we cannot simply tax our way to opulence nor can we expect the citizens to continue their present economic outputs by making high taxes even higher.

A High-Tax Threshold

WE CONSERVATIVES BELIEVE the Laffer Curve is not simply a classroom experiment or theoretical conviction; it has been proven time-and-again in economies both large and small and each nation. In the United States, recent examples from the twentieth century show the countering effects of excessively high taxation policies versus more comfortably reduced schemes.

Traditional thinking about precisely when the Laffer Curve begins its downward slope generally pins it around the 70 percent marker. That is, until the taxpayer receives only 30 percent of his earned income, government revenues will continue to rise. Yet the closer taxation reaches the 70 percent point, the rate at which government revenues increase significantly reduces. New evidence, however, suggests quite a different reality. In a study from professors at the University of California, Berkeley, the rate at which economic output begins to shrink is not 70 percent but closer to *33 percent*.[23] By studying the effects of varying tax policies on the nation's GDP, they determined that every "tax increase of 1 percent of GDP" over 33 percent "lowers real GDP by almost 3 percent."[24] To illustrate, consider the following example:

> Suppose a country's GDP is $100 billion, and suppose its tax rate is 33 percent. Then its tax revenue will be 33 percent of $100 billion, or $33 billion. Now suppose it raises taxes to 34 percent. If the [new study's] result is accurate, then this will decrease GDP by 3 percent to $97 billion. Tax revenue will be 34 percent of $97 billion, or $32.98 billion. Note that this is slightly less than the revenue at the 33 percent rate. If you experiment with other tax rates, you'll see that revenue is maximized when the tax rate is 33 1/3 percent. Moreover, as the tax rate increases to rates higher and higher than 33 1/3 percent, government revenue becomes smaller and smaller.[25]

The importance of this study comes at a time when personal and corporate economic successes are under intense scrutiny. Those responsible for the incessant spending addiction of Washington have continually tried to indemnify themselves by urging the necessity of higher taxes. All must pay their fair share, they argue, and all are required to give a little more of their earned income to purportedly balance the fiscal concerns of America—particularly the so-called "too wealthy." But this study, along with the hindsight of history, showcases a substantially different design.

During the Great Depression, in an effort to raise more government revenue, Congress increased taxes on certain imported goods by 6.3 percent.[26] Although the rate of taxation increased, the revenues from the additional tariff significantly decreased over five years, eventually leading Congress to once more lower the rate of taxation, bringing in more revenue again. More recently, in the 1980s, Congress and President Ronald Reagan drastically cut the tax rates on individuals earning at least $200,000. As a consequence, governmental revenues from those same taxpayers considerably increased, primarily a result of lower tax schemes and the use of the Laffer Curve.

The belief in ever-increasing tax policies to swell government revenues and subsequently reduce financial liabilities is an argument not supported by one of the most primary truths of economics: the Laffer Curve. WE CONSERVATIVES BELIEVE true economic stability is best achieved through lower taxes across a broader swath of the populace, not higher taxes on a small section of the wealthy—after all, working Americans are far better choosers of how to utilize their assets than the government has ever proven to be on their behalf.

The Right to Work

WE CONSERVATIVES BELIEVE a person's liberty extends beyond their interactions with government and into decisions made in their personal life. Among these choices should be the individual's right to choose whether he wishes to join a union at his place of employment and, if after deciding not to join that union, whether to still be required to pay association fees to that union.

The idea beyond the right to work (as many call it) holds that employees should not be forced to associate with groups or labor unions if they do not wish to. Right-to-work legislation is "a state law that prevents labor-management agreements requiring a person to join a union as a condition of employment."[27] Until 1947, with the passage of the federal Taft-Harley Act, federal unions and employers could agree to closed-shop workplaces wherein all employees were required to be members of that workplace's union. The passage of the law banned such conditions and gave states further authority to do the same in their respective jurisdictions.

Both the Constitution and natural law already protect the opportunity to work for an employer without being required to join a union or pay union association fees. The First Amendment's freedoms of speech and assembly, and by consequence association, prohibit the government from forcing relations between parties (in this case, for federal employees). Workers are to be free to exercise this right when determining whether to join unions or refrain from union participation. Further, natural law protects one's personal property, including any assets that person has earned through his efforts. The right of a person to retain or spend his earned money to avoid or associate with a union, coupled with his First Amendment protections, cannot be superseded by a union's policy of forced conditions of employment.

Two arguments universally made by those opposing the right to work rest on false or misleading information. First, as one Michigan State House

Representative said during that state's path to becoming right-to-work, "No one is forced to join a union. They're asked to pay their fair share of the collective bargaining process. [Right-to-work] gives them the chance to freeload and free ride."[28] The implication found in this argument (that is, those who do not join the union still benefit from union agreements with management) is that unions "spend the vast majority of their money on contract negotiations, representation, or other non-political work." But this is a great fallacy. In the same state, its largest labor union (the Michigan Education Association, representing Michigan teachers and educators) spent only 11 percent of its revenues on "representational activities" in 2012. Thus, for those both in and out of the labor union, the union only spent approximately one-tenth of all dues collected on representing them before management.

The second argument is that "no one is forced to join a union." While this is fundamentally true, it is just as fundamentally misleading. Employees working for unionized companies or the government may not be required to join the connected union yet may still be mandated to pay association fees. "Association fees, or agency fees, vary, but can represent up to 90 percent of the dues of full union members."[29] Is this non-member thoughtless enough to honestly believe it is not the same thing?

Instead, unions practice an alliance with the Democratic Party, and both unions and the Left act as each other's host. As later discussed in "Educating About Exceptionalism—Democrats and Unions," the Democratic Party is reliant on union contributions—funds that come from the collection of union dues and fees. And, just the same, unions rely on the Democratic Party with its continual adoption of union-friendly legislation (and right-to-work opposition). WE CONSERVATIVES BELIEVE right-to-work laws do not ban or limit unions' potential roles in the workplace; instead, they require unions to prove their worthiness to workers—something unions have long been able to avoid.

The Welfare Loan

Dependence and Control

WE CONSERVATIVES BELIEVE most welfare programs are designed to aid Americans in need of financial assistance or other types of support. However, the intent behind these programs is more difficult to define since it can so easily be manipulated and misconstrued.

Welfare, most fundamentally, is the undertaking of "various social insurance programs, such as unemployment compensation, old-age pensions, family allowances, food stamps," and other aids.[30] In the United States, there exists an empire of welfare programs that dwarf the entire budgets of most other countries. As of 2012, "the federal government administers nearly eighty different overlapping federal means-tested welfare programs."[31] And, even after excluding those who benefit from Social Security and Medicare, more than 100 million people in America receive some form of federal welfare. In 2011, the state and federal governments spent $1.03 trillion on means-tested welfare programs—the single biggest expenditure of the American government.[32]

Certainly, there will always be those who fall upon troubled times, and in a civilized society, we ought not to let our fellow man unnecessarily remain burdened by crippling fates. But we also must not allow our fellow man to capitalize on his hard times at the expense of others. If that befallen man seeks government assistance, from where do the resources of that assistance come? They come almost universally from the taxpayer. And from where does that taxpayer receive his assets? From his labor. Accordingly, the intent of the politician who promotes further expansions of welfare schemes is twofold.

First is the humanitarian ideal of aiding those in need and of giving to others when times necessitate. However, the second intent is far more cynical and easily deflected as a radical accusation. As noted above, out of more than 300 million Americans, over 100 million people residing in America receive a form of welfare. Surely, a third of America's population is not wholly incapable of producing additional income to counterbalance that which they otherwise receive through redistributive government designs. Instead of considering America's welfare state as amazingly unbearable, many politicians recognize it as an opportunity. "No matter how large the welfare state, liberal politicians and writers have accused it of being shamefully small" and "contemptibly austere."[33] They chastise those who condemn the reach of current social insurance and demonize them on the grounds of the first intent (that is, for humanitarian reasons). Thus, further growths of welfare become encouraged, and the politicians making such promotions gain a valuable voting bloc: those whose livelihoods depend on continued government disbursements. A vote for another politician (one who wishes to curb social expansions) is hence a vote against one's interest. Instead, it is easier for a politician to tell dependent constituents that someone else is the root of their misery and that the government will act to level the playing field—higher taxes for the successful and handouts for the dependent. It becomes a sure way for a politician to instill the fear of regression-back-to-ruin into the minds of the hard-pressed. WE CONSERVATIVES BELIEVE the true intent of welfare programs should rest firmly in aid of your fellow man and the importance of each individual's output to society's overall strength.

An Alternative Option

WE CONSERVATIVES BELIEVE fraud, corruption, over-extensions of government, and political posturing riddle the current welfare state in America.

The threats of an excessively large welfare state are more than the accompanying fiscal insolvency. Another, more looming hazard is an over-dependence on the government for one's wellbeing. While there is no doubt many among us will, at various times for various reasons, seek government assistance to help through a troubled time, a government that encourages its citizens to obtain increasingly available aid is a dangerous one. The more dependent one becomes on government resources, the less independent that same person is. With each additional individual added to the government welfare scheme, the government's reach grows stronger. If an American remains reliant on his government for his livelihood, he simultaneously loses some of his control over that government and the politicians working therein. Governments and politicians—not just in America but around the world—realize that continually dependent people will regularly make decisions that further their dependency, including decisions made in the ballot booth. Therefrom, government bodies obtain the ability to grow more audacious and expansive and are further able to demonize individuals not on the government dole.

Studies commonly show the longer one stays out of the workforce, the harder it becomes for that person to reenter it. This unfortunate truth is generally the product of rusted skill-sets and the stagnation that comes with idleness. For many, but certainly not all, this regrettable reality can translate into a continual dependence on government assistance. At first, recipients may view welfare aid as a grant or gift, one which is given to them by a benevolent government, but this attitude hastily evolves. No longer is welfare considered assistance but rather an entitlement. Thus, any person who criticizes the current state of welfare programs is attacking what is rightly the beneficiaries', and for the politicians who capitalize on the increased powers associated with constituent dependency, they are happy to agree.

If, instead, the true intent of welfare is (or ought to be) lending a helping-hand to countrymen in need, then shouldn't the purpose of that hand be to bring the individual back onto their feet? And if the government unilaterally acts as a middleman to take from those who have and give to those who have not, shouldn't those who have not, when once again standing upright, refund those who underwrote their newfound stability? For instance, every taxpayer appreciates that taxation is not a charitable contribution. Just the same, a receipt of welfare should not be the receipt of a governmental donation. Instead, social welfare programs would perhaps work best if operated as a loaning mechanism. We could still accomplish the goal of helping others, but many secondary pursuits correlated with social insurance would instantly diminish. No longer would fraud of the system be as prevalent when acceptance of government assistance is attached to a repayment plan. No longer would politicians be as capable of using welfare money as a means of garnishing and retaining voters, for, rather than receiving an award, the receiver would obtain a loan to pay back in the future. No longer would government insolvencies remain so deeply rooted, as new revenue sources would open upon repayment of the welfare loans. No longer would those whose tax monies divert to welfare programs have such an aversion for those who receive such revenues when they are eventually required to repay those funds. And no longer would governments so aptly exploit the dependency of those temporarily reliant on governmental aid. WE CONSERVATIVES BELIEVE moments will always arise when our fellow man is in need of imminent aid, and, as a civilized society, we ought to serve one another insofar as the beneficiary does not exploit the contributor's assistance and support—a welfare loan program might be a suitable program to help accomplish this lofty goal.

GOVERNMENTAL INTERFERENCE

WE CONSERVATIVES BELIEVE that in a free market economy, excessive governmental interference stifles competitive growth, even if the government is acting as a competitor itself. As a result of bureaucrats needing to please politicians far more than consumers, the persistent financing concerns confronted by the private sector are not as present in public-sector industries.

Just over a decade after the Civil War, a veteran of the conflict spoke regarding the unusual role of government in relation to the private man. In his speech, Republican Robert Ingersoll spoke of the false presumption that government can actually produce something without first having to consume something else from the people who created it:

> In the first place the Government does not support the people, the people support the Government.
>
> The Government is a perpetual pauper. It passes round the hat, and solicits contributions; but then you must remember that the Government has a musket behind the hat. The Government produces nothing. It does not plow the land, it does not sow corn, it does not grow trees. The Government is a perpetual consumer. We support the Government. Now, the idea that the Government can make money for you and me to live on—why, it is the same as though my hired man should issue certificates of my indebtedness to him for me to live on.[34]

Rather than attempting to support the people economically (a pursuit frequently sought), the government is best effective when it acts minimally in its submission to the people. A liberty-loving people never tender themselves to their government simply to become subjects of it. Instead, they cooperate with their self-created and representative institutions for the betterment of the people as a whole, allowing their government only to act through the powers delegated to it. That is, a truly free people are not dependent on the government for their financial wellbeing, but rather it is the government that is dependent upon the people for the same.

How, then, has the general American political philosophy evolved into the precise opposite? Why do so many politicians and constituents alike remain convinced that the government can serve as the remedy to personal and economic woes without regard to repeated and unremitting government failures to achieve such ends? Instead, as Thomas Paine alarmed, "how often is the natural propensity to society disturbed or destroyed by the operations of government! When the latter, instead of being ingrafted on the principles of the former, assumes to exist for itself, and acts by partialities of favour and oppression, it becomes the cause of the mischiefs it ought to prevent."[35] When combined with restrictive economic interference, those government propensities are evermore disruptive. WE CONSERVATIVES BELIEVE the best and most suitable role government should retain in free market economics is one of reasonable regulation and uninterested observation, leaving competition to the private industries acting freely therein.

Inefficient Governance

WE CONSERVATIVES BELIEVE considerable financial savings could be enjoyed by state and federal governments if it undertook private-sector work-efficiencies in public-sector positions and minimized wasteful and unproductive practices. Studies have consistently shown government industries are not only overstaffed but also underworked—an expensive combination for the taxpayer.

A striking survey administered by the Bureau of Labor Statistics (called the American Time Use Survey) underscores the reality of this claim. In conducting the investigation, interviewers sampled a large and representative number of American households over the course of a year from which they "construct[ed] a comprehensive 'time diary' for each respondent that describes activities that occurred during the entire 24-hour day before the interview."[36] Following the conferences, administrators "place each respondent's raw answers into a detailed set of activity categories, one of which is work for a primary job." The information gathered counts both work conducted from home and that formally on the job. It further excluded teachers "because of their naturally shorter work year." The results are very telling.

To begin, if the hours worked by public-sector employees simply matched those of their private-sector counterparts, "governments at all levels could save more than $100 billion in annual labor costs."[37] This realization derives from clear distinctions in the number of hours worked by each sector's employees respectively. "During a typical workweek," the review summarized, "private-sector employees work about 41.4 hours. Federal workers, by contrast, put in 38.7 hours, and state and local government employees work 38.1 hours." When calculated over the course of an entire year, a private-sector worker is on the job for about "4.7 more *weeks* than state and local government workers," and 3.8 more "workweeks than federal employees."[38] Incredibly, if the public sector worked the extra month (that is, the same length as the private sector), "governments could theoretically save around $130 billion in annual labor costs without reducing services."

Still, this data is not undermined by arguments that might suggest differences in job roles and services are to blame for the vast disparities. While occupational differences certainly do factor occasionally, "Large differences in work hours actually persist even when comparing workers with similar jobs and similar skills in each sector."[39] Thus, as Governor Mitt Romney wrote, the need for strict watchfulness of government spending and inefficiency is justified even further:

> Wherever a private sector alternative is unavailable, . . . the need to monitor and manage costs is critical because of government's natural tendency toward inefficiency, long productivity, and excessive cost.
>
> The biggest reason why government isn't as efficient and productive as the private sector is that businesses have to please their customers or those customers will go elsewhere.

> Government, on the other hand, has to please politicians who want to please voters, contributors, and lobbyists. . . . Without competition, government never goes out of business. Business rewards innovation and risk. Government rewards the status quo and the avoidance of risk.[40]

In taking steps toward fiscal solvency, perhaps the government, before asking "private-sector employees to work more to support the government, government itself should work as much as the private sector."[41] WE CONSERVATIVES BELIEVE the government, as a steward of the citizenry, is duty-bound to operate proficiently and resourcefully; simply matching the working hours of the private-sector taxpayer is a good and reasonable place to begin.

EDUCATIONAL STRENGTH

Competition in Education

Providing Options

WE CONSERVATIVES BELIEVE our children deserve an education that is not only challenging but that also graduates them with greater skill-sets than those in other developed nations, without the interference of government posturing and unionized politics. While there is no single way to guarantee this objective, the first step in its accomplishment is by eliminating the public schools' monopoly over education. By forcing the districts to compete for both funding and students, we can create a model analogous to other private industry economic schemes, those which have driven innovation and invention in various markets.

America's now infamously poor results in education cannot be fixed with one solution. The roads that have brought us to this point are entrenched and many. But there are ways to slow the regression, and, with time, reverse the course toward an upward advancement. The problem begins with, as most often, governmental intervention. Today, public schools generally obtain their funding through forced tax revenues usually derived from real property tax and federal aid. Consequently, individuals who do not have children in schools continue to pay for the public schools in their area, and the allotted revenue from these taxations provide a guaranteed source of income for this public-sector field.

Conversely, private schools act independent of the state and raise capital through tuition paid from attendees. They do not have guaranteed income nor students allocated to them through districting designs. To attract, retain, and graduate students, private institutions rely on their merits alone—through staffing decisions, facility offerings, and curriculum comprehensiveness. Although they compete against other private schools, they are at a distinct disadvantage when competing with public schools. Because private schools acquire funding from tuition, parents who wish for their child to attend one must pay both private tuition and the same tax levels as if their child was attending a public school. They generally do not receive a tax liability reduction for not utilizing the public-school system. This double hurdle is often too much for a family to jump.

Guaranteed income to a public school has negative effects on the quality of the education received and the facilities provided because it removes the school from an otherwise competitive market. The public school does not, therefore, directly compete with other bodies of education that would force the school to improve and hone its education. It does not require the district to entirely prove its worthiness to parents as a quality place to send their children. The assured proceeds permit a culture of passiveness and mediocrity, minimizing the mental challenges our students should confront and harming their stature on the world stage.

To counter this predicament, the sometimes-used school voucher program is a reasonable remedy for both leveling the competitive field and allowing the citizenry to decide how best to spend its money. A school voucher is a certificate provided to parents that they apply toward the cost of tuition at a private school if they choose to send their child there, thus offsetting the additional charge otherwise presented. In effect, it eliminates one of the two hurdles preventing many families from even considering private education. Further, it draws out the competitive nature of economics (proven time and again to benefit the consumer in free-market economics) by compelling both public and private schools to demonstrate themselves as the more credible education institution. This drives schools to remain on the cutting edge and to hire and retain teachers who best perform under higher standards while removing the lethargic and worn.

Our students, the future of America, deserve the best chance of success we can provide them. WE CONSERVATIVES BELIEVE we can afford these students a better opportunity by allowing their parents to choose which school system best suits their needs and educational beliefs.

The Influence of Unions

WE CONSERVATIVES BELIEVE public-union politics and lobbying should not hold the education of our children at their behest. As an organized labor group, its interests are, naturally, self-preservation, expansion, and the reduction of competition in the market.

An article written for the Cato Institute concerning *The Effects of Teachers Unions on American Education* lists five key objectives these unions advance (and their related consequences). They are, "(1) raising their members' wages, (2) growing their membership, (3) increasing the share of the public school labor force that they represent, (4) precluding pay based on performance or aptitude, and (5) minimizing competition from nonunion shops."[1] Of these, the last two are most troublesome, and we will explore them separately.

The notion that unions oppose member wages based on merit alone might at first seem difficult to prove. But a closer look at some general policies of organized labor groups suggests otherwise. For example, a resolution of the National Education Association (NEA) instructs that members should "exclude any form of merit pay except in institutions of higher education where it has been bargained."[2] The American Federation of Teachers (AFT), while not as explicit in its opposition to merit pay, nonetheless holds that "it is not abandoning the traditional [credential- and seniority-based] salary schedule. Failed attempts to implement differentiated pay options, like merit pay systems, identified a few teachers as 'outstanding' and paid them extra, rewarding teachers on the basis of supervisory ratings or student test scores." The examples continue, but when considering all areas of American life, shouldn't the continued employment of those who educate our children be based *solely* on merit? Or otherwise by a combination of merit and longevity, for if we enforce merit pay, a teacher's career longevity will occur because of their successful abilities.

As discussed in "Competition in Education—Providing Options," the ability of our schools to produce competitive graduates depends on the system's own ability to compete. As of 2010, public schools entertained a monopoly that was fed nearly $600 billion a year.[3] Because the monopoly persists, the goal of labor unions is now to maintain that monopoly, something most effectively done by lobbying politicians to "oppos[e] policies such as charter schools, vouchers, and education tax credits that give families easier access to nonunion schooling." Organizations representing teachers thus become less concerned with the advancement of the student and more interested in preserving their position in the educational realm. Their definition of competition is not to offer more favorable services than their competitors do; it is to eliminate the competition.

The education of future generations must be the priority of the nation's educators. WE CONSERVATIVES BELIEVE institutions that place the organization's wellbeing above the students' potential undermine the fruits of the contest and threaten the competitive edge of graduates.

Educating About Exceptionalism

Instilling Patriotism

WE CONSERVATIVES BELIEVE education is not simply about fields of study but also about instilling American values and exceptionalism in our youth. We must infuse our children with America's history, the reasons for our dominant achievements, the realization of America's overarching goodness in the world, and the idea of patriotism. Without these, America's success is not accidentally passed from generation to generation; instead, we must teach it.

Education should always begin at home and continue to grow therefrom throughout the youths of children. But in a society where family values and childrearing are becoming less commendable pursuits, the task of education often falls wholly on the backs of teachers. Our schools train millions of young Americans from all backgrounds, stories, and situations. For millions of these children, there certainly are a great number of parents who highly dedicate themselves to the success of their offspring. They attend parent-teacher conferences, help with homework, encourage extracurricular activities, and make every baseball game. The children of these parents are much more likely to succeed in school and later in the marketplace of America. Yet there are also an alarming number of parents who are unable to be as dedicated to their children's education as is optimally necessary. This may result from an overly crowded work schedule, divorce and distance separation, illness, or a host of other challenges some parents face. But much worse, there are some parents simply unwilling to participate—they do not put in an effort because it is an effort. They may prioritize sitcoms over soccer practice, gossip magazines over homework, or excessive materialistic possessions over buying a new trumpet. Regardless of alleged excuses, it is always the child who suffers and the teachers who must pick up the slack.

The basic role of the teacher in America is to ensure that, between when the child first enrolls in kindergarten to when he walks the stage at high school graduation, the student has learned enough basic skills to give him a firm footing onto which he can enter American society. But there is another purpose, too: the teacher is to promote American prosperity and allegiance, show the importance of America in the global order, and open the door to American pride. Generally, history, civics, and other liberal arts studies incorporate these goals most easily, but they can just as well appear in virtually every classroom. The mathematics teacher speaking of America's great contribution to the field; the engineering instructor promoting America's space program and its role in putting America first among nations; the health teacher supporting family values and wise personal decisions facing our youth daily; the biology teacher encouraging children to solve America's toughest health concerns; and the gym teacher asserting physical fitness to ensure a healthy foundation of smart and able young citizens to fulfill the nation's highest calling.

When the weight of infusing these callings is moving more and more onto the shoulders of our teachers (and away from the parents of many), it is doubly vital they succeed in doing so. Without proper instruction, the youth of America may not learn of American greatness. They will not understand what it means to be exceptional nor how we can continue to maintain that reality. WE CONSERVATIVES BELIEVE in exposing our children to the goodness of America through early education in both the home and the schools.

Democrats and Unions

WE CONSERVATIVES BELIEVE our youth must be instructed by those who recognize American exceptionalism and who accept America as the beacon of liberty's hope. Those who teach should understand American exceptionalism is not automatic—each generation must maintain it.

If the United States serves as the fountain from which freedom flows, then why would some disregard this reality and even act to counter our progress? And who are the people who make these motions? As Conservatives, we face a constant battering for our convictions in eternal certainties. We fight to keep an originalist interpretation of the Constitution and to protect natural law from government intrusion. We argue for less government, less restrictions on trade and commerce, and less interference with other liberty-interest rights. At the opposite end of our positions are those who want more government in our lives, with more dependency on that government, and arbitrary lines between federal and state authorities. The Left and, by consequence, the Democratic Party routinely hold these latter beliefs.

If the Left favors a more extensive role of government, then it must, in turn, convince a majority of the people that they, too, require more government. They promote personal success as being the product of government aid, and that without such assistance, one will likely not succeed. They also sponsor welfare and social programs, including universal health insurance, Social Security, Medicare, and Medicaid, regardless the costs, extent, and instability of such programs or the burdens they will place on future generations. These programs bring Americans under the financial influence of the government, in essence turning it into an ATM, one not always requiring deposits. The more people brought under the umbrella of any such programs, the more "indebted" they become to the party providing it—the Democrats. And if the Left wishes to raise new understandings about the role of government in everyday life, what better way to achieve this than through the impressionable minds of America's youths in the public-school system?

The public-school system's monopoly on education is not an accident. The two major teachers' unions claim yearly revenues over $1.5 billion—more than the Republican and Democratic Parties combined. The depth of power this level of capital permits is immense and in constant use by those unions. The Democratic Party and the teachers' unions act as two mutually dependent bodies. For one, teachers' unions depend upon legislative restrictions of private schools, charter schools, vouchers, and homeschooling, thus minimizing competition. This allows public schools to maintain their dominance with minimal resistance or contest comfortably. It is both the default schooling system and one which receives a practically guaranteed source of income from the surrounding community. On the other hand, the Democratic Party and its politicians rely on the votes of those in the teachers' unions, for the votes of teachers alone can often overcome opposing positions and politicians. The unions pay the party, the party promotes the unions; it is a vicious cycle.

And what of the children both these organizations (the government and the teachers) tasks with educating? They are placed in the middle and are thus trained to walk the line of the Democratic Party—the very party who ensures that the students' teachers' unions stay in power. This is why so many students leave our schools and, by default, are trained Liberals. For over a decade of schooling, they were educated by members of the unions who rely on the Democrats in power and by the Democrats who rely on the unions. Many of these activist-Democrats (in power and out) are the same who attempt to diminish the exceptionalism of America. WE CONSERVATIVES BELIEVE our students must be educated by professionals who value both the civil society in which they serve and America's extraordinary contributions to the world.

Defending the Homeland

WE CONSERVATIVES BELIEVE America's children deserve the exceptional country their parents were born into. We believe that in order for the miracle of America to continue, these children must understand why America is unique, why it is the leader of the free world, and how American principles and values are distinctly superior to every other model of proposed society. We must protect the relationship between the government and the people who created it, and our youth deserve to know why. This requires a non-apologetic education of America's true history, the intentions of our founders, the unwavering stability of the Constitution, and moving beyond the talking points of one-sided party politics.

Today's youth in America have more access to global travel than at any other time in history. Intercontinental travel is relatively cheap and frequent, and schools offer study abroad programs at an ever-increasing rate. All these realities are generally good. We want a citizenry who is well-cultured, who understands and sees different societies through their day-to-day workings and the various roles governments play in the lives of people around the globe. But we want these experiences to provide evidence to our youth of the exceptional nature of America. The ability of our children to see the world should open their eyes and minds to the freedoms and liberties they possess back home, from an overly powerful and intrusive government to the ability to choose their own destinies. But what happens when, for all their lives, they have been taught only of the errors of America? Of the misguided mistakes of our past? Or of the erroneous claims of American imperialism? The product is an American abroad unable to defend America. He does not know how to articulate, for instance, the security the United States provides to our allies, both through a robust military presence and a stable dollar. He does not know of the massive humanitarian aid efforts his fellow Americans provide daily. He does not know the critical role of the American financial markets and its industries' employment of so many. He does not stand up for the hard-earned and long-fought-for liberties he now enjoys—those that allow him to travel so freely. And he does not see the threat that faces our world if America does not lead and if our enemies rise in influence.

The uninformed, mislead, and ill-equipped graduate—wavering in his holdings—falls easily into the anti-American sentiment that brews in many of the nations he travels to. Perhaps this feeling toward the United States stems from our large presence around the world (both physically and economically), undisclosed envy, or from mistakes America has made in the past. Most probably, it is some combination of these and others, but for each assertion, the traveling youth should be confidently able to rebut the charges and defend his country. Instead, having been trained his whole life on the "misgivings" of American exceptionalism, he falters and flails. European-style socialism becomes attractive, American capitalism considered evil, and success demonized. He then returns to his homeland with a diminished view of America and grows to become more resentful of his country's accomplishments. As his life continues, he enters the workforce and other leadership roles with these beliefs while simultaneously hoping for a less significant America. And because American exceptionalism is not "in the bloodstream," the present reality of our uniqueness becomes muddled with his convictions of an overbearing America, and so we face a self-fulfilled prophecy of a weakened America.[4] WE CONSERVATIVES BELIEVE that for our children to live in an America that excels, protects liberties, and understands the natural rights of individuals, we must raise children to understand them as well.

Teaching and Results

We conservatives believe the teaching profession should be a highly watched-over vocation and one from which the public requires superior results from superior participants. Public teachers, as funded by the taxpayers, are inexorably linked to the public, and so answerable to it as well.

The obligatory public scrutiny of those who formally instruct our children is at least partially to blame for perceived attacks on the teaching profession. But, just as we reelect good politicians and criticize and remove (or should) bad politicians, the classroom should serve as a transparent laboratory into an educator's teaching competency. However, this workshop has not, with any real consistency, produced generally acceptable results. Recently, the Organization for Economic Cooperation and Development (OECD) provided information that measured and compared how well students from around the world were prepared to face potential future challenges. Out of thirty-four OECD nations, American students performed mediocre at best. "In reading literacy, fifteen year-old American students . . . [rank] 14th place . . .. In mathematics, U.S. fifteen year-olds . . . rank a lowly 25th . . .. [In scientific literacy, fifteen-year-olds rank] 17th place."[5] To further worsen the problem, *30 percent* of American students do not complete high school, and for those who drop out and are already financially struggling, "it becomes nearly impossible to break out of poverty during their lifetimes."[6]

Is this what one might expect from the world's leading nation? But how can we begin to turn the tide? The best and longest lasting place to ensure a student's success is universally in the family, but also of immense impact are those who teach children. A four-step approach to improving the quality of teachers at the front of classrooms could make a dramatic change. "First, make the application process to our teaching programs highly selective at the outset . . .," and second, "select only those teacher candidates who have demonstrated high levels of intellect, literacy, and numeracy. Third, open alternative pathways into teaching, particularly for individuals who have excelled in other fields."[7] This may mean devising different avenues into teaching, moving away from the strict BA/BS requirements, and allowing for individuals who have shown excellence in other sectors—through experience—to step in as well (similar to university settings). "And fourth, raise the base salaries of teachers who are beginning their careers. We spend much more than other countries on education, but in the United States, starting teacher salaries lag far behind the comparable starting salaries of other nations . . .. Teachers should be treated like the professionals they are—and low starting salaries and fixed salary progression dissuade some of our best students from choosing this essential and valuable profession."

If the United States now spends more money on public education than ever before, and if overall classroom sizes are at historic lows, why do we still have such poor results? And if we are spending more now than ever, why are teachers not being paid more and in turn attracting the best recruits? The quality of our educators and the outcomes their students produce are of direct concern to the citizenry. Criticism of the results and certain poor instructors is not a criticism of the profession. Rather, such criticism is essential to the continuation of exceptional graduates populating the workforce and families of tomorrow. WE CONSERVATIVES BELIEVE accountability of those in our school system is a vital role of the citizen, and, for their dedication to America's future, we should commend and reward teachers who perform exceptionally well.

A Bar Exam for Teachers

Adequate Preparation

WE CONSERVATIVES BELIEVE every great nation relies on its ability to educate and enlighten its youth through rigorous education schemes soundly. This necessary goal is only truly obtainable if those who teach are themselves both soundly educated and highly enlightened. The continuously poor results that America's current education system produces suggests that, in part, the existing methodology of training and selecting teachers is inadequate. The AFT proposed a new idea: a standardized bar exam for all potential teachers before they can be permitted to instruct students.

Randi Weingarten, president of the AFT, argued that "we must do away with the common rite of passage whereby new teachers are thrown into classrooms, expected to figure things out, and left to see if they (and their students) sink or swim.... It's unfair to both students and teachers."[8] Instead, she suggests "all prospective teachers in the United States take a rigorous bar exam that gauges mastery of subject-matter knowledge and demonstrates competency in how to teach it." Weingarten refers to surveys that show "many who go through traditional teacher-preparation programs feel they aren't adequately prepared to manage and teach students early in their career." This proposed bar exam would comprise of more than written exams and oral reiteration; it would require further demonstrations of mastery regarding the "candidate's ability to teach," and "must include extensive experience in actual classrooms working with accomplished teachers"—more than already mandated.

While we Conservatives do believe in enforcing higher standards of entry into the teaching profession, this recommended idea potentially carries both positive and negative weight. We agree that, as Weingarten and the AFT argue, "practicing teachers in K-12 and higher education should own responsibility for setting and enforcing the teaching profession's standards."[9] Teachers who are better prepared (whether through this proposal or other means) are less likely to leave the teaching profession (today, nearly half of new teachers exit the field within five years). America's best teachers are regularly those who have the greatest experience and exposure to educational facilities—retention of those educators is a primary requirement in providing quality education for our youth. WE CONSERVATIVES BELIEVE the failings of a weakly trained teacher should not punish students, and that new teachers deserve a proper chance to succeed in a teaching career.

An Early Evaluation

WE CONSERVATIVES BELIEVE the most qualified and thought-provoking among us should fill the ranks of those in the teaching profession. Teaching should not be the fall-back pursuit of individuals who cannot decide upon a different, more suiting career for their needs. Rather, teaching is a calling for those who recognize their special ability to educate future generations.

As discussed in "A Bar Exam for Teachers—Adequate Preparation," the AFT has suggested the implementation of a bar exam analogous to that required by law school graduates wishing to practice law. While this potential exam might have positive and negative impacts on teaching, it should not be the national exam the AFT proposed. Weingarten, the AFT's president who has worked as both a teacher and an attorney, believes this new teacher testing would work best if nationally administered. While this is not surprising considering her role in a powerful national body, it undermines the authority and sovereignty of the individual states and further chips away at the role of federalism.

Moreover, instead of an exit exam for teaching candidates, perhaps an entrance exam (similar to the LSAT for law students or the MCAT for medical students) would better make the grade. That is, raise the bar before they start learning how to teach, not right before they actually do teach. "The 'winnowing' process cannot wait until graduates have made it to the front of a classroom."[10] Typically and traditionally, additional barriers to entrance act to reduce the number of suppliers in a market. But when determining precisely who is going to teach our children, perhaps these barriers would be beneficial, minimizing those not serious about the profession and instead promoting those who hear their calling. A lower supply of potential teachers, coupled with the same demand for those teachers, could provide new educators with further leverage in negotiations with employers on matters such as salaries and other contract issues.

Another reason a nationally provided exit exam would be inappropriate rests in America's roots. Federal involvement in state education has no proper place in a republic based on federalism. If instead the bar exam was directed by the states, this would further the development of at least two things: first, the states would retain their role in determining the qualifications required for teaching candidates, beyond present prescriptions; and second, parents could determine which states' requirements best represent their own needs regarding the training of teachers and weigh the educational quality provided by each state's teachers.

All these benefits support states working as "laboratories of democracy," demonstrating how a "state may, if its citizens choose, serve as a laboratory; and try novel social and economic experiments without risk to the rest of the country."[11] But if any potential bar exam for teachers is eventually required, it should only exist in the K-12 arena, where most new teachers come from universities and not the workforce and where the ability to send one's children away to school is not available. WE CONSERVATIVES BELIEVE current practices of teacher-training can be improved, and we ought to entertain new ideas of how to accomplish that.

The Department of Education

WE CONSERVATIVES BELIEVE the education of American youths is a matter that should rest almost exclusively in the control of the states, wherein each can determine how best to challenge students without the interference of the federal government. Instead, America's educational system today heavily and thoroughly mingles with the federal Department of Education. This cabinet-level department employs over five thousand public-sector workers and maintains an annual budget of over $77 billion, yet notwithstanding, it is of itself an overexpansion of federal authority, regardless its size or value.[12]

The roles of the Education Department are varied, but as part of its mission, the department "establishes policies related to federal education funding, administers distribution of funds and monitors their use."[13] Yet the establishment of educational policies was never intended to be—nor ever was—a role of the federal government prior to recent expansions of central powers. Nowhere does the Constitution mention education, and its silence alone speaks volumes. Virtually every Framer of the new American government was a highly educated and well-regarded individual; education was of great importance to them and their countrymen. Yet in crafting the Constitution for the new federal government, they were aware of the impracticality of centralized control over most aspects of American living (hence the enumerated powers of the Constitution, which list specifically what the federal government is authorized to do). The government under the Constitution was—and is—bound by the limits placed upon it under the articles and amendments. Granting the central government the ability to regulate and "establish policy" for education schemes in the several states is inappropriate for at least three reasons: first, it fails to account for the diversity amongst the states and for the states' interests (that is, it effectively applies a one-size-fits-all approach, handing down mandates and procedures binding all states); second, the collection of educational powers in the federal government (rather than the states alone) becomes evermore tainted with the potential for political interference, forcing policies through the lens of whichever party is in the majority; and third and most importantly, the Constitution does not provide for it, let alone under the executive branch, which controls the department, further highlighting the prospective dangers of the second rationale.

Although the Constitution is mute on education, it is not silent on how to interpret such absences. The Tenth Amendment is unequivocally clear that when the Constitution does not enumerate a power, and when that power is not forbidden, the states retain the authority to act as they deem fit. Specifically, "The powers not delegated to the United States by the Constitution, nor prohibited by it to the States, are reserved to the States respectively, or to the people."[14]

Part of the purpose of the Tenth Amendment was practicality, for it would have been impossible first to imagine and then transcribe every eventuality that might befall the federal and state governments. Thus, when the Constitution makes no mention of education (a field very much in existence during the Constitutional Convention), the founders intended to leave educational decisions to the states alone. The absence of education in the Constitution was not an accident, and the vast influence over education the federal government now has never was intended. WE CONSERVATIVES BELIEVE the federal Department of Education is an overexpansion of federal power and unconstitutional by its very nature.

Scholarships and Merit

WE CONSERVATIVES BELIEVE the recent country-wide shift toward university merit scholarships both rewards educational success and creates an incentive for laborious study. While need-based aid should remain available for some, those students who continually show exceptional academic performance ought to be the central focus of taxpayer-funded scholarship initiatives.

In a country built on competition and innovation, why is our approach to education so often at odds with the real world? "Our society is built on meritocracy," said an Ohio University economics professor.[15] "What is true in real life in the job market should be true in education." With the ever-rising cost of public education at state universities, general funding for scholarships to those institutions is rarely able to keep pace. As a consequence, states have become much more particular in determining who should receive taxpayer-funded money—a tough decision for many legislators. On the one hand, arguments are made supporting those in greatest need of state tuition assistance (or need-based aid). For many poor communities, higher education is often deemed the most direct pathway out of poverty, and so financial assistance is considered necessary for breaking the mold. Alternatively, merit-based aid focuses on students' academic abilities and successes and sifts applicants through various filters to determine their eligibility. Once qualified, it grants students partial or total waivers of their tuition expenses.

For over twenty years, Georgia has remained a leader in merit-based aid by offering scholarships rooted solely in academic achievement. High grades and "strong SAT or ACT test scores" are required before being considered for full-tuition scholarships.[16] Other states, like Massachusetts, have offered free tuition to any in-state public university to high school students scoring in the top 25 percent of a state-wide test.[17] After introducing such programs, officials at these universities "say they have seen a noticeable uptick in the student-body skills. . . . Across Georgia's thirty-five public colleges and universities," for instance, merit-based scholarship "recipients are much more likely to graduate than other students."[18] In times of economic turbulence, we should direct non-reimbursable taxpayer revenues toward those most likely to utilize their awards and most likely to graduate—consistently, these students have been those who can show past academic accomplishments.

To say states should award scholarships to students exhibiting the most exceptional educational performances is not to say there is no other financial assistance available for those in greatest need. For starters, the federal government provides numerous student aid programs in many forms, including the Pell Grant, which disbursed $36 billion in the 2012 fiscal year.[19] Moreover, both public and private institutions make available student loans (loans being the method through which most college students fund their studies and one in which the federal government now takes a leading role), and thousands of organizations and individual donors provide scholarships in accordance with need, merit, or both. Yet for many, the notion of need-based tuition scholarships runs deeper, including the sources of scholarship funding. Because several states operate lottery programs to funnel state proceeds into educational schemes (including scholarships), and because those living "with low and moderate average incomes [spend] the most" on state lottery games, some call this a form of wealth redistribution not all that different from other forms thereof. That is, the poor fund the lottery and the middle- to upper-classes (whose students are most likely to receive merit scholarships) reap the benefits. But this argument carries with it an inherent distinction: a lottery player is not obligated to bet, whereas a taxpayer has no alternative. Further, because of progressive taxation, more affluent members of society are likely paying greater shares of tax, which also fund scholarships. WE CONSERVATIVES BELIEVE taxpayer-funded scholarships based on merit are more equitable, effective, and encouraging than those based solely on need.

Being Well-Rounded

WE CONSERVATIVES BELIEVE the obtainment of a well-rounded education should be a primary goal of K-12 and not the intent of higher education at universities and colleges. Those latter institutions are best reserved for specialized and focused arenas of study—not as facilities in which mediocre understandings of several academias are compulsory.

Consider an engineering student at a state university. He will, of course, enroll himself in numerous engineering and science courses. However, he will almost universally be required, as a condition of his degree pursuit, to participate in several humanities classes as well. What benefit does the engineering student acquire in taking, for example, art history or English literature? Shouldn't these studies, if deemed so important by the state, have been covered at some point in the student's twelve years of mandated education prior to college? And why isn't the humanities student required to sit through engineering courses (if, of course, the goal is well-roundedness)? After all, "our lives are governed and facilitated by technical things which make our lives comfortable and allow us to earn our livings, yet we often don't have the faintest idea how these things work."[20] Attempts to determine what constitutes "well-rounded" will inevitably include less-than-noble realities, such as increased revenues for university departments that would otherwise remain insolvent and political influences on students' core principles.

If, as is proclaimed when convenient, society deems citizens of the majority age to be adults, then we should also defer judgment to those adults in college as to what courses suit their needs. Let the engineering student focus entirely on his engineering pursuit and allow the humanities student the same deference. And what of the citizen who never attends higher education? Does he not have a chance of being well-rounded because he missed certain university requirements? We should demand that our K-12 schools produce graduates who are already fit with the groundwork to be successful in modern America. If then, after high school graduation, the student wishes to become an engineer, he can enroll in a university and intensely study engineering without the disturbance of other subject matters currently required. The more focused on a specific area of study one is, the better professional that person will become.

Requiring adult students to enroll in several distracting courses is not only time consuming, but it is also patronizing. If upon graduation the engineer becomes "interested in other fields such as history, economics, and others, [even a] local library [is] a good source of material on those subjects" not needed in one's college career.[21] WE CONSERVATIVES BELIEVE, as in so many other sectors of life, the individual can better choose what his interests and needs are far better than any state or university can.

MILITARY STRENGTH

Domestic Tranquility

WE CONSERVATIVES BELIEVE one of the chief purposes of the American government is to protect its citizens from threats to liberty and national security, a philosophy outlined in both the Declaration of Independence and the Constitution. To achieve these ends, "We the People" created a government to "establish Justice, insure domestic Tranquility, provide for the common defence, promote the general Welfare, and secure the Blessings of Liberty"—for which a strong military force is the best guarantee.[1]

Legitimate use of federal power is appropriate only within a limited scope of authority, such as creating armies and navies, conducting international affairs, and declaring war. Undeniably, "The operations of the federal government will be most extensive and important in times of war and danger."[2] We must, therefore, wield this power to protect our interests and our allies and to defeat the roots of evil wherever they may take hold. "Experience teaches us," wrote George Washington, "that it is much easier to prevent an enemy from posting themselves, than it is to dislodge them after they have got possession."[3] The uniqueness of American military capabilities means we have obligations extending beyond isolationist ideologies and may, on particularly justified occasions, preemptively strike at the heart of those seeking to undermine our peaceful pursuits and welfare violently. Yet even with the incredible power retained by the United States throughout our modern history, "we have acted with good intention—not to colonize, not to subjugate, never to oppress."[4] WE CONSERVATIVES BELIEVE the United States has steadfastly upheld the values of morality and peace, acting first to extend an olive branch in the name of liberty.

The Recognition of Evil

WE CONSERVATIVES BELIEVE the world is home to both good and evil, and overcoming the latter requires an unapologetic recognition of its existence and threat. Evil does not succumb to appeasement nor does it rest or waiver. America, as a steadfast beacon of good, must see evil for what it is and act unambiguously to resist its influence, oppression, and regression.

There are some who believe *per se* evil does not (and cannot) exist, and they instead "dismiss such a claim as simplistic and moralistic."[5] Bad acts and their consequences, therefore, are solely the product of an old society and ideology, one that draws out the animal-like instincts of man and pits brother against brother. In their eyes, so-called evil is little more than the balance between nature and nurture. "Change the society, they maintain, and people will behave" differently. The inherently violent, intolerant, and tyrannical among us are "simply misunderstood . . . [and] fully capable of joining the community of human kindness and acting responsibly, if only we would use 'carrots instead of sticks.' " To those who do not see evil for what it is, immorality is only a miscommunication of differences. We Conservatives consider this wholly wrong.

Whenever we do not recognize and defeat evil, we enable it. We cannot overcome evil by the appeasement of our enemies under the pretense of progression. Trying to elevate evil's sense of importance has never resulted in effective diplomacy, and while unfortunate surroundings and chaotic societies do often breed evil, those same tendencies can only begin through the ambitions of evil. One's condition alone is not the root of evil, and history has shown a prevalence of violence and tyranny in even the best-off in a society: "Cain killed Abel, not because of a broken home but because of evil jealousy. Pharaoh brutally repressed the Jews, and centuries later, Herod would kill their firstborn sons. These two rulers were not twisted by circumstance, but by their evil lust for power."[6]

Evil comes to us in all forms and from many places. It does not respond to friendliness; it seizes on weakness and exploits the timid. Evil is more than merely a misunderstanding of social and economic differences—a realization that must serve as the first step in the conquering of its pursuits. "There are monsters born in this world to human parents. . . . The face and the body may be perfect, but if a twisted gene or malformed egg can produce physical monsters, may not the same process produce a malformed soul?"[7] WE CONSERVATIVES BELIEVE that only through a firm stand against evil (and not appeasement thereof) will evil succumb to its shortcomings and the goodness of mankind prevail.

The Use of Soft Power

WE CONSERVATIVES BELIEVE in the employment of "soft power" as an initial measure to deter our enemies and influence global affairs. Effective and meaningful soft power depends on both a dominant military force and a nation's credibility. The "hard power" created by the military might of the United States acts as a backstop for soft power by alerting our enemies and allies of our dedication to freedom and defense.

Soft power, most basically defined, is the use of attraction and persuasion to influence others' opinions and actions. The level and degree of soft power a nation can exude rests on three resources: "its culture (in places where it is attractive to others), its political values (when it lives up to them at home and abroad), and its foreign policies (when others see them as legitimate and having moral authority)."[8] Furthermore, economic resources can, at times, be strategically used to influence others.[9] Each individual, group, or nation trying to be swayed (the target) weighs these elements, and the effectiveness of soft power rests in the target's connection to these ideals. In other words, the persuader attempts to seduce the target by showing off his or its effectiveness and conduct.

This appeal to popularity and personal affinity can be incredibly effective. And while a formal recognition of soft power in academic and political circles has only recently come about, the concept has always been present. The spread of the French language and culture across Europe in the eighteenth century, for instance, helped to maximize France's international influence; during the American Civil War, some Britons considered favoring the South but were eventually dissuaded by individual distastes of slavery, and so found the North's cause more appealing; and the lack of German contact with North America prior to World War I left little "to counteract the natural pull toward Britain."[10]

Soft power has real ramifications, but habitually, America fails to utilize its soft-power ability fully. For example, China's economy depends on American access to their markets, but we have not used that soft power to deter China from supporting non-freedom-loving nations nor to encourage it to support sanctions against our joint enemies.[11] We have failed to enter into free-trade agreements with many peace-going nations which would, in turn, bolster our influence in those areas, thus never having to step foot there. And politicians eager to show constituents photo-ops of their communications with world leaders sign empty declarations of their commitment to freedom, all the while suppressing any potential soft power initiatives that could benefit both parties. These failures of American leaders to deploy simple yet effective soft power proposals can lead to the need for hard power intervention later on.

Even with America's failure to often use its soft power capabilities, this does not mean America's enemies have done the same. Soft power depends on credibility, for if the target realizes the "seduction" is but a siren song, we lose all perceived credibility. Such a reality requires dictators to "cultivate myths of invincibility to structure expectations and attract others to join their bandwagon."[12] The worse the actuality, the better they must paint the scene and the further they must suppress the truth by curtailing the rights of the citizens. Hitler did it. Stalin did it. Osama bin Laden did it. No matter the circumstance, they used soft power to allure others to their side. Only later, once it becomes too late, do the allured understand the trap.

America is thoroughly good, and even though we have not used soft power to the greatest extent within our reach, when we have, it has been for upright causes. WE CONSERVATIVES BELIEVE soft power can play a key role in the shaping of America's foreign affairs and the future direction of our continued prosperity.

Moral Self-Confidence

WE CONSERVATIVES BELIEVE two competing attitudes divide modern American philosophy regarding military strength: those who believe the United States has a comparative moral superiority to other nations and those who are skeptical of the moral standing of our nation. Considering America's history, this is a relatively new holding, furthering the self-loathing outlook of many in American society.

While a wide divide in military moralism is a generally recent phenomenon, there had been another type of split in the American mind preceding it. Prior to the Vietnam War, "American foreign policy was divided between realists and idealists. Realists believed that the U.S. needed to exercise restraint in furthering its fundamental principles of liberty and democracy in the conduct of its foreign policy.... The idealists, on the other hand, believed in an energetic foreign policy that accepted the expenditure of considerable blood and treasure, not to mention political capital, to further American principles abroad."[13] The realists assumed unchecked military commitments undermined American statute by lowering the country "to the power politics practiced by the nations of Europe in particular," while the idealists "saw robust international engagements as an affirmation of American ideals and leading the rest of the world in the direction of raising its standards to the level of the United States." These two vantage points of military concern, although differing, shared an underlying common theme: a moral assurance in the United States serving the world as an exceptional nation. The Vietnam War, however, "shattered this fundamental consensus" and replaced it with the morality complex facing our nation today.

With American moral self-confidence, vigorous military ambitions and capabilities are considered cornerstones of "security, stability, and peace."[14] American military power can be used to defend freedom or stave off threats, ensuring the United States maintains soft power superiority while still possessing its backbone of military might. Contrarily, in the world of American self-doubt, one which views military endeavors and strength with evermore cynicism, the same confidences held by the moral-superiority division are instead viewed as likely to promote "less security, instability, and perpetual war." These skeptics thus view America's predominance in military power as a target of opportunity and so aim at the minimization of military spending, budget allocations, and leadership within the ranks. Yet no superpower—particularly one of America's stature and leading role as a worldwide peacekeeper—can survive militarily if it faces attacks on its superiority from those both outside its borders and from opponents within. WE CONSERVATIVES

BELIEVE a resurrection of domestic support for military moral righteousness—such that considers powerful armed forces necessary for the protection of liberty and peace—is central to our continued dominance in a world of innumerable threats and uncertainties.

The Defense Budget

WE CONSERVATIVES BELIEVE the safety and wellbeing of America's military men and women are vastly more important than any social program propelled by political agendas. Cutting defense spending to finance politicians' welfare projects threatens our troops' security, minimizes their disposable assets, and marginalizes the overwhelming importance of superior armed forces.

There is an often-quoted belief (usually surrounding political campaigns) that the United States spends 50 percent of its budget on the military, yet this is fundamentally inaccurate. The federal budget is deep and complicated but breaks into two distinct categories: mandatory spending (expenditures required by the federal government through law and entitlements, such as Social Security, Medicare, Medicaid, and other benefits to veterans, retirees, and the disabled) and discretionary spending (expenditures politicians may adjust, add, or eliminate, such as education, social services, and international relations). Of these two divisions, mandatory spending makes up approximately 60 percent of the annual budget, with 40 percent left for discretionary spending. Of that 40 percent, defense spending makes up about half. This thus translates into 20 percent of the total national budget.[15]

Using misleading arguments regarding national spending to advance one's political agenda is a dangerous ploy—doubly so when done regarding our national defense. WE CONSERVATIVES BELIEVE the striking of even more defensive spending jeopardizes the Army's cutting edge on the battlefield, reduces the strategic advantage of the Marines, forces our Navy to sail on outdated ships, lessens the Air Force's air-ready potential, and diminishes the Coast Guard's capacity to ward off attacks.

The Border and Terrorism

WE CONSERVATIVES BELIEVE immigration is an important factor in the growth of a prosperous and diverse people, but the insistence on looser border protections and the resulting mass migration carries problems far greater than any financial or population circumstance: easier access to American territory means easier access for all, including those who wish to harm peace-loving Americans and our civil society.

In "Immigration and Legality," concerns over illegal immigration largely rested upon financial and legal questions. But more important than those serious alarms is the possibility that other, far more dangerous realities may come to fruition. With America's stature on the world stage and our enduring pursuit of individual liberty, it is not surprising we have amassed several enemies from many corners, each utilizing different strategies to undermine the might of the United States. For some, this includes infiltrating the homeland and seeing through acts of terror like that of September 11, 2001. With an open-border approach to the outskirts of American territory, we essentially create an invitation to those seeking our demise and in turn threaten the very communities and people who make America thrive. Moreover, drug-gang violence and disputes continue to spill into states sharing borders with Mexico, a country plagued with hostility and civil disobedience and one that consistently makes the Department of State's "Travel Warnings" list, right beside Afghanistan, Iran, Yemen, and Iraq. This threat includes "paramilitaristic drug cartels that often are also involved in human smuggling, increasingly from Central American countries."[16] While financial and population issues stemming from illegal immigration are legitimate, it is clear that the problem is exponentially larger when perceived from a homeland-security vantage point.

Why, then, do so many still insist on reducing restrictions in regard to immigration to the United States and promote easy access to American lands? And why, simultaneously, do they further insist on defense budget reductions? Instead, better and more sincere efforts are required to truly lock-down our borders against those who attempt to enter through unwarranted means, and a greater dedication of financial resources is necessary to boost border personnel's ability to adequately face hostile confrontations. Also, as the only military branch presently permitted to act in a law enforcement capacity at home, we should further supplement the Coast Guard's budget to allow for an expanded role in border security in coordination with the Border Patrol, by which means we would both strengthen the capacity of the American military and better regulate movements across our borders.[17] To protect against violent threats toward American interests at home, we must first be serious about protecting the very borders within which we ought to feel safe and secure, for this is one of the principal responsibilities of our government—we cannot settle for its continued failure to do so. WE CONSERVATIVES BELIEVE financial and legal troubles associated with illegal immigration, real as they are, are significantly trumped by threats posed to our national security when violent and undermining enemies of the United States have easy access to our communities and society.

Standing with Our Allies

WE CONSERVATIVES BELIEVE in supporting America's allies through showings of commitment. We encourage other nation states who are not presently our official allies to join America in standing up for equal justice and freedom. But ties to our global partners are only as strong as our outward loyalties to them. One of the best ways to attract new global friends is to openly display our partnerships with present allies and the mutual benefits thus created.

America's commitment to its allies is more than charity, for the United States has a vested interest in maintaining peace-loving nations around the world. As the largest power capable of aiding others in their efforts to strike down tyranny and hatred, our collaboration with allies often stands as the only deterrent to those set on destroying liberty. As a co-signer of freedom, the United States owes both ourselves and our friends the protection that comes from an alliance with America. Our friends' enemies are our enemies, and these collective foes continually focus on diminishing our influence. They know that when standing with America, our allies will triumph. We must not let our enemies dictate our God-given freedoms nor our self-governing autonomy.

The United States is strong, but when standing with our global friends, we are a great deal stronger. Put simply, "We are not going to betray our friends, reward the enemies of freedom, or permit fear and retreat to become American policies—especially in this hemisphere. None of the wars in my lifetime came about because we were too strong."[18] WE CONSERVATIVES BELIEVE America must stand with its allies in steadfast opposition to our shared opponents, encourage freedom-seeking endeavors, and promote the growth of republican ideologies.

Fulfilling the Mission

WE CONSERVATIVES BELIEVE it is inappropriate to set forth a military objective, begin its fulfillment, but then withdraw before the original goal is satisfied. What is to be made of the cost in blood, body, treasure, and principle if only gaining nominal advances?

This argument may at first seem ignorant to changing battlefields and circumstances, or that it ignores the fatigue of a war-weary nation. But if we hold true to this standard (that we will not leave war without first winning war), then we should expect a much narrower scope of the wars into which we are willing to engage. If we only enter war with the intention to win, would we not first look considerably at our capabilities to ensure our eventual victory—not a rushed approach but instead a deliberate one? And does it not fall upon our elected officials to convince the electorate that a war is worthy of American involvement?

Furthermore, when the United States sets a precedent that says, "When we go to war, we stay engaged until victory," we send the same message to both our friends and enemies: count on American triumph. As in war, so too is it in life. None among us would like a friend who waivers when called upon, but all would like an enemy who never completes a task. The same theory held true in 1776 with the Revolutionary War under full swing: "The summer soldier and the sunshine patriot will, in this crisis, shrink from the service of their country; but he who stands by it now, deserves the love and thanks of man and woman."[19] To be worthy of this admiration, we must stand by our military, the mission, and our country. WE CONSERVATIVES

BELIEVE, just as did five-star General of the Army Douglas MacArthur, "it is fatal to enter any war without the will to win it."[20]

An All-Volunteer Force

WE CONSERVATIVES BELIEVE the armed forces of the United States are best manned by volunteers who willingly and on their own accord seek to serve their nation in its highest calling. An all-volunteer force, as we presently maintain, is not only more dedicated to the fulfillment of American military interests but is also more representative of the American society, one cherishing liberty and free-choice.

The conscription of men to serve in the armed forces, although constitutional, is largely unnecessary in the pursuit of retaining military supremacy. Several countering arguments favoring a draft are frequently raised (particularly at the commencement of a large military engagement), but the benefits of a volunteer force undermine each. For example, opinions denouncing an all-volunteer force include beliefs "that it might be racially unbalanced, would not provide sufficient flexibility in size of forces, and would enhance the political danger of undue military influence."[21] Yet with regard to the first and third of these concerns, "the military is not over-represented by the poor and minorities, nor is it as politically skewed as some seem to think."[22] In fact, quite a different reality exists, one in which continual studies show minorities and the poor are indeed underrepresented in the military ranks while "middle-class areas are overrepresented."[23] Even so, any potential concerns of racial imbalance and political influence "are in no way connected with the use of voluntary or compulsory means to recruit enlisted men," argued economist Milton Friedman, "and do not constitute valid arguments against abolishing the draft."[24] The second apprehension (that a volunteer force is neither sufficiently large nor flexible) "has more merit but devices exist to provide moderate flexibility under a voluntary as under a compulsory system."

A volunteer military, being manned by individuals making an affirmative choice to serve their country, has several clear and immediate benefits to the soldier and nation alike. Not only does it improve the fighting mentality of the troops, but it also lowers turnover, saving invaluable training hours otherwise spent on the constant development of recruits.[25] It furthermore allows for greater specialization and a more highly skilled force as a consequence of longer commitment times and deeper dedications. A volunteer force also preserves the choice of whether to serve in the military or to remain in the civilian body, and it enhances "the freedom of those who now do not serve. Being conscripted has been used as a weapon," Friedman continued, "to discourage freedom of speech, assembly, and protest. The freedom of young men to emigrate or to travel abroad has been limited by the need to get the permission of a draft board if the young man is not to put himself in the position of inadvertantly becoming a law-breaker."

Only under dire conditions, wherein the very survival of the union is in jeopardy, and the armed forces are wholly inadequate to confront real threats of opposition, might the conscription of men be suitable. The American Civil War, in its terrible ferocity and uniqueness, serves as one such example. In all other cases, history has shown (not only in the United States but other nations of the world) a volunteer force is far more appropriate to the needs of vibrant countries and supportive of the underlying principles upon which a free people stand. WE CONSERVATIVES BELIEVE the best-recruited ranks of America's military services are most often by men and women seeking public service to their homeland and those fully committed to the achievement of its military pursuits—goals best achieved through an all-volunteer force.

KEEPING THE ARMED FORCES STRONG

WE CONSERVATIVES BELIEVE our international peace is best preserved by a strong military, one that remains globally superior and acts only to defend American interests, promote the safety of allies, and encourage humanitarian efforts. Whereas weakness invites challenge, strength deters aggression.

In America and around the world, it is easy to find voices that attack the overwhelming superiority of the United States's military. Our military is, by every measure and capability, the leading force of strength. Through our naval, air, and ground powers, we pave the path of liberty and keep it free of real and potential threats. But what would the world look like without a strong America? Who would fill the void should the United States diminish in influence? Certainly, our enemies would enjoy greater mobility and expansion without the pressure of an American presence. Our trade routes would be more susceptible to interference and blockage. Our intelligence competencies would diminish, leaving the homeland prone to grave attacks. And our allies, who depend on America's continued support and aid, would fall prey to the evils of oppression.

As a unique force for good, the United States's military is required to defend itself and our allies, and there are many advantages to having the leading military in the world. One of these is that we needn't always use it to get our adversaries to act. The mere threat of American military force often works to sway those considering actions against the interests of the United States and its allies. And in times when our foes do not heed these warnings, our military must be able to strike unapologetically at the root of evil. WE CONSERVATIVES BELIEVE America and our allies are safer because of our continued commitments to our armed forces.

Military Readiness

WE CONSERVATIVES BELIEVE America must always be prepared to fight the wars not only of today but tomorrow as well. This requires a military on constant alert, of ever-increasing sophistication, and in receipt of steadfast dedication from the civilian leaders who control it. The United States has never fully known how, when, or from where it will face the next great military challenge, but it must nevertheless be *semper paratus*—always ready.

History has shown that predictions of where future threats will come from can be helpful but are rarely entirely accurate. They inevitably fall short in one manner or another and lack the clarity that comes with the hindsight of history. Therefore, our military prowess depends on visionary leaders who recognize that evil springs from unknown and unforeseen corners. Evil is patient and deceptive and often hides under the veil of good intentions. For the United States to defeat unanticipated dangers, our civilian and military leaderships require individuals who plan for tomorrow's engagements, receive proper funding from Congress, and have the support of the citizenry, as well as alliances with global partners to aid in our intelligence gathering capabilities. Absent these, our fighting qualifications will be limited to the narrow focus of today, simply putting out fires rather than tackling forward-thinking engagements.

In a world where America's enemies are more significant and more diverse than ever before, the security of our homeland (and those of our global friends) depends on the development of plans to confront the unknown. WE CONSERVATIVES BELIEVE that while the United States cannot always identify from where our enemies will next strike, we can be certain to be there in full-force when they do.

Mister Madison's War

WE CONSERVATIVES BELIEVE a nation goes to war with the military it has on-hand, and thus it requires consistent and continual reinforcements of its military capabilities so as to tackle both expected and unanticipated threats to liberty and peace. This necessitates commitments from forward-thinking military leaders and congressional budgeteers alike to develop operational strategies and financial outlines, providing clear boundaries within which the armed forces can function.

Examples of lax governmental policies leading to militaries unprepared for hostile conflicts riddles history. The United States itself has not escaped this historical reality on frequent occasions, including as far back as our involvement in the War of 1812 (dubbed by contemporaries as, "Mister Madison's War"), wherein British shipping vessels undertook operations to impress American sailors into the service of their king's navy. Early peace negotiations under President Thomas Jefferson proved unproductive, and embargo actions served to do more harm to the homeland than to Great Britain. Consequently, officials made the controversial decision to make war with their former brethren, and in 1812, President James Madison signed America's first declaration of war. The tiny republic of eighteen states sought to take on the world superpower that was the British Empire.

Arguing in favor of a potential war is a great deal different than arguing precisely how to accomplish it adequately. For the Americans in 1812, military abilities were considerably limited in comparison to those of their renewed foe. For example, at the start of the conflict, the United States possessed some sixteen seafaring war vessels, whereas Britain manned over six hundred. Years of indifferent and detached financing of the armed forces left it woefully under-gunned and weakened; politicians had sought short-term savings in exchange for long-term military strength. The War of 1812 would prove how dangerous such a strategy could be for a nation seeking sustained sovereignty and vigor.

After two years of fighting, neither side was very much closer to victory than at the start of the conflict, which, in consideration of America's then-fragile military position, was something of an accomplishment in itself. But as troops of the United Kingdom moved toward Maryland in August of 1814, they would march virtually uninterrupted into an undefended and deserted capital city, one which provided them full entry into a considerable number of public buildings and offices. The Senate and House of Representative buildings were burned, including the Library of Congress, as was the Treasury building and other public establishments. And, most symbolically, they also torched the White House. The inadequate preparations made by President Madison's predecessors, coupled with the difficulties of raising, training, and funding armies and navies during hostilities in the homeland, left Madison with a force not wholly suitable for even the protection of Washington.

The war ended largely as it began, with neither side able to claim a clear victory over the other. But invaluable lessons were to be learned from the conflict that would shape the structure and attitude toward the American military for decades to follow. No longer would standing armies and navies be so fervently detested by so many, and Madison himself would call for greater reliance on the armed forces for the preservation of liberty and peace: "a certain degree of preparation for war is not only indispensible to avert disasters in the onset, but affords also the best security for the continuance of peace."[26] WE CONSERVATIVES BELIEVE Mister Madison's War served to convince Americans they could no longer rely on geography or "the pacific dispositions of the American people" alone in the avoidance of war or the conflicts of commerce; instead, "the maintenance of an adequate regular force" would now function as a cornerstone of American military might and international stature—something today's politicians would be wise to keep in mind during fiscal negotiations and considerations.

PERSONAL RESPONSIBILITY

Convince by Reason

WE CONSERVATIVES BELIEVE appeals to reason and rationale are the most honorable manner of persuasion, not pandering to fear and emotion. The one who crafts his position with roots in fact, principle, and example maintains the more meritorious stance than he who plays off the shaped concerns of those to be convinced. We believe instilling irrational fears into a population is immoral, and it attempts to minimize the intellect of the very people one is trying to sway.

Throughout societal history, untamed ambition has led people to power "by exploiting human frailties, frustrations, jealousies, and inequities."[1] They prey on the weak-minded and vulnerable, attempting to divide the citizenry. They understand fear requires more attention than hope, and so utilize this awareness to drive stakes between themselves and their opposition. These "predators" offer nothing but an aggressive attack of deception, laying out a campaign of smears determined to radicalize the opponent. Generally, these motivations attract the less well-off and dependent in society and by consequence create "a sense of meaning and self-worth." The resulting class-warfare snowballs in scope, with individual success becoming increasingly chastised and reliance celebrated. A captive audience wrapped up in the aurora of a fear monger will pay no regard to the reasonable thoughts of an opponent—a reality rooting the predator's survival. He requires an audience of agreeance; deviation becomes dangerous and threatens usurpation.

Although fear is normal, it is not by itself destructive. The more we understand how fear grips us, the easier we can move through it and in spite of it. But if we are unable to control our fears (whether they be realistic or not), we become incapable of thinking clearly and making sound decisions. A predator willing to exploit another person's fear for personal gain allows the demoralized person to place his fears into another's control, without ever having to overcome their fears. The fear constantly remains in the forefront, precisely what the predator requires to stay in his position.

Conversely, to formulate persuasion in the pedigree of rationale is to carry an argumentative weight far surpassing that of the predator while having the additional advantage of being virtuous. Its creation requires a level-headed temperament and a degree of composure. It ensures all contingencies may be considered and provides a comprehensive approach to potential issues. Because, however, each of these elements is required to prepare platforms of reason, the far easier path remains that of the exploiter who works his followers into a frenzy by the employment of fright. But the one who depends on the emotions of his constituents advances nothing—"Their fear and cynicism move nothing forward; they kill progress."[2]

As the arguments of the predator are wrapped not in substance but fear, he must always maintain his elevated alarm. If he appears to be wavering, his followers lose confidence. Yet even in this moment of weakness, his followers are not automatically moved into the understanding of his rational opponent but instead are likely remaining in a limbo impatiently awaiting the next predator. *This* is the time when they are most inclined to the persuasion of reason, when the storm has passed, and their leader is fragile.

To be footed in reason is not to say one must forever remain a stoic of unemotional reflection. There are certainly times when great emotional appeals are suitable (or even needed) so long as principally based in thorough reasoning. But generally, "no one has ever served his emotions and his best interests simultaneously. When you set your mind to a task, it prevails. If passion holds sway, it consumes you, and the mind can do nothing."[3] WE CONSERVATIVES BELIEVE allowing fear to dictate reason leads to susceptibility; susceptibility leads to weakness; weakness leads to surrender; and surrender is the paralyzer of a free people.

ACCOUNTABILITY

WE CONSERVATIVES BELIEVE personal responsibility is the motor that drives progression. Only with personal responsibility can a people first obtain, and then retain, authentic liberty. It is the constant found in all great nations and, by consequence, one of the elements most commonly disregarded.

Personal responsibility is both difficult to define yet easy to understand. True responsibility has three parts. First, *acknowledgment.* Specifically, we must admit that certain decisions in our lives were not the doings of someone else. We must declare they exist and are true. Furthermore and equally important, these acknowledgments include decisions not to do something. Second, *acceptance* that these decisions (which were just acknowledged) have brought us to the place we are today. Our present reality is the product of our choices. This does not mean, however, every person will (nor should) reach the same mile-markers nor that every person is starting from the same vantage point, but rather that we each come to accept that our current position did not arrive by accident; it is the consequence of our choices. And third, after having acknowledged and accepted our decisions, we *take action* to either maintain or change course. Not all personal responsibility is in regard to adverse realizations. Sometimes it is enough to simply appreciate that while you may be comfortable with your current circumstances, there is always room for improvement. Nevertheless, having the courage to evaluate both our successes and failures provides us with insight to better inform our future decision making, resulting in a higher likelihood of continued, or new, successes.

In a society where personal responsibility is seemingly in decline, it becomes steadily more difficult for someone to stand up and take it. The failure to hold oneself accountable will, predictably, lead to the trap of victimhood, wherein the person takes comfort in blaming others. He is defeated, resistant to change, and (most dangerously) seeking someone to hold responsible. In this state of mind, he is susceptible to scapegoating his ills onto another and, most often, onto another who actually takes personal responsibility. It is easy for the scapegoater to find a successful and accountable person and then blame all his woes on him. Thus, an accountable person becomes a victim's convenient person to blame.

If, then, personal responsibility is so uncommon, and if those who do hold themselves accountable are in turn blamed for others' mishaps, why would anyone ever step up and take responsibility? This is precisely the problem that extends from toleration of blame; there is no answerability to be found. The crisis that follows, therefore, is a failure to advance, to learn from mistakes, and to seek better options. A US Navy captain summed up both the dangers of blame and benefits of responsibility when he said, "Personally, I'd like to live in a culture that allows people to candidly acknowledge mistakes and take responsibility. It's far more useful to focus on making sure the accident never happens again, rather than on finding someone to blame. As a captain, I didn't want to foster a culture that shows the lower ranks that the upper ranks try to gloss over problems to avoid blame or save their careers."[4]

Without recognizing the value personal responsibility carries, a society risks not only idleness but regression. It is unwilling (and thus unable) to appreciate the worth of mistakes (mistakes being that from which many great leaps forward have first hatched). The citizenry becomes stagnant and breeds blame; it is never fully able to capture its real potential. WE CONSERVATIVES BELIEVE in the importance of personal responsibility and accountability, not only for oneself but our country as well.

VICTIMHOOD

A Cycle of Blame

WE CONSERVATIVES BELIEVE people should be lifted out of victimhood, not remain dependent upon it. Our goal is to weave the entire citizenry into the fabric of society and for those within it to maintain productive and contributory lives. The fulfillment of the American Dream is rooted in self-reliance, personal responsibility, and the overcoming of adversity—not self-imposed victimization.

Victimhood is the next natural step that follows a consistent failure to take personal responsibility. It is a condition in which the person believes they have no control, no recourse, and no ability to conquer their misfortunes. They are in a perpetual cycle of blame. In this state of victimhood, the person believes others owe him some measure of compensation, usually in the form of money or opportunity. Most commonly, the only satisfactory place from where this reparation can come is the hands of those outside his victimhood. That is, the successful. The victim demonizes the successful and believes others' successes only came about at the expense of the victim. Because of this, he angers easily and is quick to argue with emotion rather than reason, thus allowing the aforementioned "predator" to seize upon his emotional responses and ignite the class-rivalry seen throughout man's history.

Victimhood is cancerous: it spreads quickly, is hard to contain, and is self-destructive. Because victimhood preys on success, it stunts the growth of society and encourages dependence upon others—commonly the government. The surmounting of this danger requires greater personal responsibility and independent thought. WE CONSERVATIVES BELIEVE that to retain prosperity in a nation, we must first overcome the harboring of victimhood and prize the promotion of self-reliance.

Lacking Gratitude

WE CONSERVATIVES BELIEVE self-fulfilled victimhood is erosive to both an individual's character and the society in which he lives. It encourages pity of oneself or one's class and fosters stereotypes regarding the victim and the alleged offenders.

To be in a state of victimhood is to lack gratitude perpetually. This absence of appreciation for what one does have permits the victim to justify resentment toward others who possess what the victim does not. Rather than pursue paths that would eventually allow the victim to obtain those wantings, he instead attacks the dignity of those who actually did pursue those paths. Because, in the victim's mind, society has cheated him out of what is rightfully his, he does not feel morally bound to the same rules as others and can act or lash out in a manner he deems fit.

The victim works to convince others of their alleged and common victimhood. This group then pressures its government to assault the assumed wrongdoers (the successful) and force them to "pay their fair share" in society. Somehow, the offender sidestepped the natural course of success in life (although the victim is never able to articulate exactly how) and has robbed the victim of his otherwise potential accomplishments. For that, he must pay, and this class of victims uses their political clout to serve their false justice. All the while, the victim's relative position in life has not changed, nor will it change even after punishing the "wrongdoer." But because the victim relies greatly on his emotions, it does not matter that his situation is constant. Instead, he feels better because "justice" was served. WE CONSERVATIVES BELIEVE the generalities arising from victimhood harm the entrepreneurial spirit of both individuals and societies.

A Political Opportunity

WE CONSERVATIVES BELIEVE the state of victimhood places undue restraints on a society's potential success and holds back individuals from achieving deep and lasting contentment. Instead, the society diverts enormous sums of energy and treasure to fulfill the "entitlements" of the victims, depriving both the victims and the alleged wrongdoers of what they believe is rightfully theirs.

If someone has been led to believe (either by himself or others) he is owed something, will not that person be cross if he does not receive it? Similarly, if one unjustly owes something, will not that person also be agitated for the forced distribution? When those who feel self-entitled (the victims) wish to obtain recourse, often the most straightforward and effective way to receive that recourse is through their government. Concurrently, the government is also approached by those who believe they have been wrongfully asked to contribute to something improperly (the alleged offenders). For elected officials willing to sacrifice principle and reason, and whose sustained tenure relies on the continued votes of their constituents, they will determine which of these groups carries more political sway. That is, compare those asking for more allocations versus those asking to retain what is rightfully theirs. When the class of victims outgrows the alternative, a politician has a vested interest in satisfying their longings and thus classifies new distributions as "entitlements." Anytime thereafter that another politician attempts to block these supposed entitlements, he faces the anger and wrath of those so entitled. WE CONSERVATIVES BELIEVE self-fulfilled victimhood, as often encouraged in an entitlement state, is detrimental to personal responsibility and individual liberty.

Life at Conception

Viability

WE CONSERVATIVES BELIEVE life begins at conception. We are not created at an arbitrary point thereafter nor do we believe it is moral to end a child's life following conception. Human life must not end without due process or absent irreparable harm.

The present legality of abortion upholds the practice, affirming that states cannot prevent abortions prior to the child's independent viability—that is, when the child is "potentially able to live outside the mother's womb, albeit with artificial aid."[5] Nor does the judiciary think the father should have legal recourse if the mother desires an abortion, even if he wishes the child to be born. With states able to prohibit abortions only at the time of viability, it implies the marking of true life is but little more than subjective and moveable; viability is an ever-moving point when considering the variables attached to medical changes and doctor analyses. If the standard is moveable, then the standard is futile. Who determines viability? Wouldn't pro-choice-leaning doctors have looser opinions of viability than would pro-life-leaning doctors?

The rate at which abortions occur is alarming. For some, it might be unproblematic to view statistics as little more than figures and numbers, but never should we forget abortion is the ending of life, that of a child whose only experience with our world was his death. He will never see the chance to enjoy the pleasures of liberty nor the fruits of his labor. It is adolescent, also, to ignore the alternatives to childrearing your offspring, such as adoption and the innumerable charitable foundations that focus exclusively on aiding mothers who made the right choice. WE CONSERVATIVES BELIEVE the unborn begin life at conception, from which forward point they carry legal status.

Governmental Protection

WE CONSERVATIVES BELIEVE a woman becomes a mother at conception, not at birth, and the rights of the unborn child trump the now-legal abortion rights of the mother. The mother carrying a child is not alone in her decisions, and individual reproductive rights is not a basis to abort the child—a minimum of two people are engaged, one of whom is a voiceless party.

If a pregnant mother is attacked and consequently dies, and the child she is carrying also dies, is it one death or two? Should the attacker be prosecuted for both? Surely, for the Conservative, it is two deaths, regardless of how early the mother was into the pregnancy. Two lives end, and for two people justice should now be delivered. How can a government, created by the people for their collective protection and safety, endorse the ending of unborn infants' lives within that government's jurisdiction? We know that "all men are *created* equal, that they are endowed by their Creator with certain unalienable Rights, that among these are *Life*, Liberty, and the pursuit of Happiness."[6] If our self-created government was instituted "to secure these rights," how can that very same government overlook the life-rights of the unborn? How can it hold that "no person shall be . . . deprived of life, liberty, or property, without due process of law," yet simultaneously argue that ending lives of the unborn is acceptable without due process?[7]

Our government is further based upon the duty of the citizenry to ensure their lives, liberties, and pursuits of happiness are secured. And "whenever any Form of Government becomes destructive of these ends, it is the Right of the People to alter" that government in manners that "seem mostly likely to effect their Safety and Happiness."[8] With the acceptance of abortion, has not the government become "destructive" of its role in securing the unalienable rights of life, liberty, and the pursuit of happiness? Does it not now fall upon the people to alter the government's acceptance of this calamity? As such, our elected officials ought to be vetted to ensure their pro-life beliefs and for their promises toward the wellbeing of the unborn.

But are there any permitting circumstances for an abortion? Among Conservatives, many believe that, since abortion is fundamentally immoral, there can be no conditions that allow abortion. For them, there is no litmus test for life's worthiness—once conceived, once born. For other Conservatives, who also believe in abortion's depravity, there is minor room for allowances. Usually, this will arise only in the instance of rape or when, during childbirth, the life of the mother is in grave danger and an abortion of the birthing procedure may save her life. Other circumstances further divide Conservatives on these matters and are decisions that each Conservative must make through a solemn, calm, and deep assessment. Yet regardless of potential exceptions or circumstances, we Conservatives stand clear that abortion is wrong, generally unnecessary, and immoral.

Moreover, abortion is not attached to the reproductive rights a woman has over her own body. The reproductive right she does hold is whether or not to participate in sexual relations. That right over her body is that of hers alone. But once she has become pregnant therefrom, the body over which she controls is, in fact, two bodies, one of which is not her own. Doctors strongly encourage pregnant women not to smoke, drink alcohol, or take non-prescribed drugs, and to avoid caffeine, many foods, x-rays, and saunas, all in the name of protecting the unborn child. If only one body was involved, why limit the use of these otherwise usual interactions? WE CONSERVATIVES BELIEVE unborn children are owed the protections of caring mothers and countries—something eternally avoided through the practice of abortion.

HAPPINESS PURSUED

WE CONSERVATIVES BELIEVE happiness is pursued, not given. Our founders recognized government is most useful when it takes a backseat to personal responsibility and rewards hard work. We believe happiness will not take hold when those in power presume they can guide the lives and fortunes of the citizenry better than the citizens themselves. Contentment is most secure when it is free to be individually obtained.

In America's government, there is no want of those who relish in replacing personal initiative with government mandates and handouts. In yesterday's America, our forefathers understood "there was no guarantee of fortune or comfort, only the assurance of freedom to choose the course of his life rather than have an oppressive government choose it for him."[9] But what has changed over the last centuries? Why has freedom become contingent on government corroboration? We Conservatives look for leaders who do not try to instill happiness in the lives of their constituents but rather move government aside to allow happiness to grow independently. Our Conservative leaders know "the best way to help the poor—as well as the middle class and indeed everybody—is by growing the economy and employment, and the compelling evidence demonstrates that free enterprise is the most successful system to do just that. Accordingly, we must look to measures that foster free enterprise and encourage businesses to grow, invest, and hire."[10]

WE CONSERVATIVES BELIEVE the right to choose from where one will seek his happiness is not merely a luxury associated with living in America; all mankind is created "by their Creator with certain unalienable Rights, that among these are Life, Liberty and the *pursuit of Happiness*."[11]

The American Dream

WE CONSERVATIVES BELIEVE a person fulfills the American Dream when he applies himself to his fullest capacity and achieves that which only his talents and skills can provide. The American Dream is the pursuit of happiness so cherished in the American spirit and so enshrined in our national body.

The idea of the American Dream has been present since our founding, but a book published in the early 1930s first presented and defined the term, in which the author wrote:

> But there has been also the American dream, that dream of a land in which life should be better and richer and fuller for every man, with opportunity for each according to his ability or achievement. It is a difficult dream for the European upper classes to interpret adequately, and too many of us ourselves have grown weary and mistrustful of it. It is not a dream of motor cars and high wages merely, but a dream of social order in which each man and each woman shall be able to attain to the fullest stature of which they are innately capable, and be recognized by others for what they are, regardless of the fortuitous circumstances of birth or position.[12]

Centuries before this author encapsulated what has today become a daily phrase, our founders realized the importance of this same notion—that success or failure in America was to be determined by one's pursuits and by the willingness of each person to put forth efforts to ensure such successes or failures. They believed their new nation "would be a land of equal opportunity, not of equal outcomes."[13] WE CONSERVATIVES BELIEVE the American Dream is not merely the obtainment of owning a home; instead, owning a home is often one result of having pursued the American Dream and of taking steps to guarantee personal accomplishments in the hunt for personal independence.

Voter Turnout

WE CONSERVATIVES BELIEVE every American's vote connects intimately to the political process in the United States. Casting votes is one of the few entitlements Americans justly enjoy and something invaluably engrained in the soul of America.

Even though we Americans are blessed with the circumstances to choose our leaders, very few among us turn out to do so. We vote regarding numerous things—representative officials, proposals, and taxes—but so few believe their vote to be of significance. Or worse still, so few believe in the importance of voting. Is American governance such an abstract and faraway notion as to be of no consequence to our fellow citizens? Is the electorate so fickle as to be swayed by simple advertisements and political jockeying, all the while naïve to the reality of America's real troubles? And if a single vote is so inconsequential, what would be the reaction if the government took away that vote? What would be the outcry over the non-voters' disenfranchisement after a period of not exercising their vote?

It seems improbable that we will convince more Americans to vote by providing them histories regarding the long and worthy process that eventually brought suffrage to both sexes and all races. These records are commendable and to be known, but will continue to fail in turning out larger swaths of Americans on Election Day. We should not employ a quasi-compulsory voting scheme, as seen in some countries such as Australia and Mexico. Voting is the quintessential marker of freedom and its muddling with compulsion and mandate converts it from that of a civic right to a duty. WE CONSERVATIVES BELIEVE voting is the cornerstone upon which civil society rests and recognize that "decisions are made by those who show up."[14]

Change and Effort

WE CONSERVATIVES BELIEVE responsibility begins with oneself, but its fruits extend well into surrounding spheres of influence. The free will we each exhibit is a reflection of our intentions and choices, and every intention or choice we make can result in either good or harm. All the same, our self-pitying and woeful thoughts may also brew the self-fulfillment of individual regression and victimhood. That is, when one thinks incessantly of his misery and misfortune, he demonstrates actions that only further his adversity and serves no benefit.

In every life, there is only a finite and unbeknownst slice of time we each may utilize. It is during this time we may use our free will to either promote the betterment of oneself and mankind or squander it with blame and anger. And as humans, if we find ourselves in the depths of despair and self-misery, we have the unique ability—unlike any other species on Earth—to change. It is one of the greatest and most influential tools we each possess, yet it is also one of the least-employed tools we ever use. Certainly, "At one time or another, most of us have embarked on an effort to change some part of ourselves or our lives. . . . [Yet as] a rule, these sorts of changes don't occur overnight. They take time and effort."[15] It is through this time and effort that we measure the extent of personal responsibility, for while it may be clear where each of us might improve and take control, it is a great deal more difficult actually to see it through. WE CONSERVATIVES BELIEVE personal responsibility is achieved not merely by acknowledging shortcomings but also by overcoming those individual limitations—something bettering the individual and improving his surroundings.

INTERNATIONAL LEADERSHIP

The Supreme Constitution

WE CONSERVATIVES BELIEVE the Constitution of the United States trumps, and is supreme to, treaties made by America with other foreign entities. Many have suggested that treaties, being international and binding decrees, are superior to the Constitution because they are somehow above the Constitution's restraints; we believe this is inaccurate and a misconstruction of American legal reality.

Article. VI. of the Constitution contains what has become known as the "Supremacy Clause," through which it specifies, "This Constitution, and the Laws of the United States which shall be made in Pursuance thereof; and all Treaties made, or which shall be made, under the Authority of the United States, shall be the supreme Law of the Land; and the Judges in every State shall be bound thereby, any Thing in the Constitution or Laws of any State to the Contrary notwithstanding."[1] The purpose of this distinction was to avoid the shortcomings of America's first constitution (the Articles of Confederation) and to allow general uniformity on matters of national concern. Writing in 1788, James Madison argued, "as the constitutions of the States differ much from each other, it might happen that [in the absence of the Supremacy Clause] a treaty or national law of great and equal importance to the States would interfere with some and not with other constitutions, and would consequently be valid in some of the States at the same time it would have no effect in others."[2] Without a federal body that could, through constitutional means, legislate on behalf of the entire country and supersede preexisting and conflicting state laws, the Constitution "would have been evidently and radically defective."[3]

The self-explanatory language of the Supremacy Clause describes this relationship and underlines the superiority of the Constitution over both federal laws and treaties. For federal laws to be valid, they must initially be subjected to, and overcome, constitutional scrutiny. This means that for a federal bill to be properly enacted, legislators must determine a legal source of power enumerated in the Constitution upon which to support the bill; without such a source, Congress cannot act. Alexander Hamilton wrote regarding the Supremacy Clause, "We perceive that the clause which declares the supremacy of the laws of the Union . . . only declares a truth which flows immediately and necessarily from the institution of a federal government. It will not, I presume, have escaped observation that it *expressly* confines this supremacy to laws made *pursuant to the Constitution*."[4] Hence, federal laws are only supreme in the United States if they are in accordance with the Constitution.

Accordingly, to appropriately execute a treaty, its terms must align with the governmental restraints found in the American Constitution. The federal government cannot amass more power simply by signing and ratifying a treaty. If so, the Constitution would be an empty letter and governmental moderation would be a charade. Moreover, the ability of the federal government, and the inability of the state governments, to enter into treaties is derived from the Constitution itself. How could a document (if treaties were superior to the Constitution) that permits treaty commitments simultaneously be subordinate to the treaty it allowed? Treaties involving the United States are only permissible because the supreme Constitution allows them. The United States can withdraw from treaties and still retain its Constitution; it cannot, however, renounce its Constitution and still retain its treaties. WE CONSERVATIVES BELIEVE the Constitution stands as the most superior legal document in America with regard to its enumerations, and the Supremacy Clause serves as strong evidence of this legal truth.

Globalization and Federalism

A Transformation

WE CONSERVATIVES BELIEVE attempted isolation of a country is harmful to that country's economy, standard of living, and stature. Yet in America, participating in global spheres requires a delicate balance between constitutional limits on the federal government and maintaining the proper sovereignty of the several states.

Globalization has become, in a modern sense, a transformative reality on the culture and governance of all the world's countries, regardless of whether those countries participate in international marketplaces and bodies. To truly globalize, "unprecedented levels of international cooperation" are required, as numerous contemporary examples have shown.[5] "To limit carbon emissions," for instance, "an effective regime must set standards for almost all forms of energy use worldwide. To allow for the smooth movement of capital, nations must coordinate their regulatory controls on the financial industry."[6] In essence, for the international ideals of some to work, those same individuals and groups rely on the political capital of persons representing participating countries and their ability to impose such regulations on constituents. But this dependence creates several problems for federal leaders in the United States, where the states retain a unique control of their governance, except as provided in the Constitution they composed.

In the age of expanding globalization, the American federal government has wasted no time interfering with the rights of the states through international mechanisms. Examples and questions raised thereby include:

> Do international court judgments have force in American law, invalidating otherwise valid judgments by domestic courts? Can the President and the Senate together sign an international treaty that binds the United States to either legalize or criminalize abortion . . . ? Should international and foreign laws be used to interpret the U.S. Constitution? May Congress and the President delegate federal authority to international organizations to regulate domestic conduct, for instance, in arms control and carbon emissions?[7]

Unequivocally, we Conservatives answer "no" to each of the questions posed above, yet regrettably, each is a question that has been raised by one experience or another in the relentless pursuit of globalization. But how, then, can the United States remain a key player in a "flat world" yet still retain its most important and distinctive elements: federalism and the separation of powers?

The answer is not alien to the boundaries of the Constitution, nor are federalism and the separation of powers insurmountable barriers preventing any global interactions. Quite the contrary, for they act as safeguards to overextensions of government: "These constitutional structures may prove burdensome or inefficient, but they enhance accountability and transparency in government—important features of constitutional democracy. Popular sovereignty, therefore, is to be ignored only at one's peril."[8] The following subchapters delve deeper into specific means of accomplishing appropriate globalization, yet all the while maintains the superiority of the Constitution, the separation of powers, and federalism. WE CONSERVATIVES BELIEVE international interactions with competing and collaborating nations are essential to a prosperous and leading America and can be legally accomplished through the present structure of American governance, so long as tempered by the self-imposed restraints placed upon it.

The Executing Doctrines

WE CONSERVATIVES BELIEVE the United States can compete in a global environment while still maintaining the fundamental pillars of liberty known within the founding documents and understood through natural law. For globalization to be both effective and appropriate at home, there must be legally adequate grounds upon which the United States can adopt international policies. However, by necessity, these policies must be in conformance with the Constitution and adopted through the respective channels of governance.

Authors and political commentators have suggested several means through which the Constitution can remain supreme and respected yet still allow for continued interactions abroad on matters of economic and political concern. Among these is the "non-self-execution doctrine," which suggests "treaties and other international agreements are not law *in* the United States unless or until some other domestic institution (usually Congress) decides to implement it."[9] In a constitutional approach to domestic governance, laws and regulations are not formally effective until the legislature, through bicameral procedures, passes a bill, and the executive thereafter either signs the bill or takes no action. Following that moment, the bill becomes law and carries with it the force thereof in the United States. Under the international non-self-execution doctrine, the requirements are generally the same as standard domestic law enactment, but in reverse order. With this scheme, the president, as the chief figurehead in foreign relations, agrees with foreign countries to enter into particular partnerships that will be binding on their international interactions, so long as the Senate (as specified in the Constitution) consents by a two-thirds majority.[10] But those foreign commitments are not law within the United States unless both houses of Congress move to pass legislation implementing such agreements domestically.

While non-self-executing treaties by themselves may not be effective law inside the United States, they do indeed carry significant weight nonetheless. "Even without implementation by Congress, non-self-executing treaties create *international* obligations."[11] For example, "During the Cold War, arms control agreements with the Soviet Union calling for the limitation or elimination of nuclear weapons entered the U.S. into an international legal obligation. The existence of this obligation did not, however, allow the Soviet Union or any other entity to sue in U.S. courts to require the United States to comply with an arms control treaty, or that U.S. courts are in general authorized to force U.S. compliance." America deems even the United Nations Charter as a non-self-executing treaty.

The purposes of non-self-execution are many, and they work to enhance essential supports of republican governance. On these roles, two authors have written a compelling argument regarding their importance:

> It limits the domestic legal status of treaties and international agreements, requiring something more than the President's signature and the Senate's advice and consent for a treaty or international agreement to have domestic legal effect. The doctrine shifts the decision to more broadly representative institutions. This ensures that the same institution that enacts domestic policy—Congress—will be the one to control the implementation of international agreements within the nation's borders. The treaty, in other words, does not alter the Constitution's allocation of power between the branches of the federal government over domestic policy.[12]

WE CONSERVATIVES BELIEVE this disbursement of domestic legislative authority minimizes the ability of a small body of people—the president and the Senate—to silently erode the legislative intent of the Constitution for internal affairs, and it propels accountable governance.

Presidential Deference

WE CONSERVATIVES BELIEVE that since the creation of domestic laws in accordance with international obligations should rely on the non-self-execution doctrine, there must also be a mechanism through which those global commitments are interpreted and understood. Commonly, it is believed such interpretations belong in the judiciary, but, as previously shown, an authentic application of the non-self-execution doctrine "restricts or eliminates the power of U.S. courts to give effect to a treaty or international agreement absent a specific authorizing action by Congress, the President, or the states."[13] Thus, another body or source of interpretation needs to be the determining element; we believe this ability best resides in the elected branches of government and those directly answerable to the people.

Historically, the president has served as "the chief—if not the sole—organ of the U.S. government in the conduct of foreign affairs. . . . [The] combination of delegated foreign affairs powers under the Constitution, as well as a long historical practice of presidential control over foreign affairs, has led to the development of a complex and sophisticated foreign affairs bureaucracy supervised by, and responsible to, the President."[14] While simply because one branch has become, through time, the head of a certain matter does not necessarily make that distinction appropriate, but in this instance, it probably is. Under present governance internationally and domestically, presidential understandings of international law are given great deference in judicial proceedings on global concerns. Even more, the president has "exercised the power to declare U.S. objections to international legal obligations, either by withdrawing from treaties or by challenging the rules of customary international law." The dangers of judicial review in federal courts were discussed in "Judicial Review," and the potential harms therefrom are greatly agitated should review of international law also reside in the judiciary. Under such a system, "courts are thus free, especially in the realm of customary law, to adopt broad interpretations whether or not the executive or legislative branches have approved the international law principle."[15] Consequently, unelected federal judges can impose, on their authority, international policies onto domestic legal questions. Instead, "allowing the President, the most politically accountable and institutionally expert branch of the federal government, to control the interpretation of international law substantially avoids the undemocratic nature of unwritten international law." WE CONSERVATIVES BELIEVE, therefore, and as history has proven effective and useful, granting general deference to the president on interpretations of international law furthers the republican nature of America and avoids the likelihood of unelected (and thus mostly unaccountable) officials making determinations instead—determinations that may unconstitutionally impress mandates on the American people without the consideration of the elected branches of government.

The States

WE CONSERVATIVES BELIEVE retention of state autonomy in an increasingly globalized political and economic environment is central to the continuance of American federalism and the restraints placed on federal governmental bodies. State governments should, and in fact do, play a leading role in the implementation of international obligations. Furthermore, as globalization expands, external pressures on the federal government increase, encouraging it to usurp responsibilities historically left primarily, if not exclusively, to the states—matters such as "family law, criminal law, and tax relations with local consular officials."[16] Deferring to state governments to propel international commitments both enhances the likelihood of their successful implementation and enshrines the relationship between federal and state governments as rooted in proper federalism.

Under the Constitution created by the states, foreign relations falls generally to the federal government. "Hence, Article I, Section 10 explicitly prohibits states from entering into treaties or international agreements absent congressional approval. Nor can they engage in wars or other traditional forms of international relations."[17] Yet nonetheless, states have continually served as an important (that is, crucial) party to foreign obligations found in international law applicable to the United States. When traditional state duties are evermore entering the realm of international designs, and because the Constitution tasks Washington with negotiating and crafting foreign commitments, the federal government becomes reliant on the states to ensure compliance with the new obligations. Because historical state-centered concerns involve "knowledge of local conditions and comprehensive enforcement resources—qualities lacking in the federal government—successful adaptation to globalization in areas such as crime, family, and education [require] the recognition of the primary role of the states."

A nationalized blanket attempt to implement international law obligations on the United States without cooperation from the states and an acceptance of minor variances within the states is sure to self-destruct. The pressures of globalization that smear the distinctions between the federal and state governments interfere with the valued and effective principle of federalism in America. Furthermore, centralized control over historically state matters "may actually make the American governmental system less efficient and less responsive to citizens' preferences, which may be better served by the diversity of state policies encouraged by federalism and its competition among jurisdictions. Rather than imposing a uniform rule in response to the needs of globalization, policymakers can seek and have sought ways to preserve primary state control over such issues."[18]

Some degree of diversity between the states does not serve as a hamper to the implementation of foreign commitments, and it furthers the historical autonomy of the states. Yet, if certain international obligations genuinely do require perfect consistency among the states, then the normal legislative process can be ignited, seeking the support of representatives from those very states (akin to the procedure in the domestic implementation of a non-self-executing treaty). WE CONSERVATIVES BELIEVE the federal government ought to, and in reality does, rely on the states to fulfill many of the international obligations into which it enters, for the states retain their autonomy and are more able to adapt and enforce global commitments in smaller degrees, especially with regard to matters primarily of state concern.

The Harms of Isolation

WE CONSERVATIVES BELIEVE America is the best-remaining hope for freedom in a world of constraining personal liberties. The responsibility of maintaining this optimism is in the hands of the citizen-body and, by extension, the leaders they elect. Americans first owe a duty to their nation, not to the world at large.

We believe America cannot remain the sole superpower by imposing isolationist agendas, and the threats stemming therefrom are many. Isolation removes our industries from competition with worldly markets, and when the number of participants in a market falls, the urgency to advance ahead of the competition lessens. Because competition is the driver of invention, our national output thus declines when isolated. The industries that once propelled America become second-rate to those of our outside adversaries, and we soon slip into decline. We Conservatives recognize the delicate balance of optimal self-seeking pursuits, for on the one hand we ought to always advance American interests, yet on the other cannot fall into the trap of isolation.

Fortunately, this seemingly paradoxical circumstance is not insurmountable. We can achieve both American interests first and remain an active player in the world's market, for we would not be serving America's best interests by avoiding the world's markets. Further, simply participating in the international marketplace does not prevent Americans from purchasing American goods or services; rather it makes certain our homeland industries remain on the cutting edge. WE CONSERVATIVES BELIEVE our participation in the global arena spurs ingenuity, competition, and invention—all which ensure a greater range of products, services, and qualities for the consumer, the citizen.

STRATEGIES OF POWER

WE CONSERVATIVES BELIEVE that at any given time, several strategies of power are competing to obtain global leadership and dominance. Of these, only one—that of America's—wholly propels the freedoms of liberty and ensures the natural rights of the individual.

From these strategic approaches, some suggest four are most predominant.[19] The United States employs the first such strategy, and it is "based on two fundamental principles: economic freedom and political freedom."[20] The underworkings of these two cores are not entirely different, and each empowers the other: "Individual freedom stimulates a spirit of entrepreneurship that in turn leads to innovation and enterprise." The practice of this method has, by consequence, produced the world's most powerful nation and aided numerous others in their pursuits of international influence.

The second approach is that undertaken by China. While theirs is additionally rooted in free enterprise, "it is also based on authoritarian rule."[21] When compared to the model of America and the West, "China's leaders see things quite differently. They believe that the economic vitality produced by free enterprise, combined with the stability and vision of wise leaders, unaffected by popular whim, creates the winning strategy." But even China's understanding of free enterprise is, at times, largely different from that of the American way. "Major industries continue to be state-owned and -operated. And absent from the Chinese systems is the rule of law and regulation that shapes free enterprise elsewhere."

Thirdly, Russia pursues another global strategy. "Like China, it favors authoritarian rule, but Russia's economic strategy is primarily based on energy. By controlling people and energy, Russia aims to reassert itself as a global superpower."[22] For many, it may seem inconceivable that Russia would again compete as a global leader following the fall of the Soviet Union, but "Russia's rediscovered ambition for superpower status is fueled by its massive energy reserves." And even beyond its leading amounts of oil exports, it is also utilizing science and technology to propel its position further. Moreover, Russia is allied with many nations to whom the United States and the West are opposed, most notably Iran. "Because a nuclear Iran would become a Middle East superpower, and if Russia could influence Iran, it could have even more power over world energy supplies. The same holds true with Russia's burgeoning relationship with Venezuela."[23]

The fourth and last of these approaches serves the same goal of "overcoming the West and ultimately leading the world."[24] This is the strategy of violent jihadism. Although there is no singular body that represents the jihadists, and only one country's government formally embraces its beliefs (Iran), the jihadists "share a common overarching goal: violent holy war on America and the West, the destruction of Israel and the Jews, the recapture of all lands once held by Muslims, the elimination of 'infidel' leaders in Muslim nations . . ., and ultimately, the defeat of all non-Muslim nations."[25]

This fourth strategy, "based on conquest and compulsion," is perhaps the most difficult to overcome due to the lack of central or synchronized leadership among its ranks.

These four approaches to global influence represent the predominate methods currently employed. Only one is thoroughly grounded in freedom: the strategy used by the United States and the West. "Only if America and the West succeed—if our economic and military strength endure—can we be confident that our children and grandchildren will be free."[26] Each of the latter three strategies seeks to diminish the stature of the United States, both because America functions in opposition to their ways (and is successful in doing so) and because a decreased America would serve as less competition to these other strategies. WE CONSERVATIVES BELIEVE we must prevail and remain the world's leading force of good or else make susceptible our most cherished freedoms—those of individual sovereignty and economic liberty.

The United Nations Illusion

Overreach

WE CONSERVATIVES BELIEVE the United Nations, although founded in a pool of noble ideas and expectations, has proven far from effective in achieving even the most fundamental of its endeavors and has demonstrated troubling redistributive intentions with regard to developed nations' technology and commerce. The UN, created largely to prevent war and safeguard human rights, has transformed itself into a body set on governing above the sovereignty of its member states and their citizens.

Support for the United Nations among the American citizenry has never been particularly great. A Gallup poll conducted in 2012, for instance, asked interviewees, "Do you think the United Nations is doing a good job or a poor job in trying to solve the problems it has had to face?"[27] A mere 32 percent of those polled gave the UN a "good job" grading, with 61 percent believing it was doing a "bad job." In fact, since Gallup began tracking American opinions of the UN in 1953, favorable judgments of the international body have only averaged a weak 40 percent.[28] While the original goals of the UN are commendable and likely to attract American support, its other subsequent actions and proposals have left most in the United States with a sour taste.

Today, the United Nations presents four principal purposes for its existence as an international entity: "[(1)] To keep peace throughout the world; [(2)] To develop friendly relations among nations; [(3)] To help nations work together to improve the lives of poor people, to conquer hunger, disease and illiteracy, and to encourage respect for each other's rights and freedoms; [(4)] To be a centre for harmonizing the actions of nations to achieve these goals."[29] UN sources further enumerate the broad scope of its present-day pursuits, including "sustainable development, environment and refugees protection, disaster relief, counter terrorism, disarmament and non-proliferation, . . . promoting democracy, human rights, gender equality and the advancement of women, governance, economic and social development and international health, clearing landmines, expanding food production, and more, in order to achieve its goals and coordinate efforts for a safer world for this and future generations." In essence, the United Nations holds itself to be the equal of—or, in fact, superior to—sovereign nations of the world, one permitted to function as a governing agency with the power to legislate, execute, and judge on virtually all matters of human existence. It openly admits that its scope "reaches every corner of the globe."

The ever-expanding organization is home to several other concerning realities as well. A 2011 report drafted by the UN's own Joint Inspection Unit found that those tasked with eliminating internal corruption and waste often have no professional qualifications, are improperly funded, and not necessarily independent, being instead "part of the management" and thus prone to conflicts of interest.[30] Moreover, when it discovers wrongdoing, there is minimal consistency in undertaking corrective measures. Given these insufficiencies of internal control, together with the overreaching extent of the UN's scope and various examples of its undermining of American interests, it is of little surprise that support for the organization is so small in the United States, a place where limited government, free enterprise, and accountability are enshrined. WE CONSERVATIVES BELIEVE international governing bodies ought to be of narrow scope and definition, and our involvement in them should first be with the intention of bettering American wellbeing (and consequently those of our allies), so long as consistent with the principles of American governance.

Sovereign Interference

WE CONSERVATIVES BELIEVE the United Nations, with its nearly two hundred member states, is largely unable to satisfy the interests of its greatest contributors and many players, and it frequently acts to undermine the sustained prosperity of the United States. If America is to continue leading international initiatives, then we must associate with bodies that support American pursuits of freedom and economic liberty and withdraw from those that always seek our aid but value our input only when crises arise.

The United States funds roughly one quarter of both the UN's regular budget and its peacekeeping budget, but we share voting powers with some of our greatest enemies and those seeking the minimization of America. Moreover, the troubling inadequacies of the UN, combined with its ingrained corruptive tendencies, raise legitimate questions over the value of participating in such a body. "Its efforts to address global problems such as terrorism, human trafficking, and proliferation of weapons of mass destruction," for instance, "have been weak, ineffectual, or counterproductive. Indeed, the U.N. cannot even agree on a definition of terrorism."[31]

One of the greatest areas of interest for the United Nations has become the vaguely defined "sustainable development" initiative, under which it holds environmental concerns as the purpose behind most economical and political regulations. Through sustainable development proposals, countries and citizens alike are restricted in their abilities to advance certain agendas and projects that might offend the environment's alleged balance or prospects. The UN also presses for free research and technology sharing with "undeveloped countries" by those "developed countries" that have produced such knowledge. Once shared, the creators of the technology receive no apportionment of profits or return from the undeveloped countries' use thereof, all done in an effort to redistribute capabilities and level the playing field.

While sustainable development ideologies and calls for technology sharing are troubling, the greatest threat to American strength perhaps lies in our relationship to the UN Security Council, a division of the overall United Nations organization. Tasked with international peace and security, American politicians often seek approval from this group for military action and abide by its decrees to deploy American troops absent congressional and constitutional authorization. Secretary of Defense Leon Panetta elaborated this truth during a hearing with the Senate Armed Services Committee in 2012, where Senator Jeff Sessions questioned him on the legal basis for military action:

> SESSIONS: What kind of legal basis are you looking for? What entity?
> PANETTA: Well, obviously, if NATO made the decision to go in, that would be one. If we developed an international coalition beyond NATO then obviously some kind of U.N. Security Resolution would be the basis for that. . . . We want to do it with permissions . . . by the international community.[32]

The real danger with this understanding of the powers of government is that it, in fact, harbors no understanding of those powers. In the same hearing, Senator Sessions informed the secretary that international bodies "provide no legal authority [for military deployment]. The only legal authority that is required to deploy the United States's military is the Congress and the President and the law and the Constitution." American strength depends on American sovereignty, particularly so regarding our military. WE CONSERVATIVES BELIEVE American international collaborations should exist only to the extent they maintain American independence of action and economic freedom and promote the pillars of individual and national liberty.

OVERLY REGULATED

WE CONSERVATIVES BELIEVE the risks associated with a central government that is powerful enough to regulate, and thereby control, vast concerns of American living is dangerous to domestic liberty and international relations, neither of which the United States can survive as a competing power without.

Over-regulation (whether through congressional mandate, executive fiat, judicial decree, or administrative-state rulings) suffocates economic growth and opportunity. The founders did not design the American government as a partner to private industry, and in so now doing, it may take issue with each consecutive proposal and pursuit. But as all encroaching governments have understood throughout history, such a philosophy is often the most direct route into the asset stream of commerce, regardless of the impact such a siphoning has over economic development. Rather than wait for governmental revenue to accrue as a consequence of lower taxation over broader swaths, the impatient governing bodies relentlessly hunt all corners of prosperity until those corners are dry of innovation. A once-booming beacon of success becomes a shadow of its former self when the government seeks continual interference.

The same fate has confronted countless other economies in man's history. The Spanish Empire of the sixteenth and seventeenth centuries, for instance, after its discovery and control of vast riches in the Americas, grew into the leading economic and political power of the world. "The treasure of the New World had acted like a steroid on the empire, expanding it beyond its natural dimensions."[33] But governmental lust for a share in the riches resulted in a smothering of taxes and regulations under which nothing was unaffected. With its seemingly endless source of riches, "The empire ballooned, but the Spanish mind closed in on itself. Religious fervor hardened into ceremony; the vast bureaucracy stifled ambition; a rigidly hierarchical society replicated itself in all its colonies." So iron-like were state encroachments that, for example, "In Panama or Havana, poor men needed state-approved licenses simply to beg on the streets. No human activity escaped the hand of tradition and state control. The empire had shut itself off to the idea of flexibility and change." The over-regulation of commerce in the Spanish Empire, coupled with other powers seeking control without such heavy and dogmatic burdens, would soon bring the empire to its knees and leave it in the wakes of both allies and enemies alike. Never again would the Spanish return to the prominence of its yesterdays before its own government's yearning for revenue choked the empire's most significant source of wealth: individual aspiration.

The Spanish Empire's story teaches a vital lesson: not only are limitations on governmental influence necessary for domestic strength but also for international relations in a globally competing marketplace. Remaining watchful for mankind's frequent economic sinfulness is not synonymous with ceasing economic activity altogether, nor are governmental pursuits of wealth synonymous with thieving others out of their wealth. Not a single example is extant in which evermore governmental regulations and encroachments produced economic prosperity or encouraged international business endeavors and commitments. WE CONSERVATIVES BELIEVE American fiscal strength is contingent on limitations of governmental scope and authority, as well as the endorsement of free-market philosophies and practices—all on which the strength of the United States depends, both at home and abroad.

MOVING AMERICA FORWARD

VISIONS FOR THE FUTURE

WE CONSERVATIVES BELIEVE in leaders who have visions beyond a single generation. The citizenry should elect from amongst itself leaders who represent not only their present constituents but also our collective descendants. Change is not always needed, but progress is.

What are the threats associated with short-term thinking in a society? And what happens when the citizenry only elects officials who promise riches from the state treasury or the nation's wealthy? The result universally creates at least two problems of grave significance. First, the populace, after becoming solely self-interested in their pursuits, will unlikely cast ballots for leaders who have visions for the future. To an intrinsic citizen-body, the future is but a hazy imagination far in the distance; it has no form or consequence nor requires a present sacrifice.

A second outcome associated with an overly heavy focus on the present is the inevitable fall of fiscal conservatism, leading to the rise of economic tyranny. A quote often attributed to Alexander Fraser Tytler summarizes this threat and the importance of long-term development: "A democracy cannot exist as a permanent form of government. It can only exist until the voters discover that they can vote themselves largesse from the public treasury. From that moment on, the majority only votes for candidates promising the most benefits from the public treasury, with the result that a democracy always collapses over loose fiscal policy, always followed by dictatorship."[1] WE CONSERVATIVES BELIEVE the threats against legitimate liberty are many fold, and so we must place our trust in leaders who rebel against the policies of tyranny and encroachment and who understand their duty is not just to the living but to the yet unborn as well.

Race, Sex, and Class

WE CONSERVATIVES BELIEVE in measuring individual merit by one's character and achievement with minimal regard to race, sex, or class. We look to moral absolutes to discern right from wrong, we reject public promotions centered on race, we resist movements that neutralize gender differences, and we refrain from divisions of class that are focused on distinctions of capital wealth.

Prominent Conservatives have articulated this point by making comparisons to the opposite of conservatism: liberalism and the Left. In an article by Dennis Prager, he notes that "one of the more dangerous features of the Left has been its replacement of moral categories of right and wrong, and good and evil, with three other categories: black and white (race), male and female (gender), and rich and poor (class)."[2] Through these filters, everything can be run, and every disagreement can be rooted. Rather than compare and contrast issues in an unemotional and rational manner, categorization allows the Liberal to turn everything—from the most basic and mundane matter to that of greatest complexity—into an alleged discovery of Conservative hatred. He may argue, then, that the white man who opposes affirmative action is a racist; or that the single man who opposes abortion is a sexist; or that the citizen who wants lower taxes for all is against the poor.

With these beliefs, there is no need to argue on the merits of a case; it is far easier (and all-too-often more effective) to stick to the emotional barbs that stem from an illegitimate focus on race, sex, or class. The spotlight shifts from the substance of issues to instead what the race, sex, or class of the speaker are. But when the Left focuses too heavily on distinctions of race, sex, and class, what about Conservatives who are minorities, women, or poor? If the Left believes Conservatives are generally white rich men, then where does, for instance, the Conservative black poor woman fit in? Shouldn't this be a contradiction to their underlying holding? Perhaps an even worse insult thus confronts this apparently flawed inconsistency to the intellect of the individual: demonization. Women who oppose abortion are "either not authentically female or simply traitors to their sex, just as the Left depicts blacks who oppose race-based affirmative action as not authentic blacks or are traitors to their race."[3] A white man who opposes affirmative action is thought to seek pre-1960s racial discrimination; a man who believes life begins at conception does so only from an urge to suppress a woman's right to control her own body; and the citizen who recognizes that lasting economic growth only comes from stability and low taxation inevitably wants the poor to suffer. This is the world in which many opponents of conservatism live and one against which all Conservatives have repelled.

Race, sex, and class can and should play a role in politics and decision-making insofar as the distinctions are used to remove discrimination and inequitable incidents. The problem becomes, however, drawing the line between eliminating discrimination and preventing reverse-discrimination. Instead, what has happened is the Left's realization that by employing these race-, sex-, and class-envy positions, they can illegitimize conservative arguments before they ever begin, calling Conservatives racists, sexists, elitists, etc. This instilled divisiveness prevents virtually any significant issue to be realistically discussed and explored, leaving us to become a nation of short-fused and short-sighted planners. For the Left, these mongerings work to solidify a base of the very people they suggest Conservatives are against. Unfortunately, so long as these tactics remain effective, the Left will continue to utilize them. WE CONSERVATIVES BELIEVE arguments founded on one's race, sex, or class that attempt to encapsulate another's disagreement are flawed, misleading, and immoral.

A Diverse Citizenry

WE CONSERVATIVES BELIEVE diversity among Americans is key to the continued development of our country. Diversity acts simultaneously as both the chicken and the egg—it begins and proceeds with the acceptance of individuality. But we Conservatives look largely to a person's skills, talents, and capabilities in determining the merit of their contributions; we generally do not weigh his or her race, sex, or class. Even so, if we wish to be a progressing nation, then those among us will be diverse *because* progression interlinks with diversity.

Many do not showcase today's acknowledgment of diversity in America in a positive light. For every country, diversity is meant to strengthen the roots supporting its fundamental pillars, something usually accomplished by recognizing unique differences among fellow countrymen and through the employment of various angles from which to approach competing circumstances. But instead, diversity now serves to effectively dismiss American exceptionalism by using the United States as a meeting ground for anti-American sentiment. Rather than "promote assimilation and unity of citizenship, [and] alliance to American culture," we now develop "a *cultural relativism* in which the cultures from which [diversity come] are given equal accord with the American culture. But all cultures are not equal, as evidenced, in part, by the alien fleeing his own country for the American culture."[4] General Colin Powell refined this point, reflecting during retirement that "I was an American soldier who was black, not a black American soldier."[5] WE CONSERVATIVES BELIEVE that, while seclusion breeds bigotry, diversity is advantageous insofar as it is intertwined with merit-based recognitions, serving to advance the cause of American greatness further.

Affirmative Action

WE CONSERVATIVES BELIEVE attempts to make society more dynamic through forced diversity will most usually fail and instead result in an opposite discrimination. For many, affirmative action is the source through which they launch initiatives hoping to gain the inclusion of minority races and sexes in all sectors while minimizing merit-based credentials.

Affirmative action, although branded as an anti-discrimination enterprise, is of itself discriminatory that creates impossible contradictions. For example, the Civil Rights Act of 1964 passed with provisions prohibiting employment discrimination based on the applicant's race, ethnicity, or sex. In 1991, a further amendment to the act added a " 'disparate impact provision,' which allows a claim of discrimination to be established on the basis of disproportionate racial results."[6] Liberals established this backward idea as both a futile attempt to prevent employers from committing discrimination and to further compliance with the original act itself. "The idea behind the disparate impact provision . . . was that equal *opportunity* can be measured only by equal *results*. Whenever a policy does not produce equal results, there is a presumption of racial discrimination."[7]

To countermand alleged racial discrimination and to "create" equal opportunity, certainly some form of unequal opportunity must also be enforced. Thus, ensuring a workforce or student body of diverse individuals will then also be accompanied with a consideration (and weighing) of the applicants' race, ethnicity, and sex, and turning away those who, although qualified, are of the "wrong" designation. WE CONSERVATIVES BELIEVE the ends of establishing a diverse workforce or student body may not always justify the means.

A Common Language

The Bedrock

WE CONSERVATIVES BELIEVE a common language for all Americans is central to assimilation into the national culture and promotes allegiance to the country in which we live. English has served as the bedrock language throughout American history and should continue to function as a pillar of our national identity.

The United States does not have a federally recognized language. Instead, English has stood as the *de facto* language since America's founding, emphasizing our historical ties to Great Britain. During the debates which produced today's Constitution, spoken and written English was so commonly understood as the nation's default language that contrasting arguments were virtually non-existent, and so the Constitution and other founding documents (all written in English) remain silent on the matter. Consequently, although no official language was defined, English became the primary language in which to pen legislation, executive orders, court rulings, regulations, and treaties. Yet in today's modern America, multilingual movements have slowly transformed the American language landscape away from one principally rooted in English to one that actively encourages and promotes expansions of foreign influence for immigrants and natives alike.

In the last summer of his presidency, Bill Clinton signed an executive order with the alleged intention of improving "access to services for persons with limited English proficiency."[8] Through this directive, "any group that receives any federal funding must provide its services in any foreign language that may be spoken by someone likely to receive those services."[9] As a result, rather than retaining a single language of identity, the federal government insisted on dozens. Aside from the assimilation deficiencies of such an initiative, the practicalities and costs are staggering. For example, "The total annual cost for the California Department of Motor Vehicles to provide language services is $2.2 million. Providing the same level of DMV translation services nationwide would cost approximately $8.5 million per year," a nearly four-fold increase.[10]

Yet far worse consequences reaching beyond fiscal difficulties may also result from forced multilingualism, including "the inherent danger of driving a spike between English- and non-English-speaking citizens."[11] Immigrating to the United States (or to any nation for that matter) "tests the bonds of country and citizenship unlike any other force because it involves a fundamental change of allegiance. A common language is the best way to ensure assimilation among the citizenry; it assuages concerns and sets forth a unifying medium for immigrants and new citizens to pursue happiness and prosperity. In return, assimilation encourages patriotism and a deeper appreciation for the community and homeland." Nowhere else in the world is the argument for a national language so contested and heated than here in the United States, and nowhere else is it assumed that the country, rather than the immigrant, will adapt its manner for that of the new arrival. WE CONSERVATIVES BELIEVE, as did political philosopher Alexis de Tocqueville, "The tie of language is perhaps the strongest and the most durable that can unite mankind"; in America, where we pride ourselves in our "Out of Many, One" ideology, this is evermore true.[12]

Taught by Immersion

WE CONSERVATIVES BELIEVE a unifying language is one of the most effectual ways to assimilate into a culture and one that can begin at our schools for younger immigrants. Immersion is the most direct route by which individuals may gain proficiency in American English and accordingly provides them with a substantially greater likelihood of success in the United States.

To argue for a single language is not to argue against diversity. Of the many counterarguments made against a single national language is the realism that we are a country of immigrants. But to say that America "is a nation of immigrants is to say every nation is a nation of immigrants. [Even] Mexico, the source of most immigrants in the United States today, is a nation of Spanish (and other) immigrants."[13] Instead, arguing for the establishment of a national language encourages assimilation into the country immigrants have fled to while not prohibiting the free speech of their former homeland's native language, which evidently maintained its national language. In the United States, "It is normal and healthy for ethnic groups to celebrate their diverse heritages," and in "many of these ethnic neighborhoods, the 'old language' is still spoken . . .. But neither the heritage nor home language of the individual has ever competed with the American culture for dominance."[14] Yet today's America has embraced a radically different ideology, "where aliens are taught to hold tightly to their former cultures and languages," resulting in balkanization, antagonism, and victimhood over "perceived slights."[15] "When men cannot communicate their thoughts to each other, simply because of difference of language," wrote Augustine in the early fifth century, "all the similarity of their common human nature is of no avail to unite them in fellowship."[16]

One of the most successful places for young immigrants to become fluent in American English is in their schools, where education performed in English is to be the leading tool. Nonetheless, initiatives in several states have attempted to provide daily classroom teachings in multi-language formats to compensate for those students who do not come from families fluent in English. But research has shown that "students in bilingual classes learn English more slowly than students in regular classrooms do," and examples from states that have employed such formats are demoralizing.[17] Former Governor of Massachusetts Mitt Romney recalled his experience with mandated bilingual classes in his home state: "In Massachusetts alone, the bilingual program had required that we employ hundreds of teachers to instruct youngsters in Cambodian, Vietnamese, Spanish, and Portuguese—teachers who in many cases would be otherwise unemployed in teaching because they weren't proficient in English."[18] Despite the fact that many immigrant parents "wanted their children to attend regular English-speaking classes, . . . school officials had shuttled them into bilingual classes instead." And so, even "kids who were born in America, who watched television in America, and played video games in America—thoroughly *American* kids—were being assigned to bilingual classes only to allow bilingual teachers to keep their jobs. The result that these students would be *less* fluent in English didn't seem to bother anybody."

Not only is English fluency important so as to grasp Americanism, but it is also the chief language of all international commerce and transactions. Its universality is in everything from aviation to internet code and software designs. But most importantly, English is the language of all the American founding documents, including the Declaration of Independence and the Constitution. How can one be expected to truly grasp these pillars—ones in which we scrutinize every word and silence—if he must first rely on a subjective translator? WE CONSERVATIVES BELIEVE English serves as a cornerstone of American culture and identity, and we should embrace as the national language of the United States.

Religion, Faith, and Government

WE CONSERVATIVES BELIEVE faith and government are not so conflicting that they cannot, in any manner, relate to each other. In fact, good governance intimately connects with faith, and the proper measurement of right versus wrong derives from the latter.

There are growing suggestions that faith and government are in no way interlinked. Such arguments ridicule religion's missteps and subsequently praise the alleged benevolence of mankind without religion. But what is organized religion other than man's attempt to put into practice God's teachings on Earth? Organized religion, created by man, is by itself an exhibition of the shortcomings of mankind. Just as no man is perfect, neither can an organization run by man be perfect. "[F]or all have sinned and fall short of the glory of God," and so our institutions shall also fall short of the standard of God.[19]

Conversely, faith in God is but a singular, intimate, and deep relationship between man and his creator. Faith, not necessarily religion, is the most direct connection each of us has to our maker. "Now faith is the assurance of things hoped for, the conviction of things not seen."[20] Through faith, we alone are the imperfect member of our connection with God. So, too, was it for Abel, Enoch, Noah, Abraham, Isaac, Joseph, Moses, Rahab, Gideon, Barak, Samson, Jephthah, David, Samuel, and other prophets. "And all these, though commended through their faith, . . . God had provided something better for us, that apart from us they should not be made perfect."[21]

For America "to form a more perfect Union," we must first recognize the imperfection of mankind.[22] Nothing humanity has created has reached or maintained flawlessness, and because of man's inherent ineptitude, how can he truthfully impose righteous and just standards of good or bad? Every attempted standard he proposes (when crafted from an alleged innate knowledge) will soon fail. Only standards of right and wrong deriving from God (natural law) can truly represent morality. The framers, acutely aware of this, tied together our founding documents with the goodness of God. They observed God as the source of our liberties and rights, not the government. "We should remember that the Declaration of Independence is not merely a historical document. It is an explicit recognition that our rights derive not from the King of England, not from the judiciary, not from government at all, but from God. The keystone of our system of popular sovereignty is the recognition, as the Declaration acknowledges, that 'all men are created equal' and 'endowed by their Creator with certain unalienable Rights.' Religion and God are not alien to our system of government, they're integral to it."[23] WE CONSERVATIVES BELIEVE man will forever be imperfect in his endeavors and consequently flawed in creating, by himself, scales of right and wrong; he must instead rely on the unchanging morality provided by our creator.

Marriage and the Home

WE CONSERVATIVES BELIEVE marriage is central to a society rooted in morality and to continued generational growth, helping individuals unite under transcending designs. Both society and the individual contribute to the fruits of marriage, and both greatly benefit from its existence.

It is regrettable that the case for marriage is evermore in want of support in American culture. Marriage has been, throughout man's history, the cornerstone of familial purposes. For both the individual and society, grounds are abundant from which to propel marriage. Most observable, marriage is an emotional union through which love and trust are developed and fostered. "It is also true that spouses often take care of each other and thereby reduce the caregiving burden on other people."[24] But society's main interest in marriage is neither in emotional connections nor caregiving burdens. Instead, it is in the creation and upbringing of children for the continuation of that society. If marriage did not generally produce children, "neither society nor the government would have much reason, let alone a valid reason, to regulate people's emotional unions (the government does not regulate nonmarital friendships, no matter how intense they are)." Furthermore, "If mutual caregiving were the purpose of marriage, there would be no reason to exclude adult incestuous unions from marriage." Of course, marriage can still be worthy if a marriage does not produce life, but "the institution is oriented toward child-rearing. . . . What a healthy marriage culture does is encourage adults to arrange their lives so that as many children as possible are raised and nurtured by their biological parents in a common household."

But clearly, married couples exist not merely to be objects of the state's needs—marriage also propels countless personal qualities. By its very definition, marriage makes a person more mature. "When you're single," argues Dennis Prager, "your primary concern . . . is *you*. . . . But when you get married, it's *we*. That makes you grow up. That makes you a deeper person as well, because the deepest relationship that exists in the world is that of a husband and wife."[25] Surely the existence of alternative friendships and relationships can also be acutely bonding and understanding, but in reality and practice, there is likely no other commitment that has the potential and ability to be as profoundly impactful as that between spouses, doubly so when seen as an example for one's children.

Moreover, a good marriage can make a person even happier than he or she could have been alone or coupled outside of marriage. Sharing your life with one person not only solely commits you to them but also advances a transcending purpose. Applying yourself to an effort beyond you alone is the single most effective way to guarantee lasting happiness—marriage epitomizes this notion.

Sharing your life with another is at the personal core of marriage. But those questioning marriage often rest arguments on the tragically high rate of divorce in America, consequently remaining skeptical that marriage may not be beneficial after all. But to minimize the importance of marriage based on others' divorces is instead "an argument for marrying the *right* person, . . . hardly an argument not to get married" at all.[26] For the right people at the right time in their lives, marriage may be precisely what they seek to deepen their bonds with each other and expand their individual maturity. WE CONSERVATIVES BELIEVE marriage is the foundation upon which society grows and continues, is better for an individual's development, strengthens the relationship between two loving adults, and creates the best environment under which to nurture children—all which are noble goals in a noble society.

Defending Our Stature

WE CONSERVATIVES BELIEVE America is uniquely positioned in the world to tackle the enormous obstacles confronting us both at home and abroad. Our ingenuity has led the United States to become a dominant consumer and producer as well as the leading contributor to global wellbeing. Yet many believe America's role has grown too large, that our impact on the world is too heavy, and our intentions imperialistic. Conservatives roundly reject these notions.

There are several prongs upon which those who argue against the worldwide function of the United States rest. The first of these is America's military prowess. It is often the target of anger because of its size, expansions, and global role. Some Americans and foreigners alike argue against its reach and capacity, citing that its size is unnecessary, costly, and intrusive upon other nations. Yet unlike nearly every other body of people before America, we do not go to war to colonize. The size of America's military means it is the only effective force able to reach any place in the world at a moment's notice, and this strategic advantage gives the United States the ability to deliver either military power to allies or humanitarian aid to those in need.

Further, "Our military is also charged with deterring nuclear attack whether from rogue nations or a future would-be superpower; preventing space attack and cyber-attack; protecting world shipping routes; supporting nations in their defense against insurgencies and helping failed states avoid becoming bases of terror; stopping ethnic cleansing and genocide; and maintaining the capabilities to responding to conventional wars wherever they might occur on the globe. No other nation's military takes on so many diverse missions in so many parts of the world."[27] Who will take America's place if we cannot continue to protect these interests?

Another reason for this self-loathing is America's energy consumption. Presently, America consumes around 25 percent of the world's oil production. Many argue this is an unhealthy dependence and destructive to both the global environment and other nations' standards of living. While the United States does consume around a quarter of the world's oil, it is also the birthplace of the world's largest industries (hiring the most people) and home to inventors and creators who require increased energy production to excel (and whose patents are frequently disseminated to other countries at little-to-no cost to those receiving them). Furthermore, industries in the United States must comply with endless regulations from administrative agencies (like the Environmental Protection Agency) that force American companies to restrict their emissions and outputs severely. These very same domestic companies are meanwhile competing with other nations that employ virtually no such directives on their industries (countries like China, India, Russia, and Mexico). While it is important to ensure that our environment is clean and safe for future generations, we should not self-impose restrictions that put ourselves at a significant disadvantage to other competing nations. The fact that America can still maintain global leadership in spite of these constraints is a testament to the American DNA, yet that lead is now slipping.

A third reason some oppose our scope is our economic superiority, for they see the United States as too able to impose our will on other nations through economic sanctions and find America as too focused on money-related greed. But American commercial success is the result of liberty and capitalism. Through no other monetary policy than capitalism is liberty so enshrined. It allows for risk taking, leaders and followers, and even failure.

It provides opportunity otherwise suppressed and employs the most successful workforce. WE CONSERVATIVES BELIEVE America can use its economic strength—the product of economic liberty—to deter or promote agendas without the use of physical force—a notion we ought to welcome.

Who Are the Union's Real Friends?

WE CONSERVATIVES BELIEVE deception and dishonesty are plagues forever seeking entry into republican-styled governance, for through such sins do power and eminence often develop. Accordingly, those who seek perpetual maintenance of unadulterated liberty—that which is held by the people alone—must remain vigilant against the relentless endeavors of a cunning ruling class and its selective accomplices. Pretension is as cancerous to a nation as an epidemic is to a people, something for which only a free people can operate as the remedy.

Threats to American liberty have persisted throughout the country's existence. In 1792, James Madison submitted a piece to the *National Gazette* in which he presented two alternative approaches to governing and interactions with the private citizen. Do not the following arguments still hold true hundreds of years into the future? And being so, how does that reflect on the nature of man and his general unawareness of governmental interference and deceit?

THE UNION: WHO ARE ITS REAL FRIENDS?

> Not those who charge others with not being its friends, whilst their own conduct is wantonly multiplying its enemies. . . .
>
> Not those who promote unnecessary accumulations of the debt of the Union, instead of the best means of discharging it as fast as possible; thereby encreasing the causes of corruption in the government, and the pretexts for new taxes under its authority, the former undermining the confidence, the latter alienating the affection of the people.
>
> Not those who study, by arbitrary interpretations and insidious precedents, to pervert the limited government of the

> Union, into a government of unlimited discretion, contrary to the will and subversive of the authority of the people.
>
> Not those who avow or betray principles of monarchy and aristocracy, in opposition to the republican principles of the Union, and the republican spirit of the people . . ..
>
> Not those, in a word, who would force on the people the melancholy duty of chusing between the loss of the Union, and the loss of what the union was meant to secure.
>
> The real Friends to the Union are those,
>
> Who are friends to the authority of the people, the sole foundation on which the Union rests.
>
> Who are friends to liberty, the great end, for which the Union was formed.
>
> Who are friends to the limited and republican system of government, the means provided by that authority, for the attainment of that end. . . .
>
> Who considering a public debt as injurious to the interests of the people, and baneful to the virtue of the government, are enemies to every contrivance for *unnecessarily* increasing its amount, or protracting its duration, or extending its influence.[28]

Clearly, the greatest domestic allies of the United States are those who respect the sovereignty of the people and the liberty of the individual. They are watchdogs over economic scrupulousness and require true representational governance over the American citizenry. WE CONSERVATIVES BELIEVE perilous threats to American freedom through mediums of fraud and distortion will remain close at hand as long as mankind remains naturally cunning and devious, thus requiring the attentive eyes of a liberty-loving population—the real friends of the union.

Virtue in Power

WE CONSERVATIVES BELIEVE the American experiment has proven historically remarkable not only for its grand successes but in its largely uninterrupted peaceful exchanges of power and control. The exceptional natures of Americans and, by consequence, the United States have borne the fruits of enlightenment and the virtues of good governance.

Early American politics underscores an extraordinary example of the miracle that was, and remains, the United States. After fighting and obtaining victory in the Revolutionary War, America's wartime leader George Washington was anxiously awaiting retirement at his beloved Mount Vernon estate. Yet with the new Constitution ratified in the late 1780s, his role in the recently formed presidency was all but reserved. The uniqueness of early America, in its shining new example of a republican government, meant that "the ill-defined powers of the American presidency left considerable room for honest disagreement, but one point on which all sides could agree was that it was not an electoral version of monarchy."[29] Even so, the apparent ambiguity of the presidency would undoubtedly have permitted the iconic Washington, if he had so chosen, to expand the powers of that office far beyond its intended boundaries, something potentially fatal to the republic at such a fragile moment. Some ecstatic supporters were so hopeful of his potential position in government that one rejoiced, "You are now a king, under a different name and, I am well satisfied that sovereign prerogatives have in no age or country been more honorably obtained; or that, at any time they will be more prudently and wisely exercised."[30] Yet instead, so reluctant was Washington to even become president that after his unanimous electoral election (Washington being the only unanimously elected president in American history to-date), he remarked in a letter composed on the eve of his inauguration, "My movement to the Chair of Government will be accompanied by feelings not unlike those of a culprit who is going to the place of his execution."[31]

Having fretfully sworn in and served for eight years as our president, Washington then did something even more extraordinary than that of his ascent to power: he stepped down. He allowed for the peaceful transition of government into new hands, "something brand-new in the history of the United States, [and] rare enough in the history of the world."[32] He removed himself from the public sphere and returned to working on his farm, where he wished to live as much of a private life as the world's most famous man could. Like that of the Roman aristocrat Cincinnatus more than a millennium before, who obtained near-absolute power and then immediately resigned it in favor of his farm and retirement, Washington truly was, as King George III of Great Britain said, "the greatest man in the world."[33] Rarely in history have man and moment met so perfectly than that of Washington and the country he helped shape.

Washington's story, like that of others who peacefully relinquish control and authority, help us to understand the role of civil society and virtue. Few examples exist of those with near-complete command peacefully forfeiting their prominent place—Cincinnatus, Washington, and, more recently, Pope Benedict XVI. And in America, only a few examples should exist, since we ought not to allow our officials to obtain the roles of quasi-kingships. Too often do modern politicians, rather than humbly holding Washington's lamentations of being sent to "execution," believe they have instead become the executioners. WE CONSERVATIVES BELIEVE the center of republican governance rests on the separation of powers, and that the transitioning of those powers through the electoral process is fundamental in a peaceful and productive civil society.

— — —

EPILOGUE

The Conservative Language

IT IS ABUNDANTLY CLEAR the America of today is a far cry from the America envisioned by our founders. The Constitution, designed to be "the supreme Law of the Land," is eternally under attack by those meant to be restrained by it.[1] Rather than acting under the Constitution with respect and humility (and so by consequence not serving with respect of, and humility to, the source of that authority—the people), consecutive Congresses have passed legislation extending far beyond the scope of their enumerated powers, having done so under perverse interpretations of the Constitution's aims. Presidents, too, manipulate the Constitution to best suit their ambitions and pursuits and consistently abuse their prosecutorial discretion. Finally, and most cunning in its *modus operandi*, the judiciary undercuts the legislature and executive, as well as the sovereign people, through its active role in policy making and judicial review. Its lifelong, tenured advocates promote individual and party agendas that are checked by virtually non-existent sanctions. The threats to American interests and individual liberties grow each day, and we Conservatives often serve as the only backstop by which evermore dubious governmental intrusions are blocked.

The history of the United States is one of ingenuity and persistence, of strength and independence. But today's political world is quickly transforming into a regressive state too often sponsoring the precise opposite traits. These distinctions frequently carry with them the banners of political parties, each with clear and divergent hopes and perspectives. "We have now an American political party and a European one," argued political scientist Harvey Mansfield.[2] "Not all Americans who vote for the European party want to become Europeans. But it doesn't matter because that's what they're voting for. They're voting for dependence, for lack of ambition, and for insolvency." The response from this European party—today's American Left—to the dilemmas of our country's domestic wellbeing and worldly stature has rarely been to provide sound and clear solutions (at least not in recent history). Rather, its members have discovered a much easier (and more effective) approach to executing their strategies: attacking the "American political party"—the Right. By demonizing Conservatives, Liberals have turned to the employment of strict filters of classification, filters that allow excessive and politically useful distinctions based on race, sex, and class. When opponents balk at the Left's proposals, the Liberal arsenal of disparities is often the first deployed. Regrettably, this "wolf-crying" phenomenon has minimized, or perhaps even desensitized, the impact of cases where true discrimination and harassment occur, leaving real victims unfairly marginalized.

Another proven tactic employed by the Left is "the idea that things will get better and better and progress will be made in the actualization of equality."[3] By attacking again, Liberals condemn others who have obtained more wealth or happiness than themselves, something further agitated when the Left falsely claims the economy is a zero-sum game, one with only so much capital to be owned. The result is a mutual dependence between those who have little and those who have power and education. Or in other words, "an alliance of experts and victims. . . . Social scientists and political scientists," Mansfield continued, "were very much involved in the foundation of the progressive movement. What those experts did was find ways to improve the wellbeing of the poor, the incompetent, all those who have the right to vote but can't quite govern their own lives. And still to this day we see in the Democratic Party the alliance between Ph.D.s and victims." At least for the distant future, conservative battles that attempt to turn the tide of dependence and European-style governance will remain uphill, though not impossible. "We have to take measures to teach the poor and vulnerable to become a little more independent and to prize independence, and not just live for a government check. This means self-government within each self, and where are you going to get that except with morality, responsibility, and religion?" Yet with regard to these latter three objectives, the Left largely remains convinced that morality is subjective, responsibility is secondary to conformity, and religion is archaic and unsuiting. It is only the American Right that remains rooted in all three.

Another source of political divisiveness is excessive party affiliation. For elected officials, political parties can serve as either useful collaborations or gang-like mobs. The more dividing an issue, the more reliant do politicians become on their respective parties to protect them. During America's founding, political factions (as then called) were somewhat new and indeed denounced. James Madison, although strongly opposed to factions because of their tendencies to derail authentic governance, believed them to be inevitable in a true republic:

> The latent causes of faction are thus sown in the nature of man; and we see them everywhere brought into different degrees of activity, according to the different circumstances of civil society. A zeal for different opinions concerning religion, concerning government, and many other points, as well of speculation as of practice; an attachment to different leaders ambitiously contending for pre-eminence and power; or to persons of other descriptions whose fortunes have been interesting to the human passions, have, in turn, divided mankind into parties, inflamed them with mutual animosity, and rendered them much more disposed to vex and oppress each other than to co-operate for their common good. So strong is this propensity of mankind to fall into mutual animosities that where no substantial occasion presents itself the most frivolous and fanciful distinctions have been sufficient to kindle their unfriendly passions and excite their most violent conflicts.[4]

Other founders also echoed Madison's chorus. A young John Adams wrote, " '[I would] quarrel with both parties, and with every individual of each' before joining either."[5] George Washington, near the end of his public career, said, "Let me . . . warn you in the most solemn manner against the baneful effects of the spirit of party." Thomas Jefferson declared, "I never submitted the whole system of my opinion to the creed of any party of men whatever. Such an addiction is the last degradation of a free and moral agent." Yet even with these hesitations toward party formation and allegiance, the founders, like all mankind, were imperfect, and creating parties was exactly what they "began to do, while never admitting, even to themselves, quite what they were doing." Now advance the political timeline a few centuries, and we find modern politicians and parties regularly more faithful to their factions than to their countrymen or country—one of the founders' greatest fears.

Writing in 1792, Madison further articulated the then-distinguishing traits between two competing philosophies of political thought in a piece for the *National Gazette* titled, "Who Are the Best Keepers of the People's Liberties?" This mock narrative not only carried significance in the late eighteenth century but is remarkably applicable today as well when comparing true Conservatives ("Republicans") to true Liberals ("Anti-republicans"):

> *Republican.*—The people themselves. The sacred trust can be no where so safe as in the hands most interested in preserving it.
>
> *Anti-republican.*—The people are stupid, suspicious, licentious. They cannot safely trust themselves. When they have established government they should think of nothing but obedience, leaving the care of their liberties to their wiser rulers.
>
> *Republican.*—Although all men are born free, and all nations might be so, yet too true it is, that slavery has been the general lot of the human race. Ignorant—they have been cheated; asleep—they have been surprized; divided—the yoke has been forced upon them. But what is the lesson? That because the people *may* betray themselves, they ought to give themselves up, blindfold, to those who have an interest in betraying them? Rather conclude that the people ought to be enlightened, to be awakened, to be united, that after establishing a government they should watch over it, as well as obey it.
>
> *Anti-republican.*—You look at the surface only, where errors float, instead of fathoming the depths where truth lies hid. It is not the government that is disposed to fly off from the people; but the people that are ever ready to fly off from the government. Rather say then, enlighten the government, warn it to be vigilant, enrich it with influence, arm it with force, and to the people never pronounce but two words—*Submission* and *Confidence.*

Republican.—The centrifugal tendency then is in the people, not in the government, and the secret art lies in restraining the tendency, by augmenting the attractive principle of the government with all the weight that can be added to it. What a perversion of the natural order of things! to make *power* the primary and central object of the social system, and *Liberty* but its satellite.

Anti-republican.—The science of the stars can never instruct you in the mysteries of government. Wonderful as it may seem, the more you increase the attractive force of power, the more you enlarge the sphere of liberty; the more you make government independent and hostile towards the people, the better security you provide for their rights and interests. Hence the wisdom of the theory, which, after limiting the share of the people to a third of the government, and lessening the influence of that share by the mode and term of delegating it, establishes two grand hereditary orders, with feelings, habits, interests, and prerogatives all inveterately hostile to the rights and interests of the people, yet by a *mysterious* operation all combining to fortify the people in both.

Republican.—Mysterious indeed! But mysteries belong to religion, not to government; to the ways of the Almighty, not to the works of man. And in religion itself there is nothing mysterious to its author; the mystery lies in the dimness of the human sight. So in the institutions of man let there be no mystery, unless for those inferior beings endowed with a ray perhaps of the twilight vouchsafed to the first order of terrestrial creation.

Anti-republican.—You are destitute, I perceive, of every quality of a good citizen, or rather of a good *subject.* You have neither the light of faith nor the spirit of obedience. I denounce you to the government as an accomplice of atheism and anarchy.

Republican.—And I forbear to denounce you to the people, though a blasphemer of their rights and an idolater of tyranny. Liberty disdains to persecute.[6]

Disturbing as these general trends often look, we needn't lead our country blindly. As Americans, and even more so in an age of incredibly accessible knowledge, we possess a vast wealth of hindsight to guide our course. While the United States has proven to be the greatest representation of republican-styled governance, it was not the first to try. But most republics of the past share a common weakness that soon eventuated their demise: a disdain for, and overlooking of, their roots. Consider the Roman Republic, for instance. Similar to America's creation, the Roman Republic began with the overthrow of a monarchical government, traditionally held to have occurred in 509 BC.[7] For centuries thereafter, the Romans lived under a complex political structure that embraced a largely unwritten constitution footed in precedent (somewhat analogous to the present-day United Kingdom's central government construction). Under the Roman Republic, a combination and separation of powers were utilized, one that placed republican elements of governance into a legislative assembly, aristocratic flavors into the Senate, and monarchical powers into a limited consul. Thus, depending on a Roman's vantage point, "if they turned their view upon the power of the consuls, the government appeared to be purely monarchial and regal. If, again, the authority of the Senate was considered, it then seemed to wear the form of aristocracy. And, lastly, if regard was had to the share which the people possessed in the administration of affairs, it could then scarcely fail to be denominated a popular state."[8] Yet when undertaking a sweeping observation of the Roman Republic in the ancient world, the powers of governing were uncommonly distributed.

Nevertheless, the strength of the Roman Republic slowly unraveled as a disregard of custom grew in prevalence. "Roman politics in the Late Republic was precarious, with increasingly few restraints on behaviour. The Republican system relied heavily on precedent and convention, but these were breaking down. . . . The rules of the political game had changed and it would have been difficult, perhaps impossible, to return to the old system."[9] And just as political factions have seeped cancerously into American politics, often preventing real progression to block another's personal advancements, "most of the Roman elite preferred to allow some of the major problems facing the Republic to go unanswered rather than see someone else gain the credit for dealing with them."[10]

But today in the United States, the major problems facing our republic do not always go unanswered; instead, overly ambitious politicians and parties often inflame the ill-sought pursuits. Leaders of these movements, or "masterminds" (as Conservative Mark Levin labels them), pull the country in directions that undermine its health and wellbeing, all the while providing the pretense of necessity. There are citizens among us "who delusively if not enthusiastically surrender their liberty for the mastermind's false promises of human and societal perfectibility. He hooks them with financial bribes in the form of 'entitlements.' And he makes incredible claims about indefectible health, safety, educational, and environmental policies, the success of which is to be measured not in the here and now but in the distant future."[11] And as support for the relentless leaders grow, "More and more decisions are made by the masterminds and their experts, who substitute their self-serving and dogmatic judgments—which are proclaimed righteous and compassionate—for the individual's self-interests and best interests."[12] Thus, with the mastermind deemed moral and sympathetic, any opponents who deviate from his designs are chastised while being accused of depravity and self-seeking intentions. The balance of our republic, as a result, becomes unhinged and weakened.

If our history clearly denotes one thing, it is that those in power (masterminds or not) rarely are most effectual at understanding the concerns and needs of the electorate. After having landed on the moon, Neil Armstrong spent a stint in Washington, DC, giving first-hand accounts of his experiences and findings. Upon returning from his speaking tour, he tried to sum up his time in the capital: "The future is not something I know a great deal about. But I did live in Washington for a time and learned that lack of knowledge about a subject is no impediment to talking about it."[13] Sometimes—perhaps most times—what the citizenry needs is for their representatives to do *nothing*. Allowing industries and the markets to function with only limited impediments is generally the most direct route to American prosperity. Surely, some degree of regulation and direction are necessary to prevent certain tendencies and corruptions, but those regulations should not reach the extent of restricting industries and the markets from their full potential; protect the workers and companies alike but stand not in their way of success.

President Ronald Reagan, in his first inaugural address, both summarized contemporary politics and cemented the conservative platforms from which he would lead the nation forward over the next eight years:

> Those who do work are denied a fair return for their labor by a tax system which penalizes successful achievement and keeps us from maintaining full productivity.
>
> But great as our tax burden is, it has not kept pace with public spending. For decades, we have piled deficit upon deficit, mortgaging our future and our children's future for the temporary convenience of the present. To continue this long trend is to guarantee tremendous social, cultural, political, and economic upheavals.
>
> You and I, as individuals, can, by borrowing, live beyond our means, but for only a limited period of time. Why, then, should we think that collectively, as a nation, we are not bound by that same limitation? We must act today in order to preserve tomorrow. . . .
>
> The economic ills we suffer have come upon us over several decades. They will not go away in days, weeks, or months, but they will go away. They will go away because we, as Americans, have the capacity now, as we have had in the past, to do whatever needs to be done to preserve this last and greatest bastion of freedom.
>
> In this present crisis, government is not the solution to our problem, government is the problem. . . .
>
> Now, so there will be no misunderstanding, it is not my intention to do away with government. It is, rather, to make it work—work with us, not over us; to stand by our side, not ride on our back. Government can and must provide opportunity, not smother it; foster productivity, not stifle it.[14]

The government Reagan envisioned—or better yet, reminded us of—is one which promotes individual merit and ingenuity. He echoed the sentiments of Jefferson 178 years prior when he hoped to "prevent the government from wasting the labors of the people, under the pretence of taking care of them . . .."[15] Yet today's government not only encourages victimhood, but it also suffocates righteous work ethics. Moreover, government-encouraged political correctness has seeped and spread into every corner of American living, running to such degrees that even remaining silent can be construed as a violation of some "protected comfort." But in our American republic, there is no constitutional right to feel comfortable. Indeed, a republic, by its design, is meant to be rousing and contentious, for through the frameworks of structured and limited government is liberty best endured. The acknowledgment of enforced correctness began no later than the start of our country, with Jefferson again writing (this time in 1796), "all timid men . . . prefer the calm of despotism to the boisterous sea of liberty."[16]

The reality of liberty means every man will, at some point, be left uncomfortable, but most often he will be contented with his relationship to others unless plagued by the drains of victimhood. Political correctness has another fault: transforming issues that, under any other circumstance, are of little consequence into matters of alleged national concern. And once the tide of enforced correctness is underway, it is tremendously effective at hushing opponents, for very few wish to be called vile and derogatory terms or to be harassed by an overly swayed body of people. The result is an increasingly one-sided debate in which true matters of alarm are overlooked or downsized. Thus, as credited to the eighteenth-century political philosopher Edmund Burke, "All that is necessary for the triumph of evil is for good men to do nothing."[17] WE CONSERVATIVES BELIEVE we must, by necessity, stand together to overcome great odds and to achieve our underlying principle-based goals of individual liberty, economic freedom, and American exceptionalism.

Acknowledgments

On the Shoulders of Giants

ANYONE WHO HAS CREATED a project of considerable length realizes the impossibility of doing it alone. Throughout the prolonged process, many individuals intercepted at various points and provided invaluable feedback and consultations. Without such a framework of support, this book would be infinitely less refined and much the weaker. To them, I owe a great debt for their charity and honesty.

The preceding pages are the end-result of an original manuscript filtered through many minds. From my reviewers, I asked no small feat, and each spent endless hours laboring over the pages of this book. Among these are my wonderful mother ("Mum"), who, with her uncanny attention to detail, meticulously poured over the book's manuscript to find my hundreds-upon-hundreds of errors and mistakes; my inspiring and ceaselessly patient father, the most supportive and encouraging man I know; Jeff Lacey, my only brother and a pivotal force in my conversion to conservatism; David MacKool, to whom this book is dedicated and to whom I principally credit with the unveiling of my conservative beliefs; Bob Campbell, a historical guru and role model; and, of course, my lovely wife Catherine Lacey, who so patiently endured hour-after-hour of me reading aloud all the preceding pages to ensure their flow and accuracy, and who good-naturedly suffered my frequent irritabilities related to this writing.

There are many others as well, including Todd Estes of Oakland University, who provided years of past instruction that served as pillars for the historical corners of this work—he is also the one to whom *James Madison and the Virginia Resolution* is dedicated; William Wagner of Thomas M. Cooley Law School, who gave invaluable insight into conservative interpretations of the Constitution during my law school career; Brigadier General Michael McDaniel, who helped me develop an understanding of the relationship between homeland security and homeland jurisprudence; Steve Cushard, a tremendous manager and upright man who spoke conservatism to me when I least cared to hear it; and Michael Swanigan, who relentlessly encouraged me to seek faith in God and learn to (albeit grudgingly) "let go." I am also grateful to Brian McGovern (a "Husband, father, cranky old war vet, Jesus follower, VO guy, substandard ukulelist") for his excellent and professional performance in transforming this work into an audiobook, as well as for penning the foreword to this second edition.

Several Conservative flag-bearers worked themselves into my life by their continual efforts through radio, writings, and other mediums. Chief among these leaders being Mark Levin ("The Great One"), author of several books which served as great references in the writing of this project and the launching pad for many arguments; Sean Hannity, a "good American," remarkable debater, and Conservative patriot; Rush Limbaugh, who so easily bears the never-ending barbs from those who oppose his arguments, clarity, and personality (all this "with one half of his brain tied behind his back just to make it fair"); and Dennis Prager, whose radio program and Prager University functioned as profound sources of articulate and concise conservatism.

To the men and women of America's armed forces, who have made the conversations and debates enumerated in this work possible: we remain forever indebted to your honor, respect, and devotion to duty. And finally, to the framers of America, notably the trifecta of most significant influence to me: James Madison, Thomas Jefferson, and George Washington. Without these profound leaders in America's past, our United States would be but a shadow of what it is today. To them and all the others who served beside them, we owe our eternal gratitude.

Notes

INTRODUCTION

[1] Dex Bahr, *No Christian Man Is an Island: Leading the Spiritual Quest in America's Culture Wars* (Xulon Press, 2010), 63. Quoting George Patton.
[2] Jason Barney, "We Live in a Culture of Peter Pans," *Imprimis* 42, no. 1 (January 2013): 4.
[3] Thomas Paine, *Common Sense and Other Writings*, ed. Joyce Appleby (Barnes & Noble Books, 2005), 131. Emphasis added.
[4] Alexander Hamilton, John Jay, and James Madison, *The Federalist Papers*, ed. Clinton Rossiter (Mentor, 1999), 278–79. Quoting Thomas Jefferson.
[5] Thomas Jefferson, *The Jeffersonian Cyclopedia: A Comprehensive Collection of the Views of Thomas Jefferson*, ed. John Foley (Funk & Wagnalls, 1900), 692.
[6] Elizabeth Samet, *Willing Obedience: Citizens, Soldiers, and the Progress of Consent in America, 1776–1898* (Stanford University Press, 2004), 226. Quoting George Washington.
[7] Barney, "We Live in a Culture of Peter Pans," 5.
[8] Douglas MacArthur, *General MacArthur: Wisdom and Visions*, ed. Edward Imparato (Turner Publishing, 2000), 129.
[9] Suetonius, *The Twelve Cæsars*, ed. Alexander Thomson (R. Worthington, 1883), 57. Quoting Julius Caesar.
[10] Paine, *Common Sense*, 21.
[11] Ronald Reagan, "Address to the Annual Meeting of the Phoenix Chamber of Commerce."

CONSERVATIVE HISTORY

[1] Gordon Wood, *The Purpose of the Past: Reflections on the Uses of History* (Penguin Books, 2008), 39.
[2] Paine, *Common Sense*, 17.
[3] "US Declaration of Independence" (1776), Preamble.
[4] John Scheb II and Otis Stephens Jr., *American Constitutional Law: Volume I (Sources of Power and Restraint)* (Wadsworth, 2012), 96.
[5] Although often credited to Thomas Jefferson, only variations of this quote arise in his writings. A further explanation is available at

monticello.org/site/jefferson/when-governments-fear-people-there-libertyquotation.

[6] Often credited to Thomas Jefferson, yet without an affirmative source.

[7] James Madison, *Madison: Writings*, ed. Jack Rakove (Library of America, 1999), 355.

[8] Henry David Thoreau, *Walden, Civil Disobedience, and Other Writings*, ed. William Rossi (W. W. Norton, 2008), 227. Paraphrased from a variation in this source, where, "That government is best which governs least," is Thoreau's argument.

[9] US Declaration of Independence, Preamble.

[10] William Wagner, *Jurisprudential Considerations: The Impact of Worldview on American Constitutional Law* (S & L Global, 2011), 4.

[11] Wagner, 4.

[12] "Constitution of the Commonwealth of Massachusetts" (1780), Part the First, Article XXX. John Adams was central in the authorship of the commonwealth's Constitution.

[13] Wagner, *Jurisprudential Considerations*, 5. Emphasis added.

[14] Wagner, 6.

[15] Hamilton, Jay, and Madison, *Federalist Papers*, 192–93.

[16] Hamilton, Jay, and Madison, 193.

[17] Hamilton, Jay, and Madison, 193.

[18] Mark Levin, *Liberty and Tyranny: A Conservative Manifesto* (Threshold Editions, 2009), 63.

[19] "US Constitution" (1789) amend. X.

[20] Levin, *Liberty and Tyranny*, 68.

[21] New York v. United States (June 19, 1992).

[22] J. A. Simpson and E. S. C. Weiner, eds., *Compact Oxford English Dictionary*, 3rd ed. (Oxford University Press, 2008), "democracy."

[23] Simpson and Weiner, "republic."

[24] Hamilton, Jay, and Madison, *Federalist Papers*, 291.

[25] Marvin Simkin, "Individual Rights," *Los Angeles Times*, January 12, 1992, articles.latimes.com/1992-01-12/local/me-358_1_jail-tax-individual-rights-san-diego.

[26] Madison, *Writings*, 866.

INDIVIDUAL LIBERTY

[1] Madison, 440.

[2] Hamilton, Jay, and Madison, *Federalist Papers*, 121.

[3] US Declaration of Independence, Preamble.

[4] Chester James Antieau, "Natural Rights and the Founding Fathers—The Virginians," *Washington and Lee Law Review* XVII (March 1, 1960): 45.

[5] John Locke, *The Second Treatise of Civil Government and a Letter Concerning Toleration*, ed. J. W. Gough (Basil Blackwell & Mott, 1948), 68.

[6] Thomas Paine, *Rights of Man, Common Sense, and Other Political Writings*, ed. Mark Philp (Oxford University Press, 1995), 274.

[7] Paine, *Common Sense*, 129.

[8] US Declaration of Independence, Introduction and Preamble.

[9] US Declaration of Independence, Preamble.

[10] Edward Erler, "Is the Constitution Colorblind?," *Imprimis* 41, no. 1 (November 2012): 3.

[11] US Constitution preamble.

[12] US Declaration of Independence, Preamble.

[13] US Declaration of Independence.

[14] US Constitution amend. IX.

[15] Bryan Garner, ed., *Black's Law Dictionary*, 3rd ed. (Thomson West, 2006), "property."

[16] Madison, *Writings*, 517.

[17] Paine, *Common Sense*, 129.

[18] Madison, *Writings*, 517.

[19] Stephen Halbrook, *The Founders' Second Amendment: Origins of the Right to Bear Arms* (Ivan R. Dee, 2008), 9–74 passim.

[20] US Constitution art. I, § 8.

[21] US Constitution amend. II.

[22] Hamilton, Jay, and Madison, *Federalist Papers*, 152.

[23] Hamilton, Jay, and Madison, 153. Emphasis added.

[24] US Constitution amend. XVIII.

[25] Terril Yue Jones, "Knife-Wielding Man Injures 22 Children in China," *Reuters*, December 14, 2012, reuters.com/article/us-china-stabbings/knife-wielding-man-injures-22-children-in-china-idusbre8bd06520121214.

[26] Perry Chiaramonte et al., "As Nation Mourns, Investigators Try to Figure out What Led to Tragedy in Newtown, Conn.," *Fox News*, December 16, 2012, foxnews.com/us/2012/12/16/at-least-26-dead-in-shooting-at-connecticut-school.html.
[27] Joyce Lee Malcolm, "Two Cautionary Tales of Gun Control," *The Wall Street Journal*, December 27, 2012, A13. Emphasis added.
[28] Wayne LaPierre, "More Guns Bring More Safety," *New Haven Register*, December 28, 2012, nhregister.com/news/article/guest-column-more-guns-bring-more-safety-11496326.php.
[29] John Fund, "The Facts about Mass Shootings: It's Time to Address Mental Health and Gun-Free Zones," *National Review*, December 16, 2012, nationalreview.com/2012/12/facts-about-mass-shootings-john-fund.
[30] Fund.
[31] Thomas Paine, *The Writings of Thomas Paine: Volume I (1774–1779)*, ed. Moncure Daniel Conway (Knickerbocker Press, 1906), 56.
[32] B&H Publishing Group, *The Holy Bible: Christian Standard Bible (CSB)* (B&H Publishing Group, 2017), Ecclesiastes 8:11.
[33] Richard Stevens and Aaron Zelman, *Death by "Gun Control"* (Mazel Freedom Press, 2001). See "The Genocide Chart."
[34] Hamilton, Jay, and Madison, *Federalist Papers*, 267.
[35] Jefferson, *Jeffersonian Cyclopedia*, 739.
[36] Eugene Hickok Jr., *The Bill of Rights: Original Meaning and Current Understanding* (University Press of Virginia, 1991), 124.
[37] Adolph Hitler, *Hitler's Table Talk: 1941–1944*, ed. Hugh Trevor-Roper (Enigma Books, 2008), 321.
[38] Mark Levin, *Ameritopia: The Unmaking of America* (Threshold Editions, 2012), 7.

THE LEGISLATURE

[1] Jefferson, *Jeffersonian Cyclopedia*, 977.
[2] Jefferson, 977.
[3] Madison, *Writings*, 363.
[4] US Constitution amend. IX.
[5] US Constitution amend. X.
[6] Hamilton, Jay, and Madison, *Federalist Papers*, 256.

[7] US Constitution art. I, § 8, cl. 18.

[8] Hamilton, Jay, and Madison, *Federalist Papers*, 252.

[9] Hamilton, Jay, and Madison, 252–53.

[10] US Constitution art. I, § 8, cl. 3.

[11] Wickard v. Filburn (November 9, 1942).

[12] US Constitution amend. X.

[13] New State Ice Co. v. Liebmann (March 21, 1932).

[14] William Voegeli, *Never Enough: America's Limitless Welfare State* (Encounter Books, 2012), 96.

[15] Voegeli, 97.

[16] Voegeli, 3.

[17] Voegeli, 4.

[18] Voegeli, 5.

[19] Levin, *Liberty and Tyranny*, 20.

[20] Levin, 21.

[21] Voegeli, *Never Enough*, 95.

[22] Voegeli, 6.

[23] Voegeli, 7.

[24] Daniel Horowitz, "Regarding Immigration Proposals, Beware of Your Opponents' Motivation," *Red State*, January 28, 2013, redstate.com/dhorowitz3/2013/01/28/regarding-immigration-proposals-beware-of-your-opponents-motivation-2.

[25] Levin, *Liberty and Tyranny*, 162.

[26] Levin, 173.

[27] Louis Uchitelle, "Plan May Lure More to Enter U.S. Illegally, Experts Say," *New York Times*, January 9, 2004, A12.

[28] Rush Limbaugh, "There Will Be Amnesty, Folks," *The Rush Limbaugh Show*, November 9, 2012, rushlimbaugh.com/daily/2012/11/09/there_will_be_amnesty_folks.

[29] Horowitz, "Regarding Immigration Proposals."

[30] Marbury v. Madison (February 24, 1803).

[31] Richard Brookhiser, *James Madison* (Basic Books, 2011), 225–26.

[32] Brookhiser, 226.

[33] McCulloch v. Maryland (March 6, 1819).

[34] Brookhiser, *James Madison*, 226.

[35] Madison, *Writings*, 734.

[36] Madison, 734.

[37] Alan Van Dyke, "Echoes of the Serf and the Sovereign State Still Persist," *The Wall Street Journal*, December 22, 2012, A16.

THE EXECUTIVE

[1] US Constitution art. II, § 3, cl. 5.

[2] US Constitution art. II, § 2, cl. 1.

[3] US Constitution art. II, § 2, cl. 2.

[4] US Constitution.

[5] US Constitution art. I, § 7, cl. 2–3.

[6] US Constitution art. II, § 2, cl. 1.

[7] Andrew Rudalevige, *The New Imperial Presidency: Renewing Presidential Power after Watergate* (University of Michigan Press, 2008), 19.

[8] Rudalevige, 26. Quoting H. L. Menchen.

[9] Constantinos Scaros, *Understanding the Constitution* (Jones and Barlett Publishers, 2011), 64.

[10] US Constitution art. II, § 1, cl. 1.

[11] Rudalevige, *New Imperial Presidency*, 25.

[12] Madison, *Writings*, 540–41.

[13] Rudalevige, *New Imperial Presidency*, 26.

[14] Sai Prakash, "Take Care Clause," *The Heritage Foundation*, 2017, heritage.org/constitution/#!/articles/2/essays/98/take-care-clause.

[15] Robert Delahunty and John Yoo, "The Obama Administration, the Dream Act and the Take Care Clause," *Texas Law Review* 91, no. 4 (September 9, 2012).

[16] Hamilton, Jay, and Madison, *Federalist Papers*, 415.

[17] US Constitution art. I, § 8, cl. 11–13.

[18] US Constitution art. II, § 2, cl. 1.

[19] Madison, *Writings*, 543.

[20] US Constitution art. II, § 2, cl. 1.

[21] "War Powers Resolution," 50 USC § 1541–1548 § (1973), § 1543 (reporting requirement). Emphasis added.

[22] War Powers Resolution, § 1544 (congressional action). Emphasis added.

[23] Madison, *Writings*, 586.
[24] Maine and Nebraska are the exceptions to this rule.
[25] US Constitution amend. XXII.
[26] Madison, *Writings*, 413.
[27] Garner, *Black's Law Dictionary*, "agency / independent agency."
[28] Hamilton, Jay, and Madison, *Federalist Papers*, 395–96.
[29] Hamilton, Jay, and Madison, 396.
[30] Hamilton, Jay, and Madison, 398.
[31] Matthew Spalding, "Imperial Presidency," *The Daily Signal*, June 22, 2012, dailysignal.com/2012/06/22/morning-bell-imperial-presidency.
[32] Theodore Roosevelt, *The Great Adventure: Present-Day Studies in American Nationalism* (Charles Scribner's Sons, 1919), 181.
[33] Paul Thornton, *Leadership: Off the Wall* (WestBow Press, 2010), 18. Quoting John Quincy Adams.
[34] Ronald Reagan, *The Reagan Diaries*, ed. Douglas Brinkley (Harper Perennial, 2007), xiv.
[35] Reagan, 8.

THE JUDICIARY

[1] "Oaths of Justices and Judges," 28 USC § 453 § (1990).
[2] Mark Levin, *Men in Black: How the Supreme Court Is Destroying America* (Regency Publishing, 2006), 12.
[3] Garner, *Black's Law Dictionary*, "judicial review."
[4] Levin, *Men in Black*, 23.
[5] US Constitution art. III, § 2.
[6] Warren Michelsen, "The Supreme Court and Judicial Review," *The Constitutionality Crisis*, 2016, constitutionality.us/supremecourt.html.
[7] US Constitution art. II, § 1.
[8] Thomas Jefferson, *The Writings of Thomas Jefferson: Volume XV*, ed. Albert Ellery Bergh (Thomas Jefferson Memorial Association, 1905), 486–87.
[9] Jefferson, 486–87.
[10] Levin, *Men in Black*, 24.
[11] US Constitution art. III, § 2.
[12] US Constitution amend. V.
[13] US Constitution art. VI, cl. 2.

[14] Michelsen, "Supreme Court."

[15] US Constitution amend. X.

[16] Oaths of Justices and Judges.

[17] Philip Prygoski, *Constitutional Law* (West, 2008), 11–12.

[18] *Marbury*. Emphasis added.

[19] Charles Grove Haines, *The Role of the Supreme Court in American Government and Politics: 1789–1835* (University of California Press, 1944), 209.

[20] Jefferson, *Writings: Vol. XV*, 277.

[21] Hamilton, Jay, and Madison, *Federalist Papers*, 450. This quotation is Hamilton's reference to arguments opposing his.

[22] Hamilton, Jay, and Madison, 433.

[23] Ralph Ketcham, ed., *The Anti-Federalist Papers and the Constitutional Convention Debates: The Clashes and Compromises That Gave Birth to Our Form of Government* (Signet Classics, 1986), 308.

[24] Ketcham, 298.

[25] Levin, *Men in Black*, 11–12.

[26] National Federation of Independent Business v. Sebelius (June 28, 2012).

[27] Jefferson, *Jeffersonian Cyclopedia*, 846.

[28] Hamilton, Jay, and Madison, *Federalist Papers*, 435.

[29] Hamilton, Jay, and Madison, 434.

[30] Levin, *Men in Black*, 28.

[31] John Samples, *James Madison and the Future of Limited Government* (Cato Institute, 2003), 65.

[32] Thomas Jefferson, *The Writings of Thomas Jefferson: Volume XVII*, ed. Albert Ellery Bergh (Thomas Jefferson Memorial Association, 1907), 386–87.

[33] Steven Calabresi and Robert James, "Term Limits for the Supreme Court: Life Tenure Reconsidered," *Harvard Journal of Law & Public Policy* 29, no. 3 (May 26, 2006): 771.

[34] Calabresi and James, 771.

[35] Calabresi and James, 809–818 passim.

[36] US Constitution art. III, § 1.

[37] Calabresi and James, "Term Limits for the Supreme Court," 810.

[38] Calabresi and James, 813.

[39] Calabresi and James, 815.
[40] US Constitution art. III, § 1.
[41] Hamilton, Jay, and Madison, *Federalist Papers*, 433.
[42] Calabresi and James, "Term Limits for the Supreme Court," 822.
[43] Calabresi and James, 823.
[44] Charles Warren, *The Supreme Court in United States History: Volume Two* (Little, Brown, 1922), 116.
[45] Calabresi and James, "Term Limits for the Supreme Court," 824–25.
[46] Calabresi and James, 832.

ECONOMIC STRENGTH

[1] *The Debates and Proceedings in the Congress of the United States: Third Congress* (Gates and Seaton, 1855), 170. Quoting James Madison.
[2] Jonathan Elliot, ed., *Elliot's Debates: The Debates in the Several State Conventions on the Adoption of the Federal Constitution* (J. B. Lippincott, 1836), 431.
[3] Samuel Adams, *The Writings of Samuel Adams: Volume I (1764–1769)*, ed. Harry Alonzo Cushing (Knickerbocker Press, 1904), 137.
[4] Joyce Appleby, *Thomas Jefferson* (Times Books, 2003), 144.
[5] Levin, *Ameritopia*, 79.
[6] Dennis Hedke, *The Audacity of Freedom* (Tate Publishing & Enterprises, 2011), 46.
[7] Tommy Newberry, *The War on Success: How the Obama Agenda Is Shattering the American Dream* (Regnery Publishing, 2010), 69.
[8] Garner, *Black's Law Dictionary*, "free enterprise."
[9] Walter Williams, "Free Markets: Pro-Rich or Pro-Poor," *Walter E. Williams*, May 12, 2010, walterewilliams.com/free-markets-pro-rich-or-pro-poor.
[10] Walter Williams, "Is Capitalism Moral?," *Prager University*, September 14, 2015, prageru.com/videos/capitalism-moral.
[11] P. J. O'Rourke, "Dear Mr. President, Zero-Sum Doesn't Add Up," *The Wall Street Journal*, December 28, 2012, A15.
[12] O'Rourke, A15.
[13] Simpson and Weiner, *Compact Oxford English Dictionary*, "Plagiarize."
[14] Todd Davidson and Dave Trabert, "States That Spend Less, Tax Less—and Grow More," *The Wall Street Journal*, December 14, 2012.

[15] Davidson and Trabert.

[16] "The State Tax Reformers," *The Wall Street Journal*, January 30, 2013, A12.

[17] "State Tax Reformers," A12.

[18] Davidson and Trabert, "States That Spend Less."

[19] "The New Flat Tax: Encourages Growth and Job Creation" (Heritage Foundation, January 19, 2011), thf_media.s3.amazonaws.com/2012/pdf/fs0098.pdf.

[20] "New Flat Tax."

[21] Tim Groseclose, "The Laffer Curve and New Evidence That Taxes Stifle Economic Output," *Ricochet*, September 9, 2012, ricochet.com/archives/the-laffer-curve-and-new-evidence-that-taxes-stifle-economic-output.

[22] Groseclose.

[23] Christina Romer and David Romer, "The Macroeconomic Effects of Tax Changes: Estimates Based on a New Measure of Fiscal Shocks," *American Economic Review* 100, no. 3 (June 2010).

[24] Romer and Romer, 799.

[25] Groseclose, "Laffer Curve."

[26] "Tariff Act of 1930," 19 USC §§ 1202–1683g § (1930). This act utilizes the "free and dutiable" rate, which includes goods with a tariff of zero.

[27] Garner, *Black's Law Dictionary*, "right-to-work law."

[28] Jarrett Skorup, "The Union 'Free-Rider Problem' Myth in Right-to-Work Debate," *Michigan Capitol Confidential*, December 10, 2012, michigancapitolconfidential.com/18017. Quoting Tim Greimel.

[29] Skorup.

[30] Garner, *Black's Law Dictionary*, "welfare state."

[31] Daniel Halper, "Over 100 Million Now Receiving Federal Welfare," *The Weekly Standard*, August 8, 2012, weeklystandard.com/over-100-million-now-receiving-federal-welfare/article/649589. The statistics that come "'from the U.S. Census's Survey of Income and Program Participation shows that nearly 110,000 million individuals received a welfare benefit in 2011. (These figures do not include other means-tested benefits such as the Earned Income Tax Credit or the health insurance premium subsidies included in the President's health care law. CBO estimates that the premium subsidies, scheduled to begin in 2014, will cover at least 25 million individuals by the end of the decade.)'

This is not just Americans, however. 'These figures include not only citizens, but non-citizens as well,'" according to the committee's findings.

[32] Caroline May, "Welfare Government's Single Largest Budget Item in FY 2011 at Approx. $1.03 Trillion," *The Daily Caller*, October 18, 2012, dailycaller.com/2012/10/18/report-welfare-governments-single-largest-budget-item-in-fy-2011-at-approx-1-03-trillion. "The data excludes spending on Social Security, Medicare, means-tested health care for veterans without service-connected disabilities, and the means-tested veterans pension program."

[33] Voegeli, *Never Enough*, 3.

[34] Robert Ingersoll, *The Works of Robert G. Ingersoll* (Dresden Publishing, 1900), 175.

[35] Paine, *Common Sense*, 189.

[36] Andrew Biggs and Jason Richwine, "The Underworked Public Employee," *The Wall Street Journal*, December 4, 2012, A17.

[37] Biggs and Richwine, A17.

[38] Biggs and Richwine, A17. This calculation defines a workweek as forty hours. Emphasis added.

[39] Biggs and Richwine, A17.

[40] Mitt Romney, *No Apology: Believe in America* (St. Martin's Griffin, 2010), 199–200.

[41] Biggs and Richwine, "Underworked Public Employee," A17.

EDUCATIONAL STRENGTH

[1] Andrew Coulson, "The Effect of Teachers Unions on American Education," *Cato Journal* 30, no. 1 (2010): 155.

[2] Coulson, 156.

[3] Coulson, 162.

[4] Reagan, "Address to the Annual Meeting of the Phoenix Chamber of Commerce."

[5] Arne Duncan, "Secretary Arne Duncan's Remarks at OECD's Release of the Program for International Student Assessment (PISA) 2009 Results," *US Department of Education*, December 7, 2010.

[6] Romney, *No Apology*, 215.

[7] Romney, 231.

[8] Randi Weingarten, "How About a Bar Exam for Teachers?," *The Wall Street Journal*, December 10, 2012, A21.

[9] Weingarten, A21.

[10] Romney, *No Apology*, 231.

[11] New State Ice Co.

[12] "Fiscal Year 2012 Budget of the U.S. Government," *US Office of Management and Budget*, February 14, 2011, gpo.gov/fdsys/search/pagedetails.action?packageid=budget-2012-bud.

[13] "What We Do," *US Department of Education*, February 2, 2010, ed.gov/about/what-we-do.html.

[14] US Constitution amend. X.

[15] Jennifer Levitz and Scott Thurm, "Shift to Merit Scholarships Stirs Debate," *The Wall Street Journal*, December 19, 2012, A1, A16. Quoting Richard Vedder.

[16] Levitz and Thurm, A1, A16.

[17] Romney, *No Apology*, 219. Referencing the John and Abigail Adams Scholarship.

[18] Levitz and Thurm, "Shift to Merit Scholarships Stirs Debate," A1, A16.

[19] Levitz and Thurm, A1, A16.

[20] Vernon Raque, "Well-Rounding for Liberal Arts Folk," *The Wall Street Journal*, November 8, 2012, A20.

[21] Raque, A20.

MILITARY STRENGTH

[1] US Constitution preamble.

[2] Hamilton, Jay, and Madison, *Federalist Papers*, 261.

[3] George Washington, *The Writings of George Washington: Volume III (1775–1776)*, ed. Worthington Chauncey Ford (Knickerbocker Press, 1889), 333.

[4] Romney, *No Apology*, 25.

[5] Romney, 307.

[6] Romney, 308.

[7] Romney, 308. Quoting John Steinbeck.

[8] Joseph Nye, *The Future of Power* (Public Affairs, 2011), 84.

[9] When using economic resources to persuade, it becomes more difficult to distinguish between hard and soft power.

[10] Nye, *Future of Power*, 81–82.

[11] Romney, *No Apology*, 88–91.

[12] Nye, *Future of Power*, 86.

[13] Baker Spring, "Reagan's Legacy: Military Strength," *The Daily Signal*, February 5, 2013, dailysignal.com/2013/02/05/reagans-legacy-military-strength.

[14] Spring.

[15] Douglas Elmendorf, "Discretionary Spending" (Congressional Budget Office, October 26, 2011), cbo.gov/sites/default/files/112th-congress-2011-2012/reports/10-26-discretionaryspending_testimony.pdf.

[16] Clint Bolick and Jeb Bush, "Solving the Immigration Puzzle," *The Wall Street Journal*, January 25, 2013, A13.

[17] Pursuant to the Posse Comitatus Act (18 U.S.C. § 1385), the use of military personnel to enforce laws on American soil is greatly restricted. Only under limited circumstances ("in cases and under circumstances expressly authorized by the Constitution or Act of Congress") can the armed forces be so deployed. Presently, any such authority does not exist expressly in the Constitution, and only one act of Congress permits such engagements in limited use (the Insurrection Act of 1807 (10 U.S.C. §§ 331–335)). The Coast Guard, maintaining dual domestic maritime law enforcement and international war obligations, is exempt from the Posse Comitatus Act, as is the National Guard.

[18] Ronald Reagan, *Speaking My Mind: Selected Speeches* (Simon & Schuster, 1989), 204–5.

[19] Paine, *Common Sense*, 73.

[20] Ralph Peters, *Endless War: Middle-Eastern Islam vs. Western Civilization* (Stackpole Books, 2010), 220. Quoting Douglas MacArthur.

[21] Milton Friedman, "Why Not a Volunteer Army?," *New Individualist Review* 4, no. 4 (1967).

[22] Steven Bucci, "Milton Friedman: Father of the All-Volunteer Military," *The Daily Signal*, July 31, 2012, dailysignal.com/2012/07/31/milton-friedman-father-of-the-all-volunteer-military.

[23] Tim Kane, "Who Are the Recruits? The Demographic Characteristics of U.S. Military Enlistment, 2003–2005," *The Heritage Foundation*, October 27, 2006, heritage.org/defense/report/who-are-the-recruits-the-demographic-characteristics-us-military-enlistment-2003.

[24] Friedman, "Why Not a Volunteer Army?"

[25] Friedman.

[26] Madison, *Writings*, 708.

PERSONAL RESPONSIBILITY

[1] Levin, *Ameritopia*, 8.

[2] Colin Powell, *It Worked for Me: In Life and Leadership* (HarperCollins Publishers, 2012), 27.

[3] Adrian Goldsworthy, *Caesar: Life of a Colossus* (Yale University Press, 2006), 136. Quoting Julius Caesar.

[4] Michael Abrashoff, *It's Your Ship: Management Techniques from the Best Damn Ship in the Navy* (Business Plus, 2002), 38–39.

[5] Roe v. Wade (January 22, 1973).

[6] US Declaration of Independence. Emphasis added.

[7] US Constitution amend. V.

[8] US Declaration of Independence.

[9] Romney, *No Apology*, 5–6.

[10] Romney, 10.

[11] US Declaration of Independence. Emphasis added.

[12] James Truslow Adams, *Epic of America* (Greenwood Press, 1931), 404.

[13] Romney, *No Apology*, 16.

[14] The precise source of this quote is unknown, although many variously attribute it to Harry Truman or Woody Allen.

[15] Jessie Sholl, "The Stages of Change," *Experience L!Fe*, November 2011, experiencelife.com/article/the-stages-of-change.

INTERNATIONAL LEADERSHIP

[1] US Constitution art. VI, cl. 2.

[2] Hamilton, Jay, and Madison, *Federalist Papers*, 255.

[3] Hamilton, Jay, and Madison, 254.

[4] Hamilton, Jay, and Madison, 172–73.

[5] Julian Ku and John Yoo, *Taming Globalization: International Law, the U.S. Constitution, and the New World Order* (Oxford University Press, 2012), 1.

[6] Ku and Yoo, 1–2.

[7] Ku and Yoo, 2.

[8] Ku and Yoo, 11.

[9] Ku and Yoo, 11–12. Emphasis added.

[10] US Constitution art. II, § 2, cl. 2.

[11] Ku and Yoo, *Taming Globalization*, 12.

[12] Ku and Yoo, 12.

[13] Ku and Yoo, 13.

[14] Ku and Yoo, 13.

[15] Ku and Yoo, 13–14.

[16] Ku and Yoo, 14.

[17] Ku and Yoo, 14.

[18] Ku and Yoo, 15.

[19] Romney, *No Apology*, 26–36 passim.

[20] Romney, 27.

[21] Romney, 27.

[22] Romney, 30.

[23] Romney, 32.

[24] Romney, 32.

[25] Romney, 33.

[26] Romney, 33.

[27] "United Nations," Gallup, February 2, 2012, news.gallup.com/poll/116347/united-nations.aspx.

[28] Jeffrey Jones, "Americans' Rating of United Nations Improved, but Still Low," *Gallup*, February 19, 2010, news.gallup.com/poll/126134/americans-rating-united-nations-improved-low.aspx.

[29] "History of the UN," *United Nations*, 2015, un.org/un70/en/content/history.

[30] Deborah Wynes and Mounir Zahran, "The Investigation Function in the United Nations System" (United Nations Joint Inspection Unit, August 29, 2012), 13, fao.org/docrep/meeting/027/mf796e.pdf.

[31] Brett Schaefer, "Little American Love for the U.N.," *The Heritage Foundation*, June 13, 2012, heritage.org/commentary/little-american-love-the-un.

[32] Brett Schaefer, "The U.S. Does Not Need 'International Permission' to Defend Its Interests," *The Daily Signal*, March 10, 2012,

dailysignal.com/2012/03/10/the-u-s-does-not-need-international-permission-to-defend-its-interests.

[33] Stephen Talty, *Empire of Blue Water: Captain Morgan's Great Pirate Army, the Epic Battle for the Americas, and the Catastrophe That Ended the Outlaws' Bloody Reign* (Crown Publishers, 2007).

MOVING AMERICA FORWARD

[1] Romney, *No Apology*, 59.

[2] Dennis Prager, "Why Left Talks about 'White' Tea Parties," *The Dennis Prager Show*, April 27, 2010, dennisprager.com/why-left-talks-about-white-tea-parties.

[3] Prager.

[4] Levin, *Liberty and Tyranny*, 10, 173.

[5] Powell, *It Worked for Me*, 265.

[6] Erler, "Is the Constitution Colorblind?," 1.

[7] Erler, 2.

[8] Bill Clinton, "Executive Order 13166, 'Improving Access to Services for Persons with Limited English Proficiency,'" 65 F.R. 50119 § (2000).

[9] Edwin Feulner, "Object of a Proposition: English as a National Language," *The Heritage Foundation*, February 22, 2007, heritage.org/political-process/commentary/object-proposition-english-national-language.

[10] Israel Ortega and Matthew Spalding, "Immigration Reform: The Need for Upholding Our National Language," *The Heritage Foundation*, August 2, 2007, heritage.org/immigration/commentary/immigration-reform-the-need-upholding-our-national-language.

[11] Ortega and Spalding.

[12] Alexis de Tocqueville, *Democracy in America: Volume I* (D. Appleton, 1899), 13.

[13] Levin, *Liberty and Tyranny*, 161.

[14] Levin, 174.

[15] Levin, 174–75.

[16] Augustine, *City of God* (Penguin Books, 1984), 861.

[17] Feulner, "Object of a Proposition."

[18] Romney, *No Apology*, 220–21.

[19] B&H Publishing Group, *Holy Bible (CSB)*, Romans 3:23.

[20] B&H Publishing Group, Hebrews 11:1.

[21] B&H Publishing Group, Hebrews 11:39–40.

[22] US Constitution preamble.

[23] Levin, *Men in Black*, 53.

[24] "The Case for Marriage," *National Review*, September 7, 2010, nationalreview.com/2010/09/case-marriage-editors.

[25] Dennis Prager, "The Case for Marriage," *Prager University*, June 4, 2010, prageruniversity.com/life-studies/the-case-for-marriage.html.

[26] Prager.

[27] Romney, *No Apology*, 99.

[28] Madison, *Writings*, 517–18.

[29] Joseph Ellis, *His Excellency: George Washington* (Alfred A. Knopf, 2004), 184.

[30] Ellis, 184.

[31] Ellis, 182.

[32] Brookhiser, *James Madison*, 147.

[33] Ellis, *His Excellency*, 139.

EPILOGUE

[1] US Constitution art. VI, cl. 2.

[2] Sohrab Ahmari, "The Crisis of American Self-Government: The Weekend Interview with Harvey Mansfield," *The Wall Street Journal*, December 1, 2012, A13.

[3] Ahmari, A13.

[4] Hamilton, Jay, and Madison, *Federalist Papers*, 47.

[5] Brookhiser, *James Madison*, 98.

[6] Madison, *Writings*, 533–34.

[7] Adrian Goldsworthy, *Antony and Cleopatra* (Yale University Press, 2010), 29.

[8] Polybius, *The General History of Polybius: Volume II* (Oxford University Press, 1823), 132.

[9] Goldsworthy, *Caesar*, 516.

[10] Goldsworthy, 41.

[11] Levin, *Ameritopia*, 210.

[12] Levin, 211.

[13] Craig Nelson, *Rocket Men: The Epic Story of the First Men on the Moon* (Penguin Books, 2010), 327.

[14] Ronald Reagan, "First Inaugural Address."

[15] Jefferson, *Jeffersonian Cyclopedia*, 459.

[16] Jefferson, 567.

[17] Many repeatedly credit Edmund Burke with this statement (under a number of variations), but no definitive source exists as to give him recognition properly.

Bibliography

Abrashoff, Michael. It's Your Ship: Management Techniques from the Best Damn Ship in the Navy. Business Plus, 2002.

Adams, James Truslow. Epic of America. Greenwood Press, 1931.

Adams, Samuel. The Writings of Samuel Adams: Volume I (1764–1769). Edited by Harry Alonzo Cushing. Knickerbocker Press, 1904.

Ahmari, Sohrab. "The Crisis of American Self-Government: The Weekend Interview with Harvey Mansfield." The Wall Street Journal, December 1, 2012.

Antieau, Chester James. "Natural Rights and the Founding Fathers—The Virginians." Washington and Lee Law Review XVII (March 1, 1960).

Appleby, Joyce. Thomas Jefferson. Times Books, 2003.

Augustine. City of God. Penguin Books, 1984.

Bahr, Dex. No Christian Man Is an Island: Leading the Spiritual Quest in America's Culture Wars. Xulon Press, 2010.

Barney, Jason. "We Live in a Culture of Peter Pans." Imprimis 42, no. 1 (January 2013).

B&H Publishing Group. The Holy Bible: Christian Standard Bible (CSB). B&H Publishing Group, 2017.

Biggs, Andrew, and Jason Richwine. "The Underworked Public Employee." The Wall Street Journal, December 4, 2012.

Bolick, Clint, and Jeb Bush. "Solving the Immigration Puzzle." The Wall Street Journal, January 25, 2013.

Brookhiser, Richard. James Madison. Basic Books, 2011.

Bucci, Steven. "Milton Friedman: Father of the All-Volunteer Military." The Daily Signal, July 31, 2012. dailysignal.com/2012/07/31/milton-friedman-father-of-the-all-volunteer-military.

Calabresi, Steven, and Robert James. "Term Limits for the Supreme Court: Life Tenure Reconsidered." Harvard Journal of Law & Public Policy 29, no. 3 (May 26, 2006).

Chiaramonte, Perry, Cristina Corbin, Mike Levine, and Jana Winter. "As Nation Mourns, Investigators Try to Figure out What Led to Tragedy in Newtown, Conn." Fox News, December 16, 2012.

foxnews.com/us/2012/12/16/at-least-26-dead-in-shooting-at-connecticut-school.html.

Clinton, Bill. Executive Order 13166, "Improving Access to Services for Persons with Limited English Proficiency," 65 F.R. 50119 § (2000).

Constitution of the Commonwealth of Massachusetts (1780).

Coulson, Andrew. "The Effect of Teachers Unions on American Education." Cato Journal 30, no. 1 (2010).

Davidson, Todd, and Dave Trabert. "States That Spend Less, Tax Less—and Grow More." The Wall Street Journal, December 14, 2012.

Delahunty, Robert, and John Yoo. "The Obama Administration, the Dream Act and the Take Care Clause." Texas Law Review 91, no. 4 (September 9, 2012).

Duncan, Arne. "Secretary Arne Duncan's Remarks at OECD's Release of the Program for International Student Assessment (PISA) 2009 Results." US Department of Education, December 7, 2010.

Elliot, Jonathan, ed. Elliot's Debates: The Debates in the Several State Conventions on the Adoption of the Federal Constitution. J. B. Lippincott, 1836.

Ellis, Joseph. His Excellency: George Washington. Alfred A. Knopf, 2004.

Elmendorf, Douglas. "Discretionary Spending." Congressional Budget Office, October 26, 2011. cbo.gov/sites/default/files/112th-congress-2011-2012/reports/10-26-discretionaryspending_testimony.pdf.

Erler, Edward. "Is the Constitution Colorblind?" Imprimis 41, no. 1 (November 2012).

Feulner, Edwin. "Object of a Proposition: English as a National Language." The Heritage Foundation, February 22, 2007. heritage.org/political-process/commentary/object-proposition-english-national-language.

"Fiscal Year 2012 Budget of the U.S. Government." US Office of Management and Budget, February 14, 2011. gpo.gov/fdsys/search/pagedetails.action?packageid=budget-2012-bud.

Friedman, Milton. "Why Not a Volunteer Army?" New Individualist Review 4, no. 4 (1967).

Fund, John. "The Facts about Mass Shootings: It's Time to Address Mental Health and Gun-Free Zones." National Review, December 16, 2012. nationalreview.com/2012/12/facts-about-mass-shootings-john-fund.

Garner, Bryan, ed. Black's Law Dictionary. 3rd ed. Thomson West, 2006.

Goldsworthy, Adrian. Antony and Cleopatra. Yale University Press, 2010.

———. Caesar: Life of a Colossus. Yale University Press, 2006.

Groseclose, Tim. "The Laffer Curve and New Evidence That Taxes Stifle Economic Output." Ricochet, September 9, 2012. ricochet.com/archives/the-laffer-curve-and-new-evidence-that-taxes-stifle-economic-output.

Haines, Charles Grove. The Role of the Supreme Court in American Government and Politics: 1789–1835. University of California Press, 1944.

Halbrook, Stephen. The Founders' Second Amendment: Origins of the Right to Bear Arms. Ivan R. Dee, 2008.

Halper, Daniel. "Over 100 Million Now Receiving Federal Welfare." The Weekly Standard, August 8, 2012. weeklystandard.com/over-100-million-now-receiving-federal-welfare/article/649589.

Hamilton, Alexander, John Jay, and James Madison. The Federalist Papers. Edited by Clinton Rossiter. Mentor, 1999.

Hedke, Dennis. The Audacity of Freedom. Tate Publishing & Enterprises, 2011.

Hickok Jr., Eugene. The Bill of Rights: Original Meaning and Current Understanding. University Press of Virginia, 1991.

"History of the UN." United Nations, 2015. un.org/un70/en/content/history.

Hitler, Adolph. Hitler's Table Talk: 1941–1944. Edited by Hugh Trevor-Roper. Enigma Books, 2008.

Horowitz, Daniel. "Regarding Immigration Proposals, Beware of Your Opponents' Motivation." Red State, January 28, 2013. redstate.com/dhorowitz3/2013/01/28/regarding-immigration-proposals-beware-of-your-opponents-motivation-2.

Ingersoll, Robert. The Works of Robert G. Ingersoll. Dresden Publishing, 1900.

Jefferson, Thomas. The Jeffersonian Cyclopedia: A Comprehensive Collection of the Views of Thomas Jefferson. Edited by John Foley. Funk & Wagnalls, 1900.

———. The Writings of Thomas Jefferson: Volume XV. Edited by Albert Ellery Bergh. Thomas Jefferson Memorial Association, 1905.

———. *The Writings of Thomas Jefferson: Volume XVII.* Edited by Albert Ellery Bergh. Thomas Jefferson Memorial Association, 1907.

Jones, Jeffrey. "Americans' Rating of United Nations Improved, but Still Low." Gallup, February 19, 2010. news.gallup.com/poll/126134/americans-rating-united-nations-improved-low.aspx.

Jones, Terril Yue. "Knife-Wielding Man Injures 22 Children in China." Reuters, December 14, 2012. reuters.com/article/us-china-stabbings/knife-wielding-man-injures-22-children-in-china-idusbre8bd06520121214.

Kane, Tim. "Who Are the Recruits? The Demographic Characteristics of U.S. Military Enlistment, 2003–2005." The Heritage Foundation, October 27, 2006. heritage.org/defense/report/who-are-the-recruits-the-demographic-characteristics-us-military-enlistment-2003.

Ketcham, Ralph, ed. *The Anti-Federalist Papers and the Constitutional Convention Debates: The Clashes and Compromises That Gave Birth to Our Form of Government.* Signet Classics, 1986.

Ku, Julian, and John Yoo. *Taming Globalization: International Law, the U.S. Constitution, and the New World Order.* Oxford University Press, 2012.

LaPierre, Wayne. "More Guns Bring More Safety." New Haven Register, December 28, 2012. nhregister.com/news/article/guest-column-more-guns-bring-more-safety-11496326.php.

Levin, Mark. *Ameritopia: The Unmaking of America.* Threshold Editions, 2012.

———. *Liberty and Tyranny: A Conservative Manifesto.* Threshold Editions, 2009.

———. *Men in Black: How the Supreme Court Is Destroying America.* Regency Publishing, 2006.

Levitz, Jennifer, and Scott Thurm. "Shift to Merit Scholarships Stirs Debate." The Wall Street Journal, December 19, 2012.

Limbaugh, Rush. "There Will Be Amnesty, Folks." The Rush Limbaugh Show, November 9, 2012. rushlimbaugh.com/daily/2012/11/09/there_will_be_amnesty_folks.

Locke, John. *The Second Treatise of Civil Government and a Letter Concerning Toleration.* Edited by J. W. Gough. Basil Blackwell & Mott, 1948.

MacArthur, Douglas. General MacArthur: Wisdom and Visions. Edited by Edward Imparato. Turner Publishing, 2000.

Madison, James. Madison: Writings. Edited by Jack Rakove. Library of America, 1999.

Malcolm, Joyce Lee. "Two Cautionary Tales of Gun Control." The Wall Street Journal, December 27, 2012.

Marbury v. Madison (February 24, 1803).

May, Caroline. "Welfare Government's Single Largest Budget Item in FY 2011 at Approx. $1.03 Trillion." The Daily Caller, October 18, 2012. dailycaller.com/2012/10/18/report-welfare-governments-single-largest-budget-item-in-fy-2011-at-approx-1-03-trillion.

McCulloch v. Maryland (March 6, 1819).

Michelsen, Warren. "The Supreme Court and Judicial Review." The Constitutionality Crisis, 2016. constitutionality.us/supremecourt.html.

National Federation of Independent Business v. Sebelius (June 28, 2012).

Nelson, Craig. Rocket Men: The Epic Story of the First Men on the Moon. Penguin Books, 2010.

New State Ice Co. v. Liebmann (March 21, 1932).

New York v. United States (June 19, 1992).

Newberry, Tommy. The War on Success: How the Obama Agenda Is Shattering the American Dream. Regnery Publishing, 2010.

Nye, Joseph. The Future of Power. Public Affairs, 2011.

Oaths of Justices and Judges, 28 USC § 453 § (1990).

O'Rourke, P. J. "Dear Mr. President, Zero-Sum Doesn't Add Up." The Wall Street Journal, December 28, 2012.

Ortega, Israel, and Matthew Spalding. "Immigration Reform: The Need for Upholding Our National Language." The Heritage Foundation, August 2, 2007. heritage.org/immigration/commentary/immigration-reform-the-need-upholding-our-national-language.

Paine, Thomas. Common Sense and Other Writings. Edited by Joyce Appleby. Barnes & Noble Books, 2005.

———. Rights of Man, Common Sense, and Other Political Writings. Edited by Mark Philp. Oxford University Press, 1995.

———. The Writings of Thomas Paine: Volume I (1774–1779). Edited by Moncure Daniel Conway. Knickerbocker Press, 1906.

Peters, Ralph. Endless War: Middle-Eastern Islam vs. Western Civilization. Stackpole Books, 2010.

Polybius. The General History of Polybius: Volume II. Oxford University Press, 1823.

Powell, Colin. It Worked for Me: In Life and Leadership. HarperCollins Publishers, 2012.

Prager, Dennis. "The Case for Marriage." Prager University, June 4, 2010. prageruniversity.com/life-studies/the-case-for-marriage.html.

———. "Why Left Talks about 'White' Tea Parties." The Dennis Prager Show, April 27, 2010. dennisprager.com/why-left-talks-about-white-tea-parties.

Prakash, Sai. "Take Care Clause." The Heritage Foundation, 2017. heritage.org/constitution/#!/articles/2/essays/98/take-care-clause.

Prygoski, Philip. Constitutional Law. West, 2008.

Raque, Vernon. "Well-Rounding for Liberal Arts Folk." The Wall Street Journal, November 8, 2012.

Reagan, Ronald. "Address to the Annual Meeting of the Phoenix Chamber of Commerce." March 30, 1961.

———. "First Inaugural Address." January 20, 1981.

———. Speaking My Mind: Selected Speeches. Simon & Schuster, 1989.

———. The Reagan Diaries. Edited by Douglas Brinkley. Harper Perennial, 2007.

Roe v. Wade (January 22, 1973).

Romer, Christina, and David Romer. "The Macroeconomic Effects of Tax Changes: Estimates Based on a New Measure of Fiscal Shocks." American Economic Review 100, no. 3 (June 2010).

Romney, Mitt. No Apology: Believe in America. St. Martin's Griffin, 2010.

Roosevelt, Theodore. The Great Adventure: Present-Day Studies in American Nationalism. Charles Scribner's Sons, 1919.

Rudalevige, Andrew. The New Imperial Presidency: Renewing Presidential Power after Watergate. University of Michigan Press, 2008.

Samet, Elizabeth. Willing Obedience: Citizens, Soldiers, and the Progress of Consent in America, 1776–1898. Stanford University Press, 2004.

Samples, John. James Madison and the Future of Limited Government. Cato Institute, 2003.

Scaros, Constantinos. Understanding the Constitution. Jones and Barlett Publishers, 2011.

Schaefer, Brett. "Little American Love for the U.N." The Heritage Foundation, June 13, 2012. heritage.org/commentary/little-american-love-the-un.

———. "The U.S. Does Not Need 'International Permission' to Defend Its Interests." The Daily Signal, March 10, 2012. dailysignal.com/2012/03/10/the-u-s-does-not-need-international-permission-to-defend-its-interests.

Scheb II, John, and Otis Stephens Jr. American Constitutional Law: Volume I (Sources of Power and Restraint). Wadsworth, 2012.

Sholl, Jessie. "The Stages of Change." Experience L!Fe, November 2011. experiencelife.com/article/the-stages-of-change.

Simkin, Marvin. "Individual Rights." Los Angeles Times, January 12, 1992. articles.latimes.com/1992-01-12/local/me-358_1_jail-tax-individual-rights-san-diego.

Simpson, J. A., and E. S. C. Weiner, eds. Compact Oxford English Dictionary. 3rd ed. Oxford University Press, 2008.

Skorup, Jarrett. "The Union 'Free-Rider Problem' Myth in Right-to-Work Debate." Michigan Capitol Confidential, December 10, 2012. michigancapitolconfidential.com/18017.

Spalding, Matthew. "Imperial Presidency." The Daily Signal, June 22, 2012. dailysignal.com/2012/06/22/morning-bell-imperial-presidency.

Spring, Baker. "Reagan's Legacy: Military Strength." The Daily Signal, February 5, 2013. dailysignal.com/2013/02/05/reagans-legacy-military-strength.

Stevens, Richard, and Aaron Zelman. Death by "Gun Control." Mazel Freedom Press, 2001.

Suetonius. The Twelve Cæsars. Edited by Alexander Thomson. R. Worthington, 1883.

Talty, Stephen. Empire of Blue Water: Captain Morgan's Great Pirate Army, the Epic Battle for the Americas, and the Catastrophe That Ended the Outlaws' Bloody Reign. Crown Publishers, 2007.

Tariff Act of 1930, 19 USC §§ 1202–1683g § (1930).

"The Case for Marriage." National Review, September 7, 2010. nationalreview.com/2010/09/case-marriage-editors.

The Debates and Proceedings in the Congress of the United States: Third Congress. Gates and Seaton, 1855.

"The New Flat Tax: Encourages Growth and Job Creation." Heritage Foundation, January 19, 2011. thf_media.s3.amazonaws.com/2012/pdf/fs0098.pdf.

"The State Tax Reformers." The Wall Street Journal, January 30, 2013.

Thoreau, Henry David. *Walden, Civil Disobedience, and Other Writings.* Edited by William Rossi. W. W. Norton, 2008.

Thornton, Paul. *Leadership: Off the Wall.* WestBow Press, 2010.

Tocqueville, Alexis de. *Democracy in America: Volume I.* D. Appleton, 1899.

Uchitelle, Louis. "Plan May Lure More to Enter U.S. Illegally, Experts Say." New York Times, January 9, 2004.

"United Nations." Gallup, February 2, 2012. news.gallup.com/poll/116347/united-nations.aspx.

US Constitution (1789).

US Declaration of Independence (1776).

Van Dyke, Alan. "Echoes of the Serf and the Sovereign State Still Persist." The Wall Street Journal, December 22, 2012.

Voegeli, William. *Never Enough: America's Limitless Welfare State.* Encounter Books, 2012.

Wagner, William. *Jurisprudential Considerations: The Impact of Worldview on American Constitutional Law.* S & L Global, 2011.

War Powers Resolution, 50 USC § 1541–1548 § (1973).

Warren, Charles. *The Supreme Court in United States History: Volume Two.* Little, Brown, 1922.

Washington, George. *The Writings of George Washington: Volume III (1775–1776).* Edited by Worthington Chauncey Ford. Knickerbocker Press, 1889.

Weingarten, Randi. "How About a Bar Exam for Teachers?" The Wall Street Journal, December 10, 2012.

"What We Do." US Department of Education, February 2, 2010. ed.gov/about/what-we-do.html.

Wickard v. Filburn (November 9, 1942).

Williams, Walter. "Free Markets: Pro-Rich or Pro-Poor." Walter E. Williams, May 12, 2010. walterewilliams.com/free-markets-pro-rich-or-pro-poor.

———. *"Is Capitalism Moral?" Prager University, September 14, 2015. prageru.com/videos/capitalism-moral.*

Wood, Gordon. The Purpose of the Past: Reflections on the Uses of History. Penguin Books, 2008.

Wynes, Deborah, and Mounir Zahran. "The Investigation Function in the United Nations System." United Nations Joint Inspection Unit, August 29, 2012. fao.org/docrep/meeting/027/mf796e.pdf.

INDEX

For references to individuals, see the notes section.

Made in the USA
Las Vegas, NV
18 February 2022